Achieving literacy

Longitudinal studies of adolescents learning to read

Margaret Meek
with
Stephen Armstrong
Vicky Austerfield
Judith Graham
Elizabeth Plackett

Routledge & Kegan Paul
London, Boston, Melbourne and Henley

First published in 1983
by Routledge & Kegan Paul plc
39 Store Street, London WC1E 7DD,
9 Park Street, Boston, Mass. 02108, USA,
296 Beaconsfield Parade, Middle Park,
Melbourne, 3206, Australia, and
Broadway House, Newtown Road,
Henley-on-Thames, Oxon RG9 1EN
Set in IBM Press Roman by Columns, Reading
and printed in Great Britain by
Redwood Burn Ltd., Trowbridge
© Margaret Meek, Stephen Armstrong,
Vicky Austerfield, Judith Graham,
Elizabeth Plackett, 1983

Library of Congress Cataloging in Publication Data

Meek, Margaret.

Achieving literacy.
(Language, education, and society)
Includes bibliographical references.
1. Language arts – Remedial teaching – Longitudinal
studies. 2. Literacy – Longitudinal studies.
I. Title. II. Series.
LB1631.M42 1983   428'.007'12   82-24014

ISBN 0 7100 9463 9
ISBN 0-7100-9463-9 (pbk)

Achieving literacy

Language, Education and Society

Edited by
Michael W. Stubbs
Department of Linguistics
University of Nottingham

We owe this book to our pupils, and to
Michael Simons

Contents

Contents

Editor's preface

Simply a list of some of the questions implied by the phrase *Language, Education and Society* gives an immediate idea of the complexity, and also the fascination, of the area.

How is language related to learning? Or to intelligence? How should a teacher react to non-standard dialect in the classroom? Do regional and social accents and dialects matter? What is meant by standard English? Does it make sense to talk of 'declining standards' in language or in education? Or to talk of some children's language as 're-stricted'? Do immigrant children require special language provision? How can their native languages be used as a valuable resource in schools? Can 'literacy' be equated with 'education'? Why are there so many adult illiterates in Britain and the USA? What effect has growing up with no easy access to language: for example, because a child is profoundly deaf? Why is there so much prejudice against people whose language background is odd in some way: because they are handi-capped, or speak a non-standard dialect or foreign language? Why do linguistic differences lead to political violence, in Belgium, India, Wales and other parts of the world?

These are all real questions, of the kind which worry parents, teachers and policy-makers, and the answer to them is complex and not at all obvious. It is such questions that authors in this series will dis-cuss.

Language plays a central part in education. This is probably generally agreed, but there is considerable debate and confusion about the exact relationship between language and learning. Even though the importance of language is generally recognized, we still have a lot to learn about how language is related to either educational success or to intelligence and thinking. Language is also a central fact in everyone's social life. People's attitudes and most deeply held beliefs are at stake, for it is through language that personal and social identities are maintained and recognized. People are judged, whether justly or not, by the language they speak.

Language, education and society is therefore an area where scholars have a responsibility to write clearly and persuasively, in order to communicate the best in recent research to as wide an audience as possible. This means not only other researchers, but also all those who are involved in educational, social and political policy-making, from individual teachers to government. It is an area where value judgments cannot be avoided. Any action that we take – or, of course, avoidance of action – has moral, social and political consequences. It is vital, therefore, that practice is informed by the best knowledge available, and that decisions affecting the futures of individual children or whole social groups are not taken merely on the basis of all too widespread folk myths about language in society.

Linguistics, psychology and sociology are often rejected by non-specialists as jargon-ridden; or regarded as fascinating, but of no relevance to educational or social practice. But this is superficial and short-sighted: we are dealing with complex issues, which require an understanding of the general principles involved. It is bad theory to make statements about language in use which cannot be related to educational and social reality. But it is equally unsound to base beliefs and action on anecdote, received myths and unsystematic or idiosyncratic observations.

All knowledge is value-laden: it suggests action and changes our beliefs. Change is difficult and slow, but possible nevertheless. When language in education and society is seriously and systematically studied, it becomes clear how awesomely complex is the linguistic and social knowledge of all children and adults. And with such an understanding, it becomes impossible to maintain a position of linguistic prejudice and intolerance. This may be the most important implication of a serious study of language, in our linguistically diverse modern world.

This book is a fascinating and informative report by a group of researchers and teachers who set out to teach children who have failed to acquire a useful degree of literacy, and then to discuss and reflect on their experiences. The authors say that they are presenting *a kind of evidence* about a central and constant problem in education. This is an over-modest description. Elsewhere in the book they call it *a different kind of evidence* from most discussions of literacy. They might also have said that the book provides *an essential kind of evidence* which is often unavailable because it is so difficult to collect and present.

The work does not resemble most educational research. It is a narrative, a report of truly participant research or action research, of a kind which only teachers themselves can do. One major merit of the book is that it does not conceal the personal and practical difficulties of doing such work: the time and commitment involved. Such issues are often idealized out of research reports. Another strength is that the authors' interpretations of their material are not concealed behind a superficial objectivity. They present enough of their case-notes and tape-recordings of lessons to allow readers to make their own interpretations if necessary. Readers should not be misled, however, by the narrative style. The book also contains a great deal of information about many of the central topics of teaching literacy: children's motivation, the influence of social and cultural background on learning, different methods of teaching reading, and so on. On every occasion, these topics are integrated into the detailed case-studies.

The book should be of great interest to researchers for the way in which it presents a kind of evidence on reading and writing which is not usually available. And it should also be of great interest to practising teachers, whether they intend to carry out a project of the kind the authors describe, or whether they simply wish to learn from the authors' acute and thoughtful observations. It is rare to find such a book, in which the roles of researcher and teacher are so genuinely inseparable.

Michael Stubbs.

Acknowledgments

Behind those who collaborated to produce this book were others: colleagues in schools, at the English Centre and in the Department of English in the Institute of Education. When we ran out of time, Dr Denis Lawton, Shyama Iyer and Suzanne Davies came to our rescue. We owe most grateful thanks to them all.

1
A view of the task

How children learn to read well is still almost a secret. What kind of teaching helps them is a scarcely penetrated mystery. We know some things about what children do in the early stages of learning and a great deal about what teachers do, and are told to do, in class teaching. Yet we cannot be sure that children learn to read as the direct result of being told what to do. Most expert adult readers have had no help from reading experts. Their best teachers may have been the authors of the books they enjoyed. There is abundant evidence that many children teach themselves and each other.[1] For all the money, time energy and ingenuity we have spent on reading research, we are still at the stage of saying that children learn to read when there is something they want to read and an adult who takes the time and trouble to help them.

The most important lesson children learn by becoming literate is that they can *learn*, in the way that school endorses learning. Then they join the school society of young learners who use their literacy as currency, as the medium of communication, as tools of thought and the means of deep symbolic play. The bond between the teacher and the taught is strengthened; exploration, discovery, ambition and achievement expand and flourish. The few children (and their number is not large, nor is it growing as many believe) who cannot read and write worry us because they are exiles from the society of child learners in school and are threatened, by parents, teachers and other adults, with exclusion from the wider social world outside school if they fail to become literate.

Consequently, the drive to teach children to read is intensified if they reach secondary school unable to do so. How, then, should they be taught? They have had reading lessons, or concern about their reading, for six years. What new diagnosis or remedy is possible? Even if we believe we fully understand the reasons for this delay, the learning is still to be accomplished. If the lengthening of the dole queue provides an incentive, what can a secondary school teacher do where a primary one, specially trained in the techniques of 'basic literacy' has failed? Is it inevitable that a twelve-year-old non-reader should spend his or her life in secondary school in the condition of a handicapped child? What actually happens when a teacher engages with the problems of a pupil whose reading is described as 'slow', 'backward' or 'under-achieving' so that she may help the child to reach the standard of competence consistent with what the outside world calls 'literacy'?

This book is a narrative compiled from the work of six teachers who set themselves the task of answering these questions. We began to look closely at what we were doing in reading lessons and to examine what we saw the pupils doing because no research report seemed to admit as *evidence* those things which we had to grapple with every day.[2] So we decided to record, in as much detail as we could in the busy concourse that is a school, exactly what happened when we taught an individual pupil to read and write. We planned to continue this recording until the pupils knew they were fully and freely literate in ways they could recognize and we believed to be desirable. From these observations and records we hoped to understand better and to demonstrate more clearly exactly what is involved in teaching a secondary school non-reader to read. Then we would be able to encourage others to undertake this most rewarding of all teaching-and-learning operations with fewer frustrations and more encouragement.

In order to share and discuss our individual observations of a single pupil we met as a group. Here we consulted the research and analysed our perceptions of what we had set ourselves to do. We exchanged books and materials and relied on each other for support and help. Soon we began to realize that we were giving our work a double stance, first towards the pupil we were teaching and then towards our collaborative exploration of our common understandings. As our pupils changed, so did we. As we became confident on their behalf, we began to realize that we were being forced to challenge what had hitherto been presented to teachers as evidence about what matters in secondary school reading, about the nature of the reading environment and, above all, about the pupils' and the teachers' views of each other and of the task and the texts that lay between them. What seemed at first to be a fairly straightforward undertaking became, in the space of a few months, and then for nearly four years, a many-layered activity. The original report of our work was more than twice the length of this book.

Longitudinal case studies are notoriously difficult to record. In the inevitable time-lag between the beginning of the inquiry and the final summary nothing stands still. Pupils grow older and leave school. What seems newly observed is made plain in many places at once by researchers who scarcely know of each other's existence.[3] We realized as we went on that we should have included a much closer look at writing. We strayed sometimes in search of new insights; there were false dawns and cold scents. But these also have narrative value and are essentially part of the whole story we have to tell.

There was no 'required to prove' about our undertaking, only a decision to let others know that what we actually *do* when we teach a child to read is less than half of the total picture, which also indicates what we believe we are doing, what we choose not to do, and, even more important, what we take for granted. As we shall show at every turn, our pupils' views of what learning to read means may have very little in common with our own. Learning to read and teaching reading are, in the end, ways of negotiating meanings, including what 'being a reader' means in our day and age.

Our concern is to show what we did and to explain what we came to understand. By a strictly utilitarian count of the test-teach-test kind, we have to say we failed to produce a blueprint of how inexperienced adolescents can be turned into readers beyond the risk of failure. To learn to read, the learner must gradually take over the act of reading from the teacher whose role is to mediate the responsibility for it to the learner until his experience and skill are sufficient for him to 'go it alone'. All of our pupils had different reasons for being unable or unwilling to do this. In the end, we may have learned more about reading than they did. In some ways the effort was equally painful for us all, but we now know that too much is written about what teachers *ought* to do, and how children *should* behave in reading lessons. The evidence of what actually happens is very scarce. We offer what we have found to anyone whose interests lie in teaching, learning, language, literature, child development and the social effects of literacy in the ways described by Michael Stubbs.[4]

The outcome of our narrative is to ask some of the as yet unasked questions about literacy and to point to some important lessons that have not, in the classroom sense, been taught. This may seem a poor reward for four years of hard work, but we believe that, in that time, we learned many things that, as teachers, we had hitherto concealed from ourselves and each other. As our tale unfolds you will come to know us well. We are referred to by our first names, not as a specious gesture of familiarity, but so that you can recognize us as we meet and talk. In the course of our discussions we criticize many things, including our colleagues and the institutions where we work. You have only our word for it that we do this in the same way as we try to be honest about all that happened. If you think that we sometimes take our betters to task with unnecessary vehemence, you may also see that we have been no less sparing of ourselves.

In the chapters that follow we first put you into the picture of our activities, the total reading environment of each teacher and pupil, and of the group. We examine the view of literacy mediated by the school and the teacher as representing society at large, and the kinds of negotiation that are necessary for the selection of pupils and the establishment of 'special' lessons. Gradually we narrow the focus until you see the teacher and the pupil in the closest possible proximity, the interaction in the reading lesson itself. As we move further on to see what is happening, lesson by lesson, we count on your awareness of the whole context we established earlier, of the pupils and teachers in their schools and the teachers in their discussion group in the world of multicultural London at the end of the 1970s.

There are many gaps, but as far as possible we offer you our own words in our own voices. The most significant difference between this account of teaching reading and the more official projects is that we, the teachers, are the reporters. In this way we are being judged first by the children, then by each other, and now by you.

2

Features of the starting point

As a reading teacher I was in a somewhat similar position to those primitive societies that perform ritual ceremonies to make the rains come. They know that pouring water on the ground won't really open the heavens, but they have to *do* something.

Michael Simons

A language for life

Books to me are boring. I can never get into the story. In school I don't mind reading. In school it's different, it's not so boring. You've got to sit down and shut up. I think I can get into it more in school because there's nothing else to do like looking over the wall to the Park for mates or raiding the biscuit tin. When we read in school if the story ain't so good I usually get in a bad mood or I get a headache.

There was one moment I remember most. This was the fourth year of my Junior School. It was the first day in my new class and the teacher wanted to hear us read. My stomach turned and I was getting hotter. There was about twenty people in front of me. One of them couldn't read too well and Miss said, Well, Well, now we know the people who can't read. I was next after Leigh and, I felt as though I was burning up. It was my turn nothing would come out every word I said came out with a quiver. Even very easy words wouldn't come out and she stopped me. I was never so embarrassed in my life my face was turning bright red as the teacher was saying how bad I was. She didn't seem to understand how I felt and that I was a good reader really. She seemed to be like a robot with no feelings.[1]

The eleven-year-old girl who wrote this prelude has said everything we need to say to excuse another study of reading and how it is taught. Competent readers who have no difficulties soon forget exactly how they began, and by the time they are nine they will say that you have to instruct younger children in ways that they themselves never experienced.[2] It is still not common to find the views of children offered as evidence because beginners are known to have confused conceptions of the reading process when they asked about it during their early years in school,[3] and once they have learned to read fluently they do not expect to be questioned about their difficulties. But if a child does remember clearly something about first steps in reading, the chances are that it was connected with overcoming a specific problem.

Gradually, however, studies of classroom interactions are beginning to replace single-focus observations.[4] There were very few of these in print when we began, and *Extending Beginning Reading* appeared when we had finished.[5] In this recent Schools Council Report the voices of children are heard replying to questions about their reading and what they do when they are in difficulty. In many schools, however, discussions about literacy are still conducted in the adult language of crisis which has its counterpart in the response of our young writer. The reading teacher she describes in an archetypal figure. Right at the beginning of our time as a group we knew we were looking for something as far away as possible from teaching and learning in this mode. The teacher who elicited this autobiographical vignette had taken part in discussions following the publication in 1975 of The Bullock Report; *A Language for Life*. This was also the primary incentive for our operation. For the second time this century the emotional rise in public concern about literacy, notably in its relation to the job-worthiness of young adults, the state of public behaviour in adolescents and the qualifications for entry into higher education had resulted in an official enquiry. (The Newbolt Report in 1921 dealt with the complaints of the time about illiterate school leavers.) The Bullock Report addressed itself particularly to teachers, urging them to understand the nature of the relationship of language and learning and the place of reading in the overall development of children in school. It also revealed how anxiety about literacy reaches the general public as a single feature of a more diffuse concern about defining the nature of literacy at any given time in a society that takes the literacy of its members for granted.

The writers of the Bullock Report were aware that the entire population is now expected to be more literate (however literacy is defined) as more is 'demanded' by society in general. In the world-wide move towards universal literacy, two things are happening here at once: we are increasing the level of literacy for the entire population and also extending to everyone the possibilities of becoming literate in ways that have no precedent, in subject specialisms in science, for instance, in ways related to technology, in the storage and retrieval of information by computer, and in relation to television – a relation that is more subtle than is generally admitted by those who only bewail the decrease in children's reading time. But the Bullock Report, for all its concern about the teaching of reading and the teaching of literature, could not define literacy. It also skirted the question of what a well-read person is like nowadays. Thus, for public purposes, literacy becomes what is tested by the most recent tests.[6] For all its innovative concern about adult non-readers and its nascent awareness of the growing diversity of our multicultural society, there is no close examination in the Report of how a child engages with reading as a meaningful activity, or what a committed adult actually does in teaching a child to read, either at the normal time for learning in the primary school, or as a result of the child's difficulty in conforming to the school's expectations at a particular age and stage.

When the Report considers the plight of young people who may leave school unable to read with fluency and ease, the explanation offered for their failure is the fact that most of them 'come from areas of social and economic depression'. The Report suggests that they need 'additional teaching assistance' related to the rest of their learning. The writers continue:

> It would be unrealistic to expect that conditions for learning will ever be ideal, and there will always be children who for various reasons fall behind. But a very great deal can be done to prevent reading disability by raising the quality of teaching generally and by giving skilled individual help before a sense of failure has led the child to lose confidence. (p. 275, 18.19)

Before the Report made this recommendation, we had all been giving 'individual help' to inexperienced readers. We were already convinced that 'it is not a question of "remedial methods" but of applying good teaching *in such a way* [our italics] that failure is replaced by a sense of achievement, with all that means for a child's confidence and self-respect'.[7] We wanted to know what did 'in such a way' really mean? We now needed to share experience of our teaching and the reality of our pupils' actual needs, to teach a single pupil, to read and monitor the operation and to account for what happened in order to display what kind of skills are necessary to help inexperienced readers to learn. We wanted to think of it as a investigation rather than as a research project of the kind that has generated so much unease amongst reading teachers.[8] We would attempt to reveal as much as possible of what happens from the learners' point of view and from the teachers' responses and actions to see if a way such as ours could contribute to the understanding of teaching and learning.

Reading experts or expert readers?

Teachers are the most significant variables in the process of a child's learning to read because they begin by teaching themselves and all that they believe about reading. In some ways their position is intolerable. They are at the flashpoint of every conflict about aims and methods. They are expected to read, understand and implement the findings of research reports for which they make the evidence available, but are rarely consulted about the outcomes. They are the victims of travelling salesmen with new books, gimmicks, schemes and machines. They are expected to change ignorance into knowledge and to feel responsible if a child fails. Above all, they are constantly aware of the pupils' difficulties and the multifaceted nature of any solution to their problems. It is always easier for them to envelope themselves in a profusion of specialist techniques, or to blame the pupils' environment, poor parental attitudes, truancy, generally low motivation and lack of adequate facilities in school, than to take the reading problem in hand and try to deal with it. That so many do is a matter for rejoicing. At no time did we think our group was unique in either its caring or its endeavours.

In one way it was different, however. We were about to undertake teaching usually called 'remedial' but our skills derived from another specialism: we were teachers of English. Now, English teachers have, on the whole, come late to the idea that they need a theory of literacy and a theoretical understanding of the teaching of reading. Before the advent of mixed-ability classes, the traditional English specialist used to meet well-read eleven-year-olds and take for granted the relationship of literacy to the study of literature. When we began to be concerned about those who could not read the class texts and to take an interest in the teaching of reading, we found the territory occupied by those whose studies were derived from psychology: experts in learning difficulties, diagnostic assessment, remedial methodology and child guidance, who made us feel ignorant to the point of embarrassment about techniques for behaviour modification and such specialisms as dyslexia. So English teachers had to begin at the beginning, to look at reading not as reading experts, but as expert readers who believe firmly in the importance of literacy across a wide spectrum of activity that includes literature of all kinds, mass, popular and special. Then we realized that we could offer insights and instruction of the kinds that did not appear in the reading research reports. To be considered important, however, our insights needed a different kind of validation from that offered by the results of reading tests, and to be subjected to new questions that some kinds of learning theory are not designed to answer.

So we began with a fair assumption of our own skills as readers, our background in teaching, the hospitality of a teachers' centre, tape recorders, a common aim to produce pieces of recorded actualities which are the missing dimension of most in-service education, so that evidence could be collected, collated, reviewed and built up. There was no suggestion that this evidence could be impartial. We had no time away from our normal teaching load, no funding, no more than occasional secretarial help. The group consisted of working teachers, not researchers.

We came together at the invitation of Michael Simons who was beginning his work at the English Centre in London. He says in his report:

> Ideally I wanted the group to come up with the kind of evidence that would focus teachers' attention on the ways in which each child develops his own different strategies for reading: that would reveal the short-comings of the notion that one method could provide the correct sequence for all slow, inexperienced readers.

Michael already knew that Elizabeth, Fiona, Judith, Steve and Vicky were trying, within the situations in their different schools, to concentrate on their pupils' individual strengths in approaching learning to read. Margaret was invited, by virtue of her responsibility for teaching English teachers about reading, to act as consultant and adviser to the group. For her, this was a challenge to meet teachers who were bringing as evidence their direct experience of classroom encounters in order to reflect upon it. Here is Steve's response to the invitation, recalled later:

I should stress that I was not looking for, and still less expecting to find any single method, or set of rules to be applied as a universal cure for 'poor readers' as though they were all suffering from some kind of disease, and that all that was needed was the right prescription. I knew only too well that no two pupils in this business are remotely alike, and that the recognition of an individual's difficulties and, much more importantly, his *strengths*, is always the key. Equally, however, I hoped to unearth something both generalizable and positive that might be helpful in practical terms.

and Vicky's:

I reacted with some slight surprise at being asked and some pleasure at the prospect of being involved with people working in the area I had come to be most interested in, 'the teaching of reading'. I felt I knew a little about children learning to read; there was always more to learn. The suggested longitudinal study seemed a way to explore further. In Mike Simons's first letter he said he felt there was an increasing and possibly dangerous bias towards the 'teaching of reading skills'. I was not sure of my position on this but was willing to pursue it.

It looked very simple: but we had already made some features of our starting point more relevant than others. We brought our teaching history with us, and on the whole we had been successful and skilful enough to want to help children to learn. We also had a fair amount to lose: for the first time we should be exposed to our judgments of ourselves and each other, especially when we listened to recordings of lessons. No matter how we tried to avoid it, the pupils would become 'special' to us. Although at the outset we knew each other only in the way of acquaintances with a common concern, we understood that we would change each other. We could not change the organizational structure of our schools, and poor readers have the worst records of attendance. There was no guarantee that we should see the task to the end. Our only safeguard was to take all of these things into account at the outset. We believe now that we did.

Our work together began on the 17 September 1975. We had a rough agenda, proposed by Michael Simons, our host, as a means of initiating our activities. It is interesting to look at it because it shows how a group may plan an operation as a logical sequence of inquiries and, at the same time, ignore what are clearly the realities of carrying it out. Each teacher in the group was to present a 'profile' of a pupil selected for special lessons. The subsequent lessons would be tape-recorded and brought to meetings for the group to analyse. A common undertaking would be our use of Goodman's analysis[10] — then little known in schools and not in common use — to heighten our awareness of the reading strategies and linguistic strengths of our readers. By listening together to our lessons we would discover effective learning and successful teaching, the appropriate alliance of the learners' cognitive styles and the teachers' choice of 'suitable' strategies and texts. The insistence on our need to discover what 'worked' was a good starting point because it avoided the common school practice of beginning with an assessment of pupils' failures. We were quite unrealistic in our estimation of how long it takes to prepare a reading profile, or what exactly is involved for working teachers to come to terms with the practical implications of an item of psycho-linguistic theory, especially if it is unfamiliar, and how possible it would be to detach a pupil from the social context, both inside school and outside it, if the studies were to have real significance.

Aware of her ambiguous role, her responsibility for the discussions and uncertain of the extent to which the teachers would include themselves in their accounts of lessons, Margaret invited the others to bring to the first meeting a piece of writing that described the pupil 'in any way that seemed significant' and to make notes on any activities in lessons other than English where the pupil's reading and writing showed weaknesses. This request also took little account of the realities of the school circumstances, although the terms of the request indicated a certain freedom in the matter of what might be required by the teachers.

Both Michael and Margaret ignored what they knew well from their familiarity with other working groups: sharing takes time. No new group reports confidently at a first meeting. It has to bring itself to life on a basis of common interest and concerns, mutual confidence and collaborative learning. Fortunately, as soon as we met we established the basic trust of colleagues very quickly. Each of us sensed the expertise of the others and knew that in this reservoir of experience lay skill and knowledge that we could tap and share. We acted on this awareness throughout the whole of our time together. It proved to be as important as any other understanding that came our way. It was the strongest, if unacknowledged, feature of the starting point.

We also had to learn how to express disagreement, how to tolerate alternative points of view, how to listen and when to talk; the usual conditions of working and belonging that every association of this kind has to sort out for itself. These things are as obvious as pens and note-books and taken for granted every time professional people meet to discuss things common to what they profess. But when the avowed competence is teaching-and-learning itself, then, the interactions of those involved are by no means as straightforward as they appear.

The group gathers

How did we begin after the first friendly exchanges? Margaret, anxious about her position as the only one without a pupil in school, began by asking for advice. She told the others that the next day she was due to send out her advanced students — very experienced teachers who had never taught anyone to read — to work with individual children in school. What should she tell them to do? The question: 'If you were me, what would you tell them to be sure to think about?' was designed to show that Margaret, designated as the group's consultant, trusted and respected the expertise of the others and was inviting them to show and share it. More hung on this than was apparent at the time. The thoughtful answers set the tone of the listening and talking that were to follow.

Fiona (tentatively): Talk to the child first . . .
Elizabeth: (after a pause): Don't expect the children to reveal every-
    thing to you the first time: Don't force them to read something
    hard and reveal their secrets to you. Takes a bit of time for them
    to trust you. I just let them look around for a bit.
Judith: If you go in armed with books it's a bit forbidding and they
    feel 'here we go again'.
Steve: Different kinds want different things: some want to avoid chit-
    chat and want to get down to work.
Vicky: I take in my own children's books and leave them. They go
    fast.

So we began, not with the requested profiles of the pupils, but with a discussion of what it would be good to share in the reading situation. It could be argued that we shirked the task we had come together to do. Or we can see, in these exchanges our own priorities as well as our natural uncertainties. The group is talking about itself. Almost casually, Steve said: 'They'll expect to be tested and it's good to dispel that idea,' as if that had been his own expectation about the meeting and what he had been asked to bring with him for inspection by the others. Judith said: 'Let them tell a favourite story.' Within ten minutes we were discussing what makes reading what it ought to be for children — the full enjoyment of real books, like Mervyn Peake's *Captain Slaughterboard Drops Anchor* that Judith was reading at the time.

As we listened, three years later, to that tape of our first meeting, we realized that we were making a definite statement about our approach to reading, our hopes for our pupils and the work of the group. We wanted reading to be the full, free, competent enjoyment of what had been created for pleasure as well as for instruction. This was not to deny all the other things that are consequent upon literacy, but, significantly, this came first.

In the confidence generated by this opening discussion we made a tentative discovery about what we would do for each other. Everyone except Margaret worked in a comprehensive school in an area designated 'the inner city', so there was a common understanding of the pupils' situations and an immediate agreement that we could not disregard the full social implications of our undertaking. Even if we had contemplated plucking the 'reading problem' out of the totality of the life of our pupil we could not have done so. We moved quickly to a subsequent awareness that we would become indirectly responsible for all the pupils to be studied. We would have to 'see' them in the school's set-up for teaching reading and, by implication, against the school's view of reading success and failure. So we understood, even on that first day, that whatever we longed to do we could not hope to move mountains — at most it might be desks and chairs, rooms or books — but we would validate as evidence what was common in our experience. Whatever we ideally wanted to do, in reality we should have to compromise with what was possible in the given situation. Certain kinds of research inquiry bring ideal conditions into being. Ours would not be one of these. So, another unmistakable feature of our starting point was the need to document whatever constituted reading environment in school.

By endorsing this as essential evidence we realized that we had made space in our investigation for whole areas of skill and knowledge, social, intellectual, experiential, both implicit and explicit, to which we were already committed. At first this was a matter of feeling rather than a statement, but just how these understandings ranged over the whole gamut of our reading studies becomes clearer as we proceed.

Some irrevocable decisions are made at the beginning of an enterprise, and some choices are made that make others impossible. There was an additional complication in that while pursuing investigations in a classroom, teachers instinctively protect their pupils as well as themselves. Our first intellectual engagement with what we called 'the obvious' drew us into a consideration of our own view of what we were about to embark upon.

In every undertaking that involves teaching and learning there is a cross-hatching of intentions and expectations, like the shading that gives depth to a drawing. If a teacher is to help a pupil to learn to read, she already has a view of the task ahead that stems from her experiences of earlier attempts or comparable situations. The pupil also comes to reading lessons with a view, however vague, of what reading is and what success might be like, a view shaped by previous experience and a liking for or fear of the teacher. After the first lesson encounter the teacher has a perspective that now includes her assumptions about the pupil's view of the task, which may or may not be a correct one. (For instance, the pupil may be tentative and the teacher thinks he is lazy.) By the same token, the pupil develops an idea of what he sees as the teacher's view of reading and what has to be learned if the teacher is to be satisfied. Sometimes the pupil modifies his understanding of what he thinks he should do in favour of what he imagines is expected of him. In this way, both pupil and teacher may operate a set of assumptions that are never made clear to the other person in the partnership. Where the accommodation of one viewpoint to the other is possible, success follows for both. The teacher is seen to teach, the pupil is seen to learn. Where the views of the task are in conflict, as, for example, when the child does what the teacher says without understanding what she means, confusion or bamboozlement results.

Almost none of this is ever made clear in detail. The teacher begins, the pupil responds. Where there is no estimable progress in the way the pupil behaves as a reader, the failure is attributed to the pupil's inability to understand what he is to do, or to the teacher's lack of expertise in showing what is to be done. If, however, some of these interactions could be examined, then what actually happened would be a different kind of evidence.[11] We agreed about this at the outset, as we saw that these reflexions about our work with pupils also applied to our operations as a group.

Having made some of this plain to ourselves, we should also have seen in the early stages what we had to learn more painfully later on. All our concern for our pupils, all our efforts on their behalf, had to bo directed to making ourselves redundant. The role of the reading teacher changes as the learner becomes expert. The successful culmination of reading lessons is the sharing of pleasure in texts that good readers do as naturally as breathing. Our view of the task we set ourselves had to include bringing our pupils' learning to read to the point where they would actually believe that they had taught themselves. To have said this to each other at one of our first meetings would have helped us later, but it was so obvious that we took it for granted, and then lost the insights it could have given us.

We continued to meet every third Monday, with gaps for the vacations. It is remarkable that no one missed more than one session in any term; we were never fewer than four at a meeting. The sessions were two hours long in term time, a little longer just before or after vacations. This was a realistic commitment in the lives of working teachers with families. We lost Fiona, for reasons that will emerge. The English Centre grew in importance in the lives of many teachers and became the publishing headquarters of an influential journal to which we contributed.[12] The Inner London Education Authority produced a new reading test.[13] The Assessment of Performance Unit of the DES went ahead to monitor reading standards nationally. Our pupils moved to their last years in school and left as we were putting our work together. More reading studies appeared.

You have only our word for what we learned; some of it will seem all too obvious. We cannot construe our activity as 'successful' in the somewhat simple terms we began with, but we can share some insights that, in teaching, are a special kind of knowledge, and too little regarded. The first of these is about the working of the group and how that helped to maintain the efforts of its members while they came to terms with the ways in which their actual school situations restrained their best efforts and intentions on behalf of their pupils. What a school as a community takes for granted is sometimes the greatest hindrance to any attempt to make learning to read a profitable undertaking for its pupils. We shall now explain how we found this to be the case.

3

The compromise

There is no mystique about remedial education, nor are its methods
different from those employed by successful teachers everywhere.
The essence of remedial work is that the teacher is able to give additional time and resources to adapting these methods to the individual child's needs and difficulties.

A Language for Life

When we began our investigation we agreed that we should keep as full
and faithful an account of the reading lessons as we could when they
occurred. No special provision was to be made for the teacher or the
learner in the school's normal conduct of affairs; no change in the time-
table or the daily routine of events. Nevertheless, our very awareness
that we were now to look in a detailed and particular way at our work
with one pupil threw into relief two things: the reading situation in
the school as a whole, and the ways by which pupils are chosen for
'special' lessons.

Every school has a view of literacy, not always explicit. The nature
of the provisions: lessons, books, visiting experts, materials, announces
the policy, the theoretical substructure, the concern of the institution
for reading and writing. In England the school is free to devise its own
arrangements. Heads, inspectors and advisers may discuss what must be
done for the children who need help in 'basic subjects' by referring to
the timetable and allocation of staff, while those responsible for teaching these pupils concern themselves with the provision of 'resources'. In
one school a visitor may pass a teacher sitting with a small group in
a cloakroom and report that reading lessons are given in difficult
conditions. In another a peripatetic expert may look in the book cup-
board, find very few special books, and tell the headmaster that she/he
cannot function without adequate material. The teacher who is asked
to 'help with reading' may have her group swollen by the children of

'travellers' and the intermittent attenders, as well as the rowdies from the class of the probationary teacher or the almost-retiring deputy head. Her concern is simply to 'cover' lessons. There are teachers for whom a small space, insufficient material and occasional pupils are no hindrance because they need no excuse, and there are schools where every possible provision seems to be made yet pupils make little headway. We know that children's progress is not concomitant with educational expenditure. Yet some things make a difference.

In facing outward towards the community, the school announces its view of literacy, at least partly, by the allocation of place, time, people and resources to bring it about. The school library, the provision and care of books, for example, tell a great deal about the school's view of reading. An awareness amongst the staff as a whole of the linguistic implications of the presence of second language learners in the school, the discussion of a language policy with regard to the total curriculum, reflect publicly the nature, extent and mode of these concerns. In the same way, the presence or absence of a remedial department and the work that is done there is a kind of informal statement about the needs of certain children and what the school sees as important to do for them. There is always a compromise between what is possible in the school situation and what essential for the pupils' growth. Schools differ chiefly in the ways in which they make this compromise.

The teachers in our group maintained throughout a strong loyalty to their schools. Their criticisms stemmed from a concern to explain to colleagues, parents and other ratepayers the liberating effects of literacy. Our group discussions were not simply a collective grouse about the inadequacy of understanding shown by others, nor a series of complaints about working conditions. We explained to each other how our schools made provision for reading support so that by comparing the ways in which lessons were arranged we might discover what part the organization of the school played in the success or failure of the teaching and learning.

The Bullock Report refers to three organizational patterns in secondary schools: there are *remedial departments*, where a special curriculum may be devised. Some 'slow learners' may spend much of their school time in special units which also cater for those in temporary difficulty. *Withdrawal groups* are arranged for pupils who need extra practice, usually in mathematics or reading. In a few schools there are *reading specialists in normal lessons*, a provision the Report was concerned to extend. In our schools, those who were to be given individual attention were withdrawn from other lessons. No one thought this was ideal. Our withdrawal groups had very little in common beyond the fact that the pupil came out of a class lesson for a reading lesson. Each context had its own particularities and these we had to envisage and understand.

Fiona

Fiona was the first to put us into her picture. She read to us from a prepared statement. As you read it now, you will better understand the content and nature of our early sessions together. Her secondary school is in south London; there were 1,800 boys on the roll at that time.

'It's pretty complicated. There is a remedial department which caters for boys in the first and second years. Two classes of twenty boys in each. Pupils are selected for remedial training [here Fiona's intonation rises] on the basis of their primary school profiles and an interview in the summer term before they come to secondary school. They are given a Holborn reading test at that interview.[1] There is no head of the remedial department since the previous head retired last year and the post hasn't been advertised. There are four teachers in the department, none of whom has any special training in remedial work.

The boys stay in their own remedial classrooms for the majority of lessons and are taught by the same teacher. When these boys enter their third year their literacy becomes the responsibility of the English Department. They now have to change their class base from a comparatively small building which houses only the 11–13-year-olds to the overcrowded main school building. They have to get used to many more teachers. In an attempt to accommodate these extra 'remedial' boys three teachers from the English Department have a special responsibility, so-called, for them — that's two class teachers and a back-up part-time teacher (that's me). These boys have ten 35-minute periods of English per week (last year it was fifteen) compared with the five or six periods that other classes have. As there are far more boys in school with reading and writing problems than this system can accommodate, in 1973 we started an experimental withdrawal system called 'Room 42'. This now has three teachers working for a total of thirty periods a week, one of which is me, with an official minimum of four boys in a group. Frequently two teachers are timetabled to be in Room 42 at the same time. It's quite a small room. Candidates for Room 42 have in the past been selected on the recommendation (or vilification) of their English teacher, but this tended to turn the room into a substitute sanctuary because it was found that teachers were far more likely to recommend a behaviour problem with mild reading difficulties than a boy with severe reading difficulties who could remain unnoticed in a large class.

So this year we started testing all the first year boys whose reading ages – on whatever previous test had been used – was eight or under at interview in an attempt to cope with worst cases first. This isn't very successful either, as many of these boys have improved over the summer holidays and are nine on the Neale Analysis, which we used.

Boys in the Remedial Department in the first two years are not eligible for withdrawal to Room 42. The two systems work quite separately. But those same boys may become eligible in the third year, and often do. One of our chief problems, once a boy has been put on the list for Room 42, is where to put the priorities. We're hopelessly oversubscribed. It seems most practical, in theory, to concentrate our energies on first year reading problems where we have best chances of success. Higher up the school the social problems of boys whose reading difficulties haven't been dealt with earlier make them into the kind of special cases we don't feel justified in ignoring, even if the improvement is minimal, because we found sometimes just the attitude of boys improves after they've succeeded in admitting that they have a severe reading problem instead of concealing it. Once names are decided, the boy's form teacher is asked to broach the subject, and if the boy is willing he's withdrawn from a lesson to do the Neale Analysis of Reading Ability,[2] and on the basis of *that* reading age and comprehension age boys are booked in two at a time. Emphasis is placed on inviting them to come for extra help in reading and we wouldn't insist if they hated the idea, but most of them enjoy the attention.

With one or two, the testing has to be left for a few weeks or abandoned because they refused the test situation. The Neale Analysis seems to be quite a happy test for them because it starts with questions like, "How many brothers and sisters have you got?"'

Vicky: Are they withdrawn for reading. Is that the crux?
Fiona: Well, that we try to do. Last year it was more a case of behaviour problems. The priorities were rather mixed.
M: I don't think any of us ever work in ideal circumstances. There are things in yours that could be worse. What actually makes it workable as it is?
F: A lot of things could be worse. You mean it's quite reasonable?
M: Not absolutely. But no one has a situation ideally designed for work of this kind. Yet your pupils want to come. Is it the people, the sanctuary notion?
F: We've got scraps of carpet, a few soft chairs, two plants and two gerbils and we try to make the room as relaxed as possible and unlike a classroom. It's treated as a special occasion to go. Most people seem to want to come out of the great mass of kids. It works astonishingly well. We all enjoy teaching up there.
S: What do you withdraw them from — what the kids want to miss?
F: We try not to take them out of maths, metal work or anything they particularly enjoy.

The discussion continued, overtly about the difficulty of running two separate teaching groups in one room. But other problems were emerging: *who* goes for special lessons; how the arrangements for helping a pupil who, for one reason or another, cannot be herded along with the mass of pupils, have to be designed and operated *against* the pattern of the school day. To teach a pupil in a small group or individually is to work out a compromise with a system based on the teaching of classes. Special help is not denied to any who need it; it is, however, special.

As we saw Fiona's pupil moving against a background of 1,799 other boys on his way to a room at the top of a large building where there were gerbils, plants and three teachers who liked teaching and were sceptical about reading tests, we began to understand that the organization of reading lessons carries many messages. Fiona showed how, when boys are disruptive *and* they cannot read, the school's solution is to give them extra lessons and to keep them out of the mainstream of school activity. The teacher's, Fiona's, response is to lessen the pressure of school, to change the quality of the environment, if only a little. Then the pupil's behaviour changes before anything has been done about his literacy. ('You'd behave in Room 42.') Thus, Fiona contends, if the messages conveyed by Room 42 were part of the school's view of reading and the teaching of literacy, segregation would be unnecessary, and perhaps all those who needed help, and not simply the badly behaved, would get some. The problem of negotiating the return of the exiles to their class group would then be solved.

All of this, our first encounter with other learning problems such as tests, the teachers' responsibility for diagnosing difficulty, the 'normal' standard of reading required for work in an 'ordinary' lesson, and the difficulty of persuading our colleagues not to solve behavioural problems by excluding pupils from learning situations, came out after Fiona's presentation of the context of her work. Here is part of the discussion that followed:

Steve: Do you go by what the kid wants to miss?
Fiona: No, we don't. We try not to take them out of something they're particularly fond of . . . or fairly basic things, like maths. I don't take them out of metalwork.
S: What did you say about the size of the groups? What happens . . .
F: In practice, we're supposed to have a group of not less than four. . . . I do have three sometimes. But there's someone else in the room too.
Vicky: Unless you're working together . . . is it difficult? If you're doing something at one end . . .
F: If someone's doing something with a tape recorder, it can bring problems. Mostly it works fairly well. They want to get on with what they are doing and they concentrate pretty hard. You can have two groups . . . we've divided the room with a locker block so you can get into the shadows a bit.
S: How long is that period of time? Is it a lesson limit?
F: I don't think the concentrated struggle can go on for a double period. . . . I have to break it, with conversation about the last lesson, what they did at the weekend . . .
S: But they are officially with you for a double period?
F: Yes, seventy minutes . . . they come for a double period once a week . . .
Eliz: And always the same group?
F: Well, I switch them around now and then, according to the way the relationship develops. If something bad happens, I change it.
E: It's good to keep them together . . .
F: Sometimes they help each other quite a bit.
Judith: Were you suggesting that there are children in the first and second forms who could do with the help you give in Room 42 who don't get it because they are supposed to be getting help in these remedial classes?

F: It isn't so much that . . . they do in the remedial forms get more
reading help because there are only twenty compared with thirty
in ordinary classes and their lessons are concentrated on their
problems in the basic skills. But it does mean that because the two
systems are run separately that they come into the third year, and
we've had nothing to do with them before and they are completely
dark horses. They emerge as behaviour problems with all those other
changes they are facing. We've got a galloping problem before we
know where we are.

J: How do you see that being resolved?

F: The two systems – there should be one system that should work
throughout the school. But I couldn't say what it should be. I'm
extremely muddled as to the virtues and drawbacks of withdrawal
systems. There *are* big drawbacks, I know that. Some kids are
positively disadvantaged by being taken out of lessons all the time.

V: But if they *seem* to be in remedial classes . . .

F: Some children find that to have their day disrupted from the rest
of the class . . .

V: I find they get into a rhythm. They are disrupted at the beginning
. . . then they discover it's *their* time, it's when *they* come.

F: It might be interesting to try a withdrawal system throughout the
school . . . is that what you do?

J: No, we have the same system, with remedial streams . . . all the way
through. The withdrawals come from the mixed ability streams
. . . [Judith breaks off] .

M: asks, Have you a picture in your head of where you will meet the
character who walks on to that scene?

J (continues): I have a vision of it as a place where people are glad to
go, for a rest from other demands being made on them. Teachers
always feel that pupils should be working for forty minutes of
every lesson. It's difficult for us to accept that a rest is important.

F: But you do feel a pressure because you seem to see them so little . . .

M: The pressure then is on the teacher rather than the pupil . . .

F: I hope it is, to a certain extent . . .

M: It's tricky. You feel you can't let them relax too much because of
what has to be done, and they're so thankful that they're not meeting what look like arbitrary demands, especially in fields where they
can't operate satisfactorily, that this meeting is important . . . let's
think about it . . .

J: That links up with the business of the children coming because
they have admitted their problems and they don't have to keep

up a front . . .

F: There are some children who will come and refuse tests and take a
   few weeks until they admit they have problems. They've spent the
   previous years running errands for the teacher and doing anything
   that has kept them out of the actual reading and working situation . . .

M: One of the things we have to remind ourselves about experienced
   readers is that they take a rest from time to time. But that's easy
   for them because they aren't afraid that when they start again they
   will have forgotten how to do it. Look too at the very successful
   young readers. When they are reading, they actually get a rest from
   adult interference. Those who can read are in a private world. Adults
   are so happy about it they leave them alone . . . they don't have to
   meet other social demands. The non-reader always has to meet
   social demands because he hasn't the legitimate excuse of living in
   a secondary world . . .

J: I've been going into first forms this week. Children who can read
   take a book from the class library and *know* that as long as they go
   on reading no one's going to come and nag them. They're free, as
   you say. If a child can't read, he's going to get a book and pretend.
   Then someone's going to sit beside him, or his attention is going to
   wander because the book holds nothing for him and he's going to
   be exposed again and vulnerable to an adult's nagging.

M: Even subtly, especially in the one-to-one situation, where the pressure is intense. I'm devoted to the idea of one-to-one, but Fiona
   is making me think about the small group, or the pair, where the
   pressure is lifted a bit . . .

J: Could we sell the idea that in learning to read the pupil would be
   relieved?

V: That's why I feel passionately about reading. It was my great escape
   from adults in childhood . . . it was the great let-out. It's a driving
   force in my keenness . . .

J: You get praise too. But you've lost that anxiety.

M: We'll be back to this. People emphasise useful doing and getting
   from reading. But what's wrong with self-indulgence too? There's a
   kind of reading that goes on early that isn't like reading at any other
   time and we know that's what these kids have missed . . .

At this moment the group is drawn back into a discussion of their own
pleasure in reading. A concentrated stretch of listening, in this case to
the problems of organization as described by Fiona, always brings the

group back to a heightened awareness of what the inexperienced pupil is missing. It is as if the most important issue is the redefinition of the intensity of the pleasure, the difference of this kind of experience from anything else which keeps before us the reasons why we will persist, whatever the odds, to persuade children to share it. When Vicky then relates that her daughter won't come to tea because, 'My eyes are stuck to the page', we all understand, and we know that this is precisely what our pupils have never experienced.

Fiona's summary of her situation makes the conditions of the compromise quite clear. First, the school demands that pupils should learn to read, but offers restricted means. Then, the help is divided between the responsibilities of 'remedial' teachers -- in this case for two years only – and the English teachers who are responsible for the long-lasting failures. Fiona would like the pupils in difficulty to be fully helped as soon as possible. By their third year in the school the problem has become more complicated. She wonders if a more unified approach to the problem would help. Like all good teachers, she will make the best of an inadequate situation. Compare at this stage the provision made for reading ('some bits of carpet, a few soft chairs') with a science laboratory, a business studies room, a geography room, a music room. The notion of giving inexperienced readers a comfortable place to read seems to pander to the notion that these children are 'having it soft', when that is exactly what a real reader would expect. There is no especial virtue in a hard chair for reading, except that it makes the puritanical onlooker agree that the reader is then 'working' hard.

Elizabeth

Elizabeth talks from her notes.

'It's an eight-form entry – mixed – basically unstreamed. We test all the first year entrants with the Young Reading Test[3] which has a low top score, and very easy beginning part, so there won't be anyone who can't score. It's a written test so they can do it in their classes . . . and having done that we'll take about 100 of the 240 first-year kids. Grouping them, we've got fourteen groups in the first year; it varies from a group of four that comes every day, to groups which come only twice a week for 'practice'. These have sixteen kids with two teachers. In the second year we've got about fifty kids. Third year, I'm not sure, about thirty-five. And we've got one group of fourth years.

   We've got two full-time teachers and three part-timers. There isn't a remedial department. It's all done in the English Department . . . we've got one very big classroom which we all work in. We've tried to arrange it like a primary classroom so that it's all in corners and areas . . . and armchairs . . . and carpet. We have the children for – some come once a day, the others have three lessons a week. They can come out of any lesson – we won that concession, but I try not to take them out of practical lessons because they do really enjoy that, also I try not to take them out of maths. . . .

   Perhaps it's better if you ask questions. I'll know what you want to know.'

Judith: Have you always . . . not had a remedial stream?

Elizabeth: Never since I've been there . . . they got rid of it quite a while ago.

J: And that . . . does that have full staff approval?

E: I believe there are mutters in corners, that it would be better if we got rid of those children we can't cope with.

J: What do you mean 'got rid of'? Into a remedial stream?

E: Yes, there are people who think it isn't their job to teach these children. But on the whole I think most people do agree with us. The Head would very much oppose going back to a streamed situation so it's not likely to happen. I find that the big advantage is – and I discovered this when I went on a course for remedial teachers – if you are in the remedial department you are under the care and protection, if you can call it that, of the psychological services, whereas if you're in the English department you're in the charge of the English inspectorate, which is a better thing to be. The school psychologists seem to be so obsessed with tests. On this course I went to, they said that if you came across a child who couldn't read you could give him this battery of tests, which are fourteen in number . . .

M: It's complicated . . . that implies a philosophy of defectology . . . that a child's learning is made up of skills based on how your eyes and ears practise looking and hearing.

E: The advantage of being in an English department is that you tend to be talking about reading . . . and although I'm not suggesting that all of our department is devoted, radical, keen on working-class culture or anything . . . the basic ideas are there. People know what they're talking about when you talk about children reading their own stories, and reading, and that kind of thing. They see

reading as pleasurable, as a whole activity and not something that
you break up into little bits to practise.

M: What about that?

J: I must say that I think this is how — what we're teaching them for.
It gets rid of Fiona's problem of not seeing the children in the first
two years.

E: A remedial department suggests that a child is defective in everything . . .

F: That's just ridiculous . . .

M: You can see . . . it has an interesting history . . . there was a time
when the comprehensive schools began, and a wider range of children came to secondary schools, for the first time people who taught
in grammar schools found themselves faced with children who
couldn't read. They thought that this needed an expertise they
lacked. The people who had, in other schools, taken on slow learners
and non-readers, who understood the need for special help, got
specialist status as remedial teachers, by becoming specialists in teaching the backward, the retarded, the slow learners. The people who
taught these teachers were, for the most part, psychologists. These
teachers had to become specialists in the problems that the subject
specialists didn't want to know about. . . . It was good that they got
recognition in this way. But now it's more complicated. 'Remedial'
suggests that something is to be remedied, and when you discuss it
with them you are told that the child needs remedying . . . or the
parents, or the home. But there's recent evidence in the journals that
this is changing.[4]

Vicky: I can't decide about it either because — um — we have withdrawal groups. It is all right not to have the children in remedial
groups if the school is well-organized and well run. But those who
are not very confident find it difficult to read, write and talk in
class. Our school is formally run; not terribly imaginative. There's
a big turnover of teachers. So these children are just swept along
with their class . . . not only do they go to different classes throughout the day, but throughout the year there are teachers leaving and
new ones coming in. . . . If you could only find them a quiet place
with someone caring for them and looking after them responding to
them. I think they largely get left out at the moment. I worry about
their needs.

E: I'm talking about just one child in each class . . . whom you can
hardly find a book for and who can hardly sit down and write a
word on his own. About eight children a year.

V: There's a stigma when you have a remedial class. There's a stigma when you have a withdrawal group. You lose on both. Which do you lose on more?

Steve: Flexibility is the key feature of the withdrawal scheme. If the rest of the school is streamed or not, the remedial department is run for half of the timetable and the children are stuck there. It probably requires something rather momentous to haul a kid out or put another one in . . . whereas with withdrawal, you can say 'perhaps he should come out for a bit into my class . . .'

E: Or you have a flexibility which says 'if you're doing something you like and are getting on well with you needn't come to reading until it's finished'. That's what I like.

M: But you are in a team with a philosophy: this feeds into what you want to do. Vicky's point is a relevant one. If the kids have no one else except the person who stays fixed whatever else sweeps on, there they have at least a sheet anchor.

S: After a great working party produced a paper *we* had it all worked out – it hasn't happened – although it was voted for overwhelmingly – that the children should have the bulk of their teaching in the lower school with one person. . . . Mornings always in the tutor-group base with the tutor who would teach a given range of subjects. The change from primary school to secondary school, the size of the school, the rushing round the building . . . it's still a plan. It hasn't happened yet.

Elizabeth's situation is felt to be a good one, although everyone understands the kind of compromise she too is asked to make. She sees the success of the enterprise in her school as the English teachers having achieved the agreement that mixed ability teaching should remain just that, despite the 'muttering in corners'. The flexibility of the withdrawal pattern is praised, but no one suggests that what is flexible for Elizabeth is desirable for all. For uninitiated teachers this pattern may look like the sloppiness of 'unstructured' teaching, especially if a pupil can miss a reading lesson. Judith wants to know most about the situation because it seems to be nearest to what she would like for herself. But no one is deceived about how the child views the situation. Extra help carries with it the stigma of failure. The compromise is, one must do what one can despite this. For all its shortness, Elizabeth's report has some fundamental statements. Above all she feels supported by her headmaster and her head of department. One of Margaret's colleagues who had visited Elizabeth at work, said 'That place must help a lot to make the lessons good.'

Vicky

Vicky talks next about her all-girls school:

'A five form entry school ... well, it's really a four form entry because one form didn't materialize this year ... four forms spread across five forms. 90 ... so, the classes are like groups. I think a sympathetic ear is leant to us at divisional office ... there's no remedial class at all. The way the pupils for reading lessons are selected ... there's a first year mistress and the head of a local infant school ... she does group work, like I do, and because she knows about primary schools, she goes round the different primary schools. They have a look at them in school to see if they will need help later on in secondary school. I don't quite know how they do this ... they get some profiles ... they talk to the teachers and get some opinions, and so when the children come to our school in September there is a list ... a proportion of the children are on a list ... and in the first or second week we call them in, in groups of about five. We do it very informally because she (the infant head) doesn't believe in tests and I'm not sure that I do really, either ... less and less anyway. The children select a book from her room and sit down and write something about their holidays ... and then we call them up and hear them read and look at their writing ... and that's all ... that's how we select them.'

E: It's just the ones you've already got on your list?
V: Yes.
J: Just to recap. That list is made after the visit to the primary school?
V: The head of the coming first year, and this ex-head of an infant school ...
J: You need not necessarily have seen their primary school profile?
V: No, we haven't seen them at all. She might have seen them, but I doubt it very much, in fact I think she does it off the cuff. She's a great believer in her instinct and experience and so on ... she likes to take ...
S: We have about seventy or eighty primary schools. I wondered what kind of an operation this was ...
V: I think it's about twelve or fifteen ... She thinks her experience as an infant teacher is helpful ... she knows about the very early stages of reading, and I just take children. I don't mind. She takes the hard core ...

What happens is that after a year, if she hasn't got anywhere with them, I take them on in the second year. I quite enjoy this. I've got a funny sort of mixture. In the first year they seem not to be so bad. . . . I might be able to feed them back later . . . in the second year I have a mixture of very poor readers and some who are ticking over. It varies tremendously. Then we do get recommendations by individual teachers (remember it's a small school) who come up and say they're worried about so-and-so. We say, well you know, I've got this group and it's full, and you go and talk to another teacher . . . and there's one other thing that's rather disastrous. We are in fact three remedial teachers – there's a Polish lady who's been here for a number of years, and . . . she's retired and teaches part-time to supplement her pension. She's rather out of touch with . . . you know . . . methods, and she has a strong Polish accent. She's officially a remedial teacher. She'll only take children who 'want to learn'. In fact, she's carried by the school. There's no other way of describing it . . . because no one would like to distress her. Coming to the school is her only contact with the outside world. That's a fact of life. . . . This is another way they're fed in. English or Humanities teachers just come up and suggest so-and-so. . . . The maths department say they mustn't come out of maths . . . English and French are the chief subjects for withdrawal . . . occasionally other things. Not DS or games.

F: Do they mind missing French?

V: The French department is so relieved not to have them around . . .

F: We have some boys in the fifth form who are absolutely miserable at always having missed modern languages.

V: We're always torn on this one . . . that's the problem of the withdrawal group . . . what they're missing . . . the whole school situation is the problem. They're just reluctant to come to school.

Vicky's teaching benefits from the close contact that is possible in a small school: a word at lunch-time, the passing round of good work, advice sought and given on the spot. Vicky's base is a prefabricated classroom in the playground which she greatly enjoys. It provides the relaxed atmosphere of Room 42 and other quiet corners. The overriding concern is, are the right children being withdrawn? In the depressed inner city area where her school serves a multicultural and multiethnic neighbourhood where transience is common and many genuine Londoners are not white-skinned, the teachers talk about the threat of closure or amalgamation with another school and accept that the children have low ability and what they call 'little motivation'. School refusal is common. 'A heavy bottom end' is a usual description of classes to be taught. Vicky sees the pupils' depressed view of their capabilities emphasized by the tacit responses of their teachers. She knows that collaborative help would make a difference so that some of her compromises would be unnecessary. For example, her tandem operation with the 'expert' headteacher who takes 'the real non-readers' makes Vicky's position an invidious one, yet this good forceful lady needs her specialist status too. The idea that the person who teaches beginners should teach the failures is a compromise with unexamined assumptions. Vicky does not want to compromise with the school's low expectation of the pupils' success. The situation improved when a new head of department changed the depressed view which both the teachers and the children had of themselves.

Steve

Steve now takes up the tale:

'There is no remedial department in the school. What remedial work there is, if you want to call it that, is organized for English by the English department and in Maths by the Maths department. Just in passing – the Maths people do it by having extra teachers into lessons – we do it by withdrawal. The organization of the intake is now completely mixed ability, 11-form entry, completely mixed groups so there's no question of children "going down". Apart from withdrawal to us there is only one possible reason in the whole school for any child being away from the family group and that's if they go to the sanctuary unit, which is sort ... of ... twenty kids out of the whole school, so these are fairly exceptional – emotional problems or whatever ... um ... There are one or two premisses underlying the rationale for the way we do things. One is that the children should, as far as possible, be with their tutor-set so that if they need any extra help they should be withdrawn for not too great a length of time, and that in the time that they are withdrawn they should have as much individual help as possible ... and also that there are a lot of resources around waiting to be tapped for teaching the children.

Involved in the scheme are most of the teachers in the English department – about fifteen of them, and about twenty outside adult helpers, many of whom are parents of children in the school, and about forty to fifty sixth formers, so it's a teaching force of about eighty which administratively is an enormous headache: my headache. That's why I'm here, really. It's my particular function to timetable and organize all this.

As far as possible a withdrawal group is taught by the class's own English teacher, and this is always true of the first year. So, to take the first year, each of the eleven classes has five periods of ordinary class English a week, and a bit of drama which may or may not be taught by their own English teacher . . . and also four withdrawal periods for the half-dozen or so children that the teacher feels he'd like to give additional help to. A group of about six then. But the teacher is also helped in that by at least one or two volunteer adult helpers, and one or two sixth formers, so that the teaching is no more than one to two, and is often one to one. As the year goes on the sixth formers fall off as their exams come along. . . . The basic rationale is that it doesn't have to be a reading expert, or even a trained teacher to help these children in the majority of cases . . . that any sympathetic, caring, relatively grown-up person with a bit of time to spare, prepared to get to know a child . . . see him reasonably regularly, if only once a week perhaps, can do something useful. It isn't specially reading . . . we call it "Extra English", It can be reading, writing, or spelling, whatever the individual child comes to get help for. In the group situation it's rare that we're going to be together "reading round". It's all off in ones and twos, doing whatever the teacher thinks is appropriate . . .'

Fiona: Do they, sorry, get the same helper, or sixth former every time they come?

S: They get the same *teacher*. The teacher is with the class. This is fundamental. There's a teacher with six in the room, four times a week — thirty-five minutes at a time. This individual attention happens to be intense, so we don't withdraw for double periods. . . . This means they're only out of four single lessons a week. In the second and third year it's only three single lessons. But I would argue that because they're getting very intensive individual attention and probably are having to work very hard, that's long enough . . .

V: Because of the settling-in time, and so on, it's really a bit shorter . . . meeting your tutor and adjusting . . .

S: It takes a week or two for anyone who starts off just by coming in to latch on to a particular child and get something regular ongoing with that particular one . . .

V: It seems very short to me. You don't find it short?

S: I don't think it is, actually, I mean . . . very often that thirty-five minutes will be spent in three different activities. If you are hearing a child read one-to-one, or are reading to him, or whatever, taking it in turns . . .

V: Is there time for a child finding a book and reading to himself for a bit . . .

S: That's what can happen . . . well . . .

V: I don't know, it seems to me . . . well, anyway, I always find it very short.

S: It's a question of what you're used to. I would find a double period, especially with young lads, very, very long . . .

F: How much control is there by the teacher in charge over the methods used to teach them?

S: The teacher in charge is the one who sees the child not only for those four withdrawal lessons, but all the English lessons as well. . . . The lesson will start and the teacher will say: 'Mrs X will you take John for today', and, 'John has been reading this book. He's got to such and such a page. Perhaps you'd like to finish the book with him and then he might like to write something for you when he's finished.' Very often, it's surprising . . . how people who are non-teachers get into the swing of it and can simply be left. I honestly can say to a lot of them, 'Mrs X will you take John for today?' and know that the time will not be badly spent. I don't believe, in fact, also, that if he . . . especially in the initial stages when Mrs X doesn't know John very well, that if they just talk to each other . . . for the first session that isn't a waste of time. In school the one thing that is lacking for any child is . . . relaxed time and a relaxed atmosphere in which to talk to an adult.

F: Is there any opportunity for the helpers and sixth formers and teachers to talk about any methods they might have in common?

S: Yes, we have meetings: we've got one on Wednesday that will involve . . . the teachers and the adult helpers . . . we have had meetings to which the sixth formers were invited as well. Their free time marks what they can do. We have their meeting at the beginning of term when they come to me and say I'm free at such and such a time for private study. They give up two, or at the most, four, of these periods to work with younger children. I behave a bit like a computer trying to fit them all in with other children . . . with a class from their own house, if that's possible, as they might already know the younger ones . . . and that sort of thing. It doesn't always work. The sixth formers are in a very good position. Some of them are very good at it and they're in a good position to build up an informal but constructive relationship with a child just because they're not in the position of teacher. The adults who come in do the same, because they can be more . . . whatever figure is appropriate, as opposed to a teacher-figure.

J: How do you select the children who are taught?

S: In the case of a withdrawal group that is taught by the English teacher, it is now solely up to the class teacher to recognize if there are poor readers, writers, in their English class, and take them into their own withdrawal group. But mostly English teachers get together to discuss individual cases, what's needed. That's where it becomes administratively difficult in a big school . . . even with quite a big department. It's all done by teachers in the English department who know each other well enough anyway for this to work. And it does, just about, although it takes some time to get going at the beginning of the year.

S: We used to have a mass reading test at the beginning of the year. Last year was my first year at the job, and we had it — the Schonell test — it produced a lot of ridiculous results. So we abolished it and everybody felt they could easily locate, within a couple of weeks of the first year arriving, or pinpoint accurately whoever it was who ought to have extra help. That was flexible enough for it to be changed if they discovered somebody who had slipped through the net, or who had arrived late . . . they can come straight into the group. There's no . . . sort of . . . official borders — like you've got [to Judith] about who's going to deal with this child and why. There's only this one system . . . they go into the extra English groups they need . . .

The impression left by Steve was that here was a school, known to have considerable social problems and every disadvantage of the inner city, where a large department had mobilized a more general awareness of the needs of pupils with reading and writing difficulties so that the larger community of parents and Margaret's seconded teacher-students from the Institute could be involved, and the sixth formers used their special kind of confidence to break down the barriers that so quickly grow between the experienced reader and the others. Steve carried forward the point that had been growing in importance in everyone's mind since Fiona had talked of carpets and gerbils, and

Elizabeth had indicated that a certain loosening of constraints is necessary for this kind of teaching. The context is crucial. A pupil does not automatically become a different person because he goes into a different classroom, but the way he is construed, assumed to be, when he is learning to read, can in fact be backed up by the environment and the reception he meets when he goes for 'Extra English'. If the walls declare his incompetence, with their vowel charts, so kindly meant, the pupil gets the message. If lots of people are helping in a co-operative enterprise, some of the stigma must go. See how often the claim is made that only when the pupil can relax will the business of being a reader begin properly.

Judith

All through these statements it was clear that Judith was uneasy, even angry, and the moment of her declaration was more than a piece of simple reporting. The school in which she teaches part-time is in an area richly settled by what the Bullock Report calls 'families of overseas origin'. Indeed, the white children are now in the minority. Most of the pupils were born in London. The school has a reputation for good innovative teaching and pastoral concern, so much so that the dispute we are now to document could have arisen only where teachers take their responsibilities seriously.

The contraposition of the remedial departments of school and the English departments is a consequence of mixed-ability teaching and a swing away from the hospitalization of low achievers in specially segregated rooms. It threatens the specialism of the remedial teachers, as Margaret described above and brings into sharp contrast certain methods of teaching reading. In Judith's school the remedial department has defined its role clearly. This is reflected in the organization of the school. The operations of the English department, based on a different view of what reading is and is for, challenge both this view and this role.

Judith recounts the situation from her point of view. She knows she will be heard sympathetically, that she has no need to overstress her position; indeed, her tone on the recording is measured and, where she is explaining the school's organizational pattern, unemphatic, as if she were concerned to stand back in order to be fair and detached. But, as will become clear, she disapproves of the constraints that are put upon her and the position she is forced into.

There is no need to ask if Judith's account is 'correct'. This is the situation as she sees it and her response is to what she sees. She was to have begun, as the others have done, with a description of how the school meets its obligations to slow learning children and inexperienced readers. A meeting between the English department and the remedial department had been arranged, and we had promised Judith that she should tell us what happened at the meeting. We had actually believed that a dialogue between the two departments would have offered a fruitful exchange of ideas. We were wrong.

The account comes from the tape of the group meeting. 'They' is used often to refer to the teachers in the remedial department.

M: We were going to hear from Judith about her encounter with the remedial department. Isn't that right?
J: I was going to. But it didn't take place.
M: So it has yet to happen?
J (very formally): I was refused admittance. Can you credit that? I came in on my day off because the meeting was on a Thursday, which is the day I don't teach . . . and . . . I went up with my head of department and . . . we were told that . . . it had been arranged between the remedial department and J.G. [Judith's department head]. It would be improper – I think that was the word used – certainly, 'difficult' to include me.
E: Did she [i.e. J's department head] go in?
J: She went in . . . the whole point was to discuss the English department's subjective assessment of the children in their classes and the remedial department's results of their tests. As I was going to take some of the children, it was very pertinent that I should be there . . . and as I was involved in the classes in the first year, I was asked to be 'on call'. I spent the whole morning in the staffroom waiting to be summoned to give my comments on selected children – which I was in the end. The whole thing was hugely disappointing and very upsetting, really. Such a . . .
V: Battle lines were drawn . . .
J: Such a non-productive way to go about things. So nothing came of that . . .
M: Are the children in the middle of this kind of fight?
J: Yes, very much so.
M: How do you think it affects them?
J: Well, there are two children in particular whose form teacher and English teachers didn't see eye-to-eye on. The remedial department

tested those two along with everyone else and decided that they were to be brought from the form to which they had been allotted, down to the remedial department. The English teachers strove to keep them. But because the form teacher had decided they were trouble-makers, she backed the remedial department, and we, the English department, lost. This means I lose touch with them because I'm not allowed to withdraw children from the remedial department. I can withdraw from only the ordinary streams. One of these two children was the one I'd decided to do my study of and had already started taping. He was going to be marvellous because his voice on the tape was clear and he was a really bubbly child who talked all the time. Although I had surreptitiously tried to get hold of him, it was just too difficult. Isn't it unbelievable?

S: Absolutely.

M: So that means, remediation is ordered on grounds of behavioural difficulties?

S: Effectively . . .

J: If they are difficult children, and enough members of staff complain about their behaviour, whether they are considered to be 'bright under-achievers' or whatever word is used, they will go into a class of backward children. In fact, we have been very unsuccessful in asking for children the remedial department have wanted to take out of ordinary classes.

M: Is there a pattern in it?

J: The ones who have remained are quiet children whose teachers say they are no trouble. That's the only pattern you can detect.

S: Is it possible for there to be . . . I mean, given that you're going to have a remedial department . . . and given what we would regard as the obvious criteria for someone being allocated to a remedial department, is it possible that quiet children who would meet these criteria are nevertheless in the main stream of the school and being withdrawn from you. Is that what's happening?

J: (pause): The children I have . . .

The children who . . . You see it's very difficult. We have both a remedial department and a withdrawal system . . . after they have juggled around with the streams, they then juggle around with withdrawing. The remedial department, as such, withdraws the children who, on the tests they are given at the beginning, come out to be fairly bright — who have higher IQs, but who aren't reading very well, whose reading age is below eight. They're called the 'under-achievers', you see. And that's the only *type* of child that the withdrawal reading unit, which is attached to the remedial department, touches.

E: Are you saying that those children are in the remedial department?

J: No.

V: They're withdrawals.

J: They're withdrawn.

S: They're yours.

J: No, they're not mine, there are two withdrawal classes to the remedial department.

E: So they only give *special* help to children they consider to be underachieving?

J: The remedial department do.

V: But that's only withdrawal. They have remedial *classes* as well. Presumably they . . . have them?

E: But aren't these children in remedial classes?

J: No, these are children withdrawn from the ordinary streams. I'm sorry. I haven't made it very clear.

E: And you withdraw yours as well?

J: *Then*, from the tests that they use, are thrown up a number of children with low IQs and low reading ages who are in the main stream of the school and who, for one reason or another, they haven't got room for in the remedial department or aren't interested in grabbing . . .

There are only one or two that they somehow get worked up about and pull down at any cost. But there are some that are left and . . . there are also children who really haven't started to read at all. There's one child who has just come from Barbados who can't read at all, whom they also won't touch. I have those children.

V: What about your classes. Do they have anything to do with them at all?

J: I construct my own timetable and I gave myself a chance to help with one of the remedial first form streams and was told that as they were a small group anyway, they didn't need any extra help. It was an inefficient use of my time, they said, to go into them.

V: The English department has nothing to do with the remedial classes?

J: No, no.

E: What are the criteria . . . what exactly are the tests on which they devise their remedial classes?

J: They give them three tests . . . one of them is Raven's non-verbal to work out the IQ.[5] The other is the Schonell word list . . .

E: Very up-to-date!

J: Quite the worst of the worst, and the other is a Schonell sentence completion test.

E: How come that a child who can't read at all doesn't land up with them?

J (pause): Well . . .

V: The thing would be — if he had a low IQ and a low reading age he would be functioning at the appropriate level and therefore didn't need their help.

J: Let me see. It's very difficult . . . on that day I went in for the meeting that didn't take place as far as I was concerned, I was handed a sheaf of notes and . . . put into the headmistress's study and asked to digest these things. They were simply the test results. I couldn't understand them as they stood. I copied them down . . .

At this point Judith reads out to the group the scores given to a boy who had done the battery of tests. The summary is given thus:

T. falls into a group which is underachieving in reading. His poor attendance may well have hindered his progress in reading development. On the other hand his frustration in reading could have contributed to his poor attendance. There is no sign of visual impairment. Recommendation: T should join the reading unit for bright underachievers. These lessons should be in addition to the English lessons ['that's the sop to our department'] . . . His course should be highly structured and as intensive as possible. Success in this unit may well help his attendance and help to lower his frustration level in other subjects. [J: 'of which they know nothing — they haven't made any inquiries'.] Then it says, 'The lady who takes his withdrawal unit has had success with poor attenders in the past.'

E: So there aren't absolute rules for taking children to that unit?

J: They say they take the underachievers . . . bright children who aren't reading as well as they should be. They leave anyone else for me.

E: That's a cinch isn't it?

J: For them, yes.

S: What proportion of the total intake are allocated to the actual remedial department?

J: There are six ordinary streams in this current first year, with an average of about thirty in each — 180. Then there are forty in the remedial streams, twenty in each class, approximate . . .

S: So what happens is, those forty sort of get classed as sort of remedial children who have to spend half a week at least . . .

J: They're allotted to those remedial streams solely on their primary school records, *solely* . . .

E: So they don't do these tests?

V: Sorry, these ones you are referring to are withdrawals.

J: Yes, they do the tests . . . there's said to be a slight movement . . . but very slight.

S: But how many are they taking into their own withdrawal unit?

J: I've got notes on that.

V: Can I just ask one thing. What is the headmistress's view of this? Are you left to fight it out amongst yourselves?

J: She delegates it to her second who is much in support of the remedial department's approach. We have little support . . . you know. He regards their neat scientific results as more impressive . . . than our comments. Sixteen from the first year are the first batch for withdrawal. When they graduate, which is the term that's used, they leave the reading unit, having had their reading age bumped up by several years, then they'll take some more.

M: Is there any evidence that they're trying to find out what it says in the Bullock Report — that you can increase a child's reading age by short sharp application of specific procedures, but that this isn't long-lasting?

J: The remedial department doesn't follow-up any pupil who is sent back.

V: They bump them up and bump them back?

J: It's difficult to say. One wants the observations of their teachers afterwards.

M: One of the important things to discover about any child in this situation is his history of failure. If this procedure puts him in hazard again that would be an important piece of evidence. I don't know how we can do anything about the past, but at least we can't take refuge in excusing ourselves because something happened before we came on the scene. It does seem however, that the set-up is organized so that these children have to meet new hurdles, especially if the first thing that happens to them is that they are fought over; and they are assigned to people whose intentions they're not very clear about. The argument is that they should stay in their class so that they get all the social benefit of that . . . and that this is more important than that they should have short sharp applications of a reading kit. . .

J: I should have found out how often these remedial groups are with-drawn. . . . I have a feeling it's every day for a double period – five hours a week. I'll have to check on that.

E: What basis is there for thinking that there is a direct correlation between reading ability and intelligence? Supposing that either of these is well measured?

M: The evidence is the other way . . .

E: My experience is the other way: it just doesn't work like that . . .

M: They would argue that it's the discrepancy between reading age and intelligence that they've looked at . . . and the underachiever has the higher IQ than reading age . . .

E: Yes . . .

M: If you choose another pupil, Judith, from which category will he or she come? He won't be a remedial pupil, sorted out from the primary school record, will he? He can't be one of the groups with-drawn to the remedial department. That's the debatable land . . . so what does that leave you with, those who can't do it at all . . .

E: I can't see how anyone who can't do it at all isn't put into a remedial stream . . . that's what baffles me. If you've got a remedial stream, that's where the chosen non-readers are . . .

J: Let me tell you whom the remedial department recommended me to have . . .

M: Recommended to Judith is what I'm writing down . . .

J: And for what reasons. [Pause.] Someone was described as 'cul-turally impoverished' . . .

M (sardonically): Well, it's good to have it said, I suppose.

J: And was given to me. In fact, I'm not doing anything with her because I don't consider her to have cultural impoverishment.

M: Did you get that defined?

J: She is apparently the child of elderly parents and she truants a great deal . . . she has a weak heart (does that contribute to her cultural impoverishment?) . . . she's a nice hardworking girl . . .

V: Judith, just as an offshoot of this, what about the ESN recom-mendation thing . . . does this feature . . . in the selection and the tests? Do they get them? What's the position of the remedial depart-ment? Is there . . . what do they . . . there can be quite . . .

J: You mean children dropping out of the *school*?

V: Recommended as ESN . . . because all these tests must throw up . . . you know . . .

J: I'm sure they do . . . they throw up the full range.

V: But there's not a policy , , , do they try to keep them in, or send them out?

J: I'm sure they try and get rid of them . . . but I really don't know.

V: They try and send them to other schools . . . it's quite a feature in our place.

M: Meaning that . . .

V: The other remedial teacher . . . makes quite a point of recommending children very strongly for ESN schools . . . and . . . I feel that quite often it's not the right treatment for them . . . not the appropriate thing to do. You know . . . it can fall on someone's back that they think it's their job to get them away . . . or they take it on themselves; and, I'm in the middle of some of this at the moment. I get the ones who are recommended ESN and are virtually written off by my colleagues . . . they could probably cope quite well.

J: To come back to your question. I think I get the ones . . . I'm fairly casual . . . I don't mind whom I get because I don't believe in their tests. I'm sure amongst the children who come to me are those who are bright, those who are dull . . . you know . . . so *they* [the remedial department] think they've got the bright ones, which is probably a *good* thing, because at least they won't give up. The children I've got are the ones they can't sort of . . . say . . . they've got perceptual difficulties . . . that's another word they use a great deal. . . . If they can pin a label on any child, and they think they've got a way of dealing with it . . . they take them . . . if the child is elusive in any way, then I get him.

M: I'm writing down: Judith gets pupils whose difficulties are not defined . . .

J: Yes, that's probably it . . . and to answer your question about why a non-reader is not in the remedial department . . . in the first place. Well, they only take 220. Some children coming . . . one child I have is straight from Barbados, so he has no records at all . . . others have had teachers who have not wanted, perhaps or not even found it necessary to say that their reading is almost non-existent . . . who have always provided the child with an optimum reading situation where . . . they haven't felt it necessary to put in the record 'this child doesn't read'. There are hardly any children who just can't read at all.

M: Do you see that when you set up this kind of inquiry you are actually working from a base of having decided what reading is? If you think you've got that safe, then it's the child that doesn't fit the definition . . . rather than . . . doing what in fact reading involves doing. The one thing that will remain stable for remedial teaching

is a notion of what reading is, irrespective of what the child can do.
It must be a tricky situation for any department to get itself into . . .

E: Do you mean that the child you were going to work with had had
to change his class?

J: Yes.

E: That's terrible . . . that really is wicked.

J: I must try to get hold of copies of the letters — two sides of fool-
scap, that two of his English teachers . . . wrote . . . to try to keep
this one child in his class. One child's form teacher and his drama
teacher . . . they were really impassioned letters, and still they
wouldn't. He can't read at all, and when I first saw him he said he
didn't want to read. He wasn't at all ashamed of it . . . he could get
a job where he didn't need to read, and by the end of the hour . . .
the other child with him said: 'I can't believe you Robert . . . what
do your Mum and Dad say when you say that . . .' at the end of the
hour he said he would like to be able to read. He dictated a smashing
story which I've got here and then read it back. That's what I've got
on tape . . . obviously he was defensive at first, but was quite willing
to muck in when he saw it was going to be quite relaxed . . . but he
is now being taught in a very formal way . . . straight from the front
by a rigid class teacher . . .

M: What you're saying is that the vested interests of certain teachers in
a particular kind of teaching is one of the things we have to look at.
If change comes from reflexion on experience, which seems to be
normal procedure, then how do you operate to make people flexible
enough, so that anything, no matter what it is, even if it is the
opposite of what you're doing, can be organized to the pupil's
advantage?

How do you get it across? I don't mean we want to make everyone think as we do . . . we don't all think alike, and even if we did,
we'd do different things. But what interests me is: what kind of
notion is persuasive to make you look, just look, again, at your
practice? Nothing more than that . . . because it would seem that if
nothing makes a difference, if you're just determined to do, even
if it means treating a child in this way, then I'm in a kind of despair . . .

F: Are they threatened by what they think are trendy progressive ideas
in the English department?

J: You mean, the remedial department are?

M: But they may think *they're* the progressives and the others are the
sloppy, non-structured, non-rigorous teachers . . .

V: What are the influences on them? Have they degrees in psychology ... or what? What is making them take these particular attitudes?

J: The lady who does the withdrawal unit reading is a very pleasant person. She claims she knows that phonics and S.R.A. are best. The books are all 'readers', no real books. There are boxes of material and charts of sounds on the wall. She has decided she can do that ... and the evidence of the tests shows improvement. The head of the remedial department is totally inaccessible.

Margaret came to speak at one of our meetings about the Bullock Report – and the remedial department came and one left during the talk. The others left before the questions.

V: Their feelings must run so high about it.

As we have already said, the view of reading held by Judith's colleagues in the English department have been published for all to read.[6] What seems like an ineffectual internal squabble is in fact a radical theoretical difference. At this stage in our inquiry, Judith has uncovered a problem that is tacitly acknowledged in Elizabeth's situation, skirted around in Vicky's and dealt with differently in Fiona's. In Elizabeth's and Steve's schools, where the mixed ability teaching of English is assumed to include a responsibility for the non-readers, the conflict with a group of specialist remedial teachers fades away. In Fiona's there is a kind of demarcation dispute. In Judith's situation the conflict is in the open.

We struggled hard to follow Judith's account, because, however she tried to make it clear to us, however objective she tried to be, she clearly found the situation intolerable – a set of compromises that she felt were disabling the pupils because of the deep-rooted conflicts in teaching philosophy and teaching practice.

Judith clearly resents the tug-of-war over certain pupils. The underachievers need special help, but Judith sees their removal to the remedial department as a passage 'downwards' which threatens the pupils' views of themselves as competent learners. The remedial department threaten Judith's view of her own competence and experience as well as her conviction about the pupil's abilities. The impermeability of the situation is its most distressing feature. Judith also raised an issue which we had yet to face. What happened to newly-arrived West Indian pupils? In Judith's school there is a small trickle of these children who join an established London community. They are dialect speakers. Often their educational background is unknown and having to fit into a London comprehensive school is a tough assignment. Reading may be part of a much bigger problem. Do the facilities of a remedial department stretch to dealing with it, or has the English teacher to take this on? How valid are test results in this case? Here is another nexus of the language-linked difficulties of inner-city children.

At this point we all read Roger Gurney's book, *Language, Reading and Remedial Education*[7] and, even at the risk of further delay, forced ourselves to take stock of the compromises teachers are always bound to make.

A good opportunity to do this came when the English Centre in Steve's school held a divisional meeting to discuss ways of organizing the teaching of reading. We produced a summary account of our discussions of the situations in our five schools, distributed these at the meeting, and asked for comments to be sent to us. Although about fifty teachers attended we had only three written responses to our paper. These were accounts of other modes of organization. The meeting itself revealed all the conflicts that Judith had reported. The invited speakers represented the extremes of current practice in remedial reading for secondary pupils. One described the tidy administration of tests, special materials, graded operations, machines and calculated scores in a physically separate remedial department. Others emphasized a need for sympathetic concern for the reader as a person, the establishing of a trust situation where reading could go on as part of a total way of behaving. In the general discussion, there were no compromises, only statements of extreme positions.

This meeting may have come too soon in our work as a group, but, already alerted by Judith, we were shocked by the depth of feeling that 'remedial' work arouses. We had no intention of making a statement of policy or of urging a particular kind of practice. At most we wanted to say: see how we all talk about 'withdrawal groups' and yet in five schools the patterns are different in each. We were scarcely beyond the initial stage of describing how our classes were arranged, yet we tapped the root of some deeply and passionately held convictions that stretched back into cultural and philosophical assumptions about educational thought and behaviour.

So we were forced to confront what we instinctively knew; a series of unexamined compromises follows in the wake of a teacher's decision to help a child to read. The first is the most serious; the teacher's intentions are confronted by the view of reading the school *really* holds, irrespective of the one it professes. In each of our five schools there is provision for extra care. The time-table announces it, there are places for it to go on and teachers to give it. But the image of 'remedy' dies hard, and the makeshift appearance of the provision does not suggest that there is a widespread concern to mobilize resources for literacy. Whatever the reading teacher's view of the task of teaching a pupil, the school as an institution modifies it at once. Individualized instruction needs more than goodwill and good practice, so it is not surprising that programmes 'carried out with rigour and precision' [8] are rare.

Although group discussions seemed to focus on practical matters of organization, it became clear that their salience extended beyond notions of administrative convenience. To talk about the ideal length of a withdrawal lesson is to tackle the question of how to maintain the continuity of a pupil's membership of a learning group. Again and again, we tried to weigh up the advantages of taking a pupil out of a lesson. We agreed that some inexperienced readers attracted too much attention in a way that fluent readers escaped. We regretted the fact that our pupils were made to forgo the kind of lessons, such as learning another language, that are the mark of seniority. Continuous concern about pupils — for both their individuality and their membership of a group — entails a constant striving to put into the relationship a kind of wholeness that can compensate for the fractured curriculum and unsuccessful school life that is the lot of those whose difficulties are always judged in terms of their reading ability.

From this account it is clear that we all felt the need to lessen the tension experienced by our pupils. We dare not say 'relax' when it is clear that, to learn to read they must work hard and reading lessons are difficult. But effort need not be linked with discomfort; Fiona's room 42, Elizabeth's dark corners and Vicky's Portacabin announce the tutorial relationship that, in other kinds of schools, is taken for granted. We seem to emphasize the need to soften the image of school for those who have never discovered that reading, while it can be productively and powerfully social, is also something essentially private. A serious aspect of reading is another kind of withdrawal, an absence from the normal social contact of everyday life into the quasi-social relationship of reader and author. This is the lesson many never learn. If withdrawal systems offer a place which symbolizes this relationship, then, in Vicky's terms at least, something is gained.

The tutorial model of reading lessons distends the school pressures but increases the strain for the teacher and the learner in that it demands from both a rigorous attention to the matter in hand. The tutor organizes the programme, the learning design, the short-term and long-term goals, and is answerable for these. The pupil complies and comes to meet the challenge offered by the task. Yet the lesson itself can be relaxed, collaborative, reflexive, as in the most effective teaching we had ourselves experienced as students. That was the model in our heads. In examining the best teaching we knew, we saw in it, whatever external constraints there were, no compromise with the notion that the learner finally has to take the task in hand for himself or herself. At the same time no effective learning is confined to lessons. It has to become action knowledge elsewhere.[9] For our pupils, reading lessons would never be enough; there had to be some continuity between what happened in school and what went on outside. The notion that pupils learn to read in reading lessons is itself a compromise. Unless one is a reader in the world of adults and readers, the learning is neither effective nor complete.

So we found ourselves again discussing our notions of reading and this became the thread of our subsequent explorations. It was as if we needed to come back after what were really exhausting sessions to a belief that it was all worthwhile. We see the lead into this from Judith's conflicts with the views held by her colleagues and the underpinning claimed for them. There is no doubt that every reading teacher adopts a psychological stance. All teachers need psychological allies and specialist help. But behind every psychology is a view of man, and part of Judith's unease arises from the fact that she actually sees her pupils in a different light, as human beings, for whom the notion of 'under-achiever' is inadequate. Too often teachers have to compromise with a prevailing school view of children as systems of deficit, whether as 'second language learners' or 'dialect speakers', and reading then becomes the way in which these deficits are 'remedied'. We need and appreciate the considerable skills of those who have professional expertise in dealing with children whose difficulties are acute and prolonged. But there is nothing specific about these skills that makes them different from the other competences of good teachers. They can be learned, examined or judged by other professionals in the same field. Again, collaboration would make compromise unnecessary.

There is no suggestion that uniformity of practice would eliminate the problems we faced. Indeed, any attempt to standardize procedures would increase local difficulties. But there is no doubt that we were working, for the most part, in unnecessary isolation and having to bear responsibilities which could profitably have been shared with other colleagues in our schools.

Two other issues engaged us at this stage. Must reading help be 'expert' help, or will Steve's caring adult or older person, with supervision, and the necessary continuity, be better than no help at all? Has the wider community, by designating schools as places of teaching and learning, renounced a necessary responsibility? Steve's situation is an attempt to keep up the continuity of school and the outside world. In all of the others, as Vicky said, school stands for something demanded of the pupils, not for desires that they necessarily generate. If their view of reading is in no way consonant with that presented by the school, then a still greater *rapprochement* is necessary. The pupils' most significant compromise is that they should let themselves be taught and willingly and actively learn. This means, agreeing that the school conditions are at least good enough to let them begin. We are not sure that they are. Most schools simply mobilize the resources that are to hand, and make them carry a view of what learning to read is all about.

Judith's conflict and our need to discuss it interrupted the planned progression of our work. We went on helping pupils and recording lessons, their responses and strategies, as well as our own. But at some point in each meeting we would return to our views about reading, almost as if we had to reassure ourselves that we were really inviting our pupils to join us in something we cared about rather than imposing on them some kind of obligation they refused to acknowledge. So we have to discuss this next.

4

Reading, without tests

The process of becoming literate can have marked — but commonly
unsuspected — effects on the growth of the mind.

Margaret Donaldson

English teachers have to make considerable leaps of imagination to
understand the case of the child who cannot read. We confessed to each
other that, in our early days of teaching inexperienced readers, we were
like those who try to understand the plight of the blind by walking
with their eyes shut. Even more difficult for us to understand at any
significant level is that some people really do not want to read and do
not mind if they read very little. A powerful addiction to print, well-set
habits of confirming and extending experience and awareness by means
of books and journals, as well as talk and writing, encourage teachers
to take for granted that everyone wants to possess the mastery of
language and learning that is the consequence of literacy. It is an
assumption we rarely query, yet our failure to do so results in the cross-
purposes of much work in school.

Embedded as they are in the development of language, and firmly
linked to ways of learning that have evolved over the centuries since
the invention of the alphabet, reading and writing are not learned like
speech. Yet a child learning to talk is still the best argument we have for
the belief that most people who are not grossly impaired, mentally or
physically, can become literate. The development of speech also reminds
us that reading and writing have private as well as public manifestations.
There is more to both than a teacher can ever know, and they function
for those who master them in relation to intention and desire. So, our
chief problems lay with what we least understood: children who did
not want to read because they had no idea what reading was *for*, and
little idea of what success would be like, in the private or the public
realm. We came early to an appreciation of our cultural alienation, but

counted on talk with our pupils as our way back to the tap roots of their experiences in order to begin transforming these into discourse they could *see* on a page, as well as hear in their inner speech.

We talked about reading as often as we met, as if we needed to come to a deeper, fuller realization of the nature of the skills we held in common and to discover ways of 'enskilling' our pupils so that they were not set at odds with their own culture. In these discussions we discovered how much we had taught ourselves, and how many lessons came from encounters with texts where the author had begun by giving us a lesson on how the book was to be read. Think of the beginning of *Treasure Island*:

> Squire Trelawney, Dr Livesey, and the rest of these gentlemen having asked me to write down the whole particulars about Treasure Island, from the beginning to the end, keeping nothing back but the bearings of the island and that only because there is treasure not lifted, I take up my pen in the year of grace 17–, and go back to the time when my father kept the 'Admiral Benbow', and the brown seaman, with the sabre cut, first took up his lodging under our roof.

and consider the shift in time and place that it brings about in the reader, movements in thinking that are both ordinary and fabulous[1]. Then consider how you would *teach* such an encounter. The lesson is: submit to the spellbinding. But what if the pupil doesn't know how to? Where are the roots of understanding how a story works? Who taught you?

As a group we shared similar backgrounds of class and schooling. Successful readers from an early age, and nurtured for the latter part of our school lives in the grammar school tradition of 'arts' subjects, our convictions about reading had been shaped by what we read. The sustained nature of that reading – long books in textured prose, in foreign languages, in libraries, for examinations – the breadth and scope of the confidence it brings, had resulted in educational privileges that gave us access to books, and, even more important, to adults who helped us to believe that our feelings and opinions mattered. We had learned how to turn literature into experience. As our interests now extend beyond our undergraduate disciplines, we read and write in response to all kinds of discourse. We are rarely deterred by print, even the most abstract or technological, if we are bent on pursuing some information or idea. We see this as a remarkable freedom that allows us to reflect on our world and a power we would give to our pupils, with both hands. Just as we were admitted into 'readership' in our youth, so would we welcome them.

To many of the children we teach, however, our background in reading and the books that give us pleasure and knowledge are not only unknown but alien. This is not an elitist value judgment that suggests we are the guardians of the literary heritage. Quite the reverse. We observe that some things mediated to us by print come to our pupils just as meaningfully in other ways — visual, oral, social. We give these things their full meaning. That we had all chosen to move out of the kinds of schools where we had been pupils is not without importance. Nevertheless, we believe that every child should have the right and access to all forms of literacy, not only those we represent, and should be helped and invited to share in and to choose from whatever is there to be read.

We often talked with our pupils about reading and realized that their prime view of being able to read was a utilitarian one, a necessary skill for getting a job, a kind of clerkly competence ('good spelling'), or a means of gathering practical information. We acknowledge the social reality of this view at this time, but we also believe it is a perspective formed not entirely from our pupils' estimation of their prospects, or from a judgment of what reading is 'worth'. Rather, it stems from an acceptance of a value placed on them as people by their teachers, and made clear by the books they are given to read. We learned, with regret, that teachers themselves sometimes set the exclusive conditions of acceptance into the group of readers, the readership, and make sure that some pupils are always denied entrance.

There is no test, no standard, no agreed functional minimum of clerical skills which society recognizes as the basic requirement for a literate life in our time. Government officials, writers of post office prose, educators, employers and investigators always seem to suggest that there is a standard, a benchmark. Examinations are seen as mediating such a standard at different levels. But while we understand the need for a public definition of literacy and know that we want our pupils to meet these standards, reading also means something else.

In all discussions we seemed to be straining away from this basic species minimum view of literacy. Somehow we could never be satisfied with helping pupils to read only so that they would not be society's victims, people of whom 'demands' were being made. We came back, again and again, to a determination that what we wanted to ensure for our pupils was assurance, freedom, autonomy as learners. Literate as we are, we *enjoy* reading as something more than getting information as we move about in a print-laden world. Our security also comes from knowing how to sort out what we need *not* read, what we can ignore. Most especially, we realize that print can nowadays make knowledge easy to avoid.

As a group we read a great deal; we shared materials from journals and drew on the resources of the English Centre and the Institute of Education. We quickly discovered that reading research is dominated by the investigations of pupils' failures. We felt bound to look at studies of dyslexia but we found nothing to show a necessary connection between failure to read as a single entity and brain defect.[2] As there seemed to be no pedagogic consequence of this emotive topic that was not already part of what we would regard as normal teaching procedures, it proved a blind alley. From experience we knew that the poor long-term effect of specific remedial teaching reported by Pumphrey[3] is confirmed by most schools. The most disheartening outcome of the reading studies that deal with pupils' difficulties is the small amount of attention paid to what inexperienced readers actually *can* read.

The Bullock Report itself has an ill-concealed dichotomy in its approach to reading. On the one hand, there is a strong case made for the necessary embedding of reading and writing in the development of language and thought; on the other (notably in chapter 6), there is a model of reading development based on operant conditioning and the reinforcement of 'skills'. This latter view was fairly prominent in the first edition, now revised, of the course in Reading Development offered by the Open University. The Open University view is that 'there are various skills which are specific to print and these need to be taught however we choose to define reading'.[4] The later material says that 'from the teaching point of view *there is something to be said* (italics added) for grouping language and reading together as part of a broader curriculum element − the development of thinking skills',[5] but the new alliance does not make clear what more is involved. The main thrust of this training is that reading is most useful when in operation for the retrieval of information. Elizabeth and Vicky had done the course in its early form, Elizabeth selectively and Vicky with the thoroughness that characterizes all she does. Both reported that there was no easy match of what they had learned about the training of 'skills' to the needs of the pupils they were teaching.

We read attentively David Moseley's *Special Provision for Readers − when will they ever learn*[6] and found that it expresses what many teachers often feel. We agreed with him that 'with skilled individualised teaching almost all children can achieve at least a minimum standard of literacy', although we saw that he still looks for a standard to be defined by a test result. As a summary of research his work is invaluable, although by no means impartial. His distrust of English teachers as a body, and his misinterpretation of James Britton's 'expressive' function of language are dismaying. But the frankness and openness which lets him admit 'we don't know exactly why remedial teaching works, but we have reason to believe that it is something to do with a sense of being valued and gaining confidence', is encouraging. David Moseley has consistently maintained that it is impossible to make decisions about investment in reading which are not political decisions. We approve his insistence that a community which wills universal literacy as an educational and social goal must will the means by which it may be attained. His belief that the teaching of reading can involve more people than teachers has its manifestation in our report on the practice in Steve's school.

Investigations which include the teachers' part in the research operations are notoriously few. Of these, Joan Tough's studies in Leeds are the best known,[7] and rightly, as all over the country teachers were asked to participate. This gave them a sense of being significant investigators and an awareness of children's language that nothing else could have done. *Listening to Children Talking* appeared in the summer term of 1976. Margaret studied the work in detail and saw the videotape material. She found that the role of the teachers was to implement and perform the activities that had been agreed as the necessary means by which children's linguistic powers are extended. It was collaborative research in that it acknowledged the power of the teacher. But the teachers were to feed back material, not to recreate the theory. Gordon Wells's criticisms echoed our own.[8]

This article came at an important time in the life of the group. We had learned to trust each other; we were trying to see the material we were collecting from lessons in the collaborative pattern we had established, teaching the children and learning with them in school, teaching each other and revising ideas in the group. Margaret was anxious that the others should question rather than accept what was being offered in the realm of ideas, as in our discussions of our reading we moved fairly close together.

Our theoretical sources included the insights drawn from Connie and Harold Rosen[9] whose phrase 'the voice on the page' we adopted. James Britton's definition of reading, his use of Kelly, and the LATE studies in comprehension which stand behind it offered us a model which put the child as reader firmly in the forefront of our thinking.[10]

His conviction that 'children learn to read to read stories'[11] together with Margaret Clark's investigations in *Young Fluent Readers*[12] which we read later, sustained us when our choice of material was attacked as 'too literary'. It was to James Britton that we owed our first sight of Jane Torrey's report on John.[13] The Newsons, in *Perspectives on School at Seven Years Old*, confirmed that our stance should be behind the head of the learner. In describing reading as 'a necessary condition of liberty', they show how the beginnings of reading failure cannot be explained in isolation. They also agree that success is dependent on 'a sense of personal worth'. They quote Kelly in their insistence that 'no one need be the prisoner of his biography'. They found that everyone they interviewed in the course of their investigations recognized the moment when a child appears to have 'got the hang of it'. They add, 'Yet the sense of a lucky moment of fusion between something in the teaching and something in the learner increases the ambiguity which surrounds the process of the teaching of reading.'[14]

It is clear, however, that we came together on the theoretical level in our reading of Kenneth Goodman's 'Reading as a Psycholinguistic Guessing Game' and Frank Smith's *Understanding Reading*.[15] The reason is simple. These authors present reading as a process taken in hand by the users of language. The emphasis is on the learner and on the definition of a different role for the teacher, to 'respond to what the child is trying to do' when he tries to make sense of the text. From the miscues in the pupil's reading aloud the teacher discovers the linguistic processes that work for the pupil in reading. The whole emphasis then shifts from failure to success. The difference that this makes in practical terms is that the learner is invited from the outset to behave like a reader and to take on the task for himself. The notion that children who cannot read cannot handle language and the ideas expressed in language is firmly rejected. Put thus, the guessing game seems simple to the point of naivety. But as far as we could gather, this invitation — to behave like a reader — had never actually been extended to our pupils.

Some of our last discussions as a group were about the books that had stayed with us throughout our years together. Vicky described reading Kenneth Goodman:

V: It gave me confidence to let them go on reading, even when they backtracked, even when they went round and stumbled or made mistakes ... whereas before [pause] I thought you had to read what was on the page. It made me realize what was possible and what was actually happening, I think.

M: When did you read that article Vicky?

V: I've gone back to it several times since. I read it first when I was doing the O.U. course.

M: But it wasn't central to the course as you did it. It was an appendix.

V: It was an article at the back. But it was one of the most crucial things I read . . .

E: I agree, Vicky. That was one of the few things on that course that really . . .

V: And I was never the same afterwards.

M: But it was actually an alternative to the view of reading you were being taught.

V: But a lot of the things we were taught were peripheral, word games, eye movements and things. But you had to look closely at your own reading.

E: It was one of the few things we had to read that was actually human. D'you know what I mean?

V: It was a very positive view that children *can* read rather than the other view that they can't and you have to do something about it. . . .

E: Yes, we did the tests and assessments. . . . Even the parts of the course, that are specifically about children, learning to read were very mechanistic. The article seemed to be about real people . . . a description of what someone had seen happening . . . Most of them weren't. They were head counting . . . you know . . .

V: I had that article duplicated and given to all the English Department.

S: The other very human piece is Ronald Morris.[16]

E: That was one of the first things we read together.

S: Peter G and I are putting together a little pack of articles . . . after our course thing . . . articles that are helpful. It boils down to Morris, the Goodmans and Frank Smith's Twelve Easy Ways . . .

J: I remember *Hearing Children Read* by Elizabeth Goodacre, chiefly for the way she described the 'frustration level'. We seemed to be there a lot.[17]

A number of books appeared as we carried on. *A Question of Reading* by Moon and Raban[18] offered the teachers in junior schools the encouragement of the Smith and Goodman position and roused more antipathy from those who insisted that its 'guessing' techniques gave teachers a way out of properly organized instruction. Some of our colleagues in other schools made case-studies of selected pupils,[19] especially those whose linguistic competences seemed to belie their reading performance. Margaret's students kept logs of lessons and increased the bulk of the observational data of secondary and adult pupils. Margaret Donaldson and Jess Reid joined those concerned with 'the possibilities of meaning'. Margaret Donaldson put Vygotsky firmly at the centre of her *Children's Minds*. 'The hope then is that reading can be taught in such a way as greatly to enhance the child's reflective awareness, not only of language as a symbolic system but of the processes of his own mind.'[20]

We also watched Moira Mackenzie, of the Centre for Language in Primary Education, make videotapes of early reading lessons. We discussed with her the work of Marie Clay.[21] Roger Gurney tackled the problem of remedial reading, which, from the child's viewpoint he called 'a state of suspended animation'.[22] As our work came to an end he began a detailed investigation of the grey area between reading aloud and silent reading.[23]

Compared with our minute investigations, the work of the Schools Council covers the whole area of reading research. We read the reports as they appeared. Frank Whitehead's exhaustive study of *Children and their Books* confirmed the role of the teacher in influencing children's reading matter.[24] Eric Lunzer and Keith Gardner's view of meaning in reading as 'an emergent pattern of relationships [which] depend on experience of life and language' cheered us as much as their enthusiasm for SRA reading workshops conflicted with our most strongly held beliefs about what reading is for. We took some comfort from the (not unexpected) discovery offered by readability studies that what sometimes seem to be readers' problems are, in fact, the author's inadequacies as a writer.[25]

Thus, as months went by, we found ourselves linked to writers and teachers who did what we were concerned to do — looked at the child, the task and the material — and sought to educe the teaching method from the context situation. Perhaps in our anxiety to look forward we were less than explicit about the friendly ghosts: the pioneers of 'Breakthrough', who knew that writing is power,[26] Edmund B. Huey who, in 1903, was writing about 'inner speech', 'meaning in itself . . . in reading any sentence that makes grammatical sense, and this quite independently of anything the sentence tells' and the readers who 'grow into it as they learned to talk with no special instruction or purposed method.'[27] George Dennison's case studies were an early inspiration, and he strengthened our resolve by his insistence that 'if you cannot add to the intelligence of childhood, at least do not destroy it.'[28] As he acknowledged Tolstoy and A.S. Neill, Carl Rogers and Jean Piaget, so do we.

We had one further conviction about reading: that our earliest and most abiding lessons had been derived from stories. So we agreed that we should select narrative material, and wherever we could, we would work from books written by authors who genuinely wanted to tell a story. This may seem an obvious and simple statement, but it flies in the face of much current practice which offers children reading books (called, oddly, 'readers') of such linguistic poverty that the real author's voice is never heard. Despite Margaret Clark's warning that a teacher may have 'too little appreciation of the effects that her initial approach to the reading situation may have on children's later progress', beginners still struggle with material that gives them a view of reading that disenchants them, a fact confirmed again and again by our pupils.

We were persuaded by Barbara Hardy, Denys Harding, James Britton, R.L. Gregory and Donald Winnicott that narrative is natural discourse.[29] James Moffett confirms this when he shows that the progress of children's thinking in language is dominated by the narrative mode until late in childhood.[30] Children who learn to read without the help of adults discover first how a story works. Good readers are speedy because they are confident they can tackle long stretches of text, and this confidence is bred in listening to stories and in reading them. The more you read, the more fluent you become, obviously. 'What happens next?' is the curiosity that compels us all. The author's invitation to us to enter into the story (a lesson that has to be learned but is never taught) establishes a quasi-social relationship that all good readers understand and inexperienced readers scarcely glimpse. By means of the conventions of narrative the reader's attention is sustained in a way that never happens in books of information organized for speedy assimilation.

In addition, skilled readers see no break in the way they organize their view of the world outside and the world in their heads. As Applebee shows, storying in one's head and on the page, language and thought, are inextricably linked.[31] Bettelheim, Singer and others make it clear that the inner world of personal storying is the mainstay of an integrated personality.[32] Despite the fact that they were splendid storytellers, our pupils found it difficult to give equal importance to the stories in their heads, the narratives of television, and a factual narrative about an actual experience told, for example, by a friend. They did not understand that, whatever the text, the reader brings his meanings to it. If a reader has never discovered that his understandings and what he tells himself are relevant to his reading, he is bound to find it difficult to make text *mean.* You will meet Trevor with his splendid sense of story — a natural approach to reading he had come to discount. Chris is short-winded in stories. Tom's strength emerged when he told a story. Sharon could not sort out the world of the book because she could not see its relevance to the stories she told herself.

As we looked at our emerging views on reading, they seemed to hang in festoons around our thinking and our teaching. Society has a view of reading, researchers have theirs, the school has one, or more than one, and professional educators have lists of definitions. Sometimes one view is foregrounded, sometimes another. Then suddenly, as a teacher, you have to decide for yourself, as Margaret asked the group to do. Judith's English department, in the teeth of opposition, wrote the document that set out their point of view and Judith contributed to it. Elizabeth wrote a piece for her colleagues and Margaret for hers. Vicky made a selection from her tapes and Steve urged us on with pertinent questions.

Judith wrote a chapter in the Clissold Park post-Bullock document *The Meaning of Reading.*[33] The introduction takes the bull by the horns and says:

> The whole business of backwardness in reading in the secondary school is so worrying that if one can find some way of isolating part of the problem, working on it intensively, and then checking up on it, one has the reassuring feeling that something definite is being done, that the impersonal figures that the tests throw up must be giving relevant and helpful, even full information. This is all very well if one believes that learning to read is simply learning to master the decoding process, but we want to put it to you that there is very much more to it than this, and that is what we try to explain to you in the following paper.

Judith writes about the slow reader whose hesitation makes it difficult for him to grasp the sense of what he is reading in meaningful units if he is concentrating on isolated words. She explains how the predictive skills of the fluent reader are more successful than the phonic decoding process, and how 'there are children who are alert (and brave) enough to dismiss their teacher's precepts because they can rely on their own intuitions or detect information in the text more useful than that to which the teacher is directing their attention'.

One thing more emerged quite clearly: good teachers *read.* In addition to all the studies of reading and the books written for children, we read what gave us pleasure and profit. The print habit, once established, never fades in real readers. That was the biggest puzzle of all for our pupils.

Judith offers some direct application of this point to promote and encourage children to read with understanding and enjoyment. She says the ideas come from the primary school. In fact, they are features of all reading instruction *before* schools began to insist that the ability to read is to be able to decode new text.[34] If you know the text before you read it – songs, TV jingles – you make your own rules about how print works. Judith insists that what is read must provide an inbuilt incentive to the child to continue reading because he must find out what happens next. Children are similarly motivated to read each other's work and *seem to overcome enormous visual difficulties* (handwriting, spelling, punctuation idiosyncrasies) in order to read their friends' stories. If children's own writing is accorded the respect it deserves, says Judith, symbolized, perhaps, by being typed out or made into a book, it can also provide vigorous incentives and learning possibilities. Judith sees that the slow reader's chances are improved, 'when he can trust his own knowledge of the language he speaks and the world he lives in and use this knowledge to help him to read with understanding'.

Pushed by her head of department to make her view plain for others, Elizabeth produced a discussion document for her colleagues. She plunges in: 'If we really do want kids to have a real desire to learn, and to take on the process of learning for themselves, we should take their work more seriously.' (Where do you read that in a psychology text book?)

We need to focus on *what* they read, and not principally on their reading skills. When they write for us, we need to pay attention *to what they have to say*, and not chiefly to spelling, handwriting and punctuation. Children are only likely to master these skills effectively when they see that they serve their own purposes, as well as ours. The opportunity to share with others what you think and feel, what you have learnt and how, should be an integral part of school life. Then, perhaps, real purposes for reading and writing might develop . . .

Elizabeth then goes on to write about 'how reading works'. Her account owes something to Frank Smith, but the tone and conviction are fully hers:

A child does not first learn a lot of rules and then work out the meaning of a text with them; he uses his previous knowledge and experience of books and stories to predict, anticipate and guess his way through a book ... taking on the task of real reading from the start, that is, the task of making it make sense.

Elizabeth does not say the meaning is in the child's experience. It is his knowledge and experience 'of books and stories', i.e. both text and utterance, the oral and written forms help him to *locate* the meaning and assimilate and accommodate it.

I have often seen an expression of hopeless incomprehension come over the face of a child as I explained to him some highly logical (to me) way of making reading easy. What is logical to the teacher is not necessarily logical to the child; it may merely be one more proof that he's too stupid to ever understand how it works. Our kids often associate reading with failure and humiliation ... the social stigma of not being able to read is immensely strong and we should not under-estimate its influence on our kids.

In suggesting modes of operation to her colleagues, Elizabeth insists that self-confidence and success allied to reading real books and writing for real purposes are necessary. As we look at this now, it seems obvious. But it was a crusading stance at that early stage in our work because the post-Bullock emphasis was still on teaching rather than learning. To give children 'success from the start' we have to take what they bring to the task. Yet prevalent notions of children's inadequacy make it difficult for teachers to be convincing about this.

Elizabeth's writing carries the conviction of practice:

The complete beginner may use only his writing as a text, or only books he has had read to him many times. Most children will need some introduction, perhaps even a detailed one, looking at pictures and speculating about the story. If he knows about the story before he starts, he will be able to detect his own miscues and to correct them. This process of seeing where *and why* you went wrong, then putting it right, is an absolutely vital one, and it is one we cannot do for the children; they must do it for themselves. Our job is to lay the groundwork and then give the child only the information he wants.

Here Elizabeth is moving towards an awareness of the learner's difficulty in predicting his or her way through 'new' text. The teacher's patience is most stretched when children are practising by reading aloud. 'Sometimes a child will preface a pause for thought with "Don't tell me", obviously knowing all too well my inability to let him stop and think for a moment ... the habits of "get it word perfect" and "don't guess" die hard. We should never let reading become a meaningless chore.'

Elizabeth's piece shows an understanding that teachers want to give children a way to make reading easier, but that there is no way other than helping them to become readers by reading, even if it is with an enormous amount of support. Her paper ends with suggestions for assessing progress based on the view of reading she has set out and which involve the teacher in a closer look at what the child can do to further his own purposes, self-confidence, expectations and strategies in both reading and writing.

Elizabeth not only says with conviction born of experience many of the things confirmed by Smith and Goodman. She also shows how a teacher takes on one view of reading rather than another and communicates this to the learner. 'We should be interested in what they are reading and not just in the degree of skill which they show in doing it. We should read to them often and use the best books we can find.' These convictions have roots that run deeper than learning theory. Elizabeth begins with a view of reading which offers the highest possible standards. There is no suggestion that her pupils, however inexperienced, are to be 'tied to the functional demands of work and citizenship'.[35]

Vicky's view of reading comes from watching herself at work. She made tapes of each lesson for a period of eight weeks, then edited these to make a master tape of her interaction with a pupil. No one in the group had tried to present a child on tape before this point.

So that we could hear Sharon clearly, Vicky edited much of herself out — a step we discussed at length — so we brought Vicky back to these early days to say how she thought she saw reading. Already her commitment to the Smith/Goodman position has been stated. From the master tape it is clear that Vicky wants Sharon to enjoy reading stories and Sharon clearly knows that this is something Vicky minds about because she does it with her own children. Sharon is curious about Vicky's children and her relationship with them. Clearly, if reading is important, then Sharon knows she will have a claim on Vicky's attention if she attempts it.

Vicky sees reading as a source of pleasure and power, a means of gaining confidence in moving about the world. She knows that, to teach Sharon to read, she has to change her attitude to the task which she now regards as something connected with either tests or comics, and the troublesome school. Vicky shares her pleasure in reading with Sharon and others in a group when they read a play together. This also allows the pupils to become fluent by transferring the natural language of speech to a written text. Vicky encourages Sharon to compose a story so that she will interest an audience as a real writer does.

No one worked harder than Vicky in these early stages to examine the ways in which she invited her pupils to take on the role of a reader and a writer. She offers Sharon a view of herself and her family as a reading community and invites Sharon into reading on the same terms of confidence and familiarity. Sharon need only take a firm step towards reading and Vicky will go with her all the way. Right from the start, Vicky shows Sharon what success would be like. But Sharon, as we shall see, has such an inhibiting view of reading that it will not let her get to first base. We meet Sharon and Vicky again as we discuss the early encounters of teachers and pupils.

Steve had to come to terms with his view of reading when he accepted an invitation to work with another group at the English Centre for the duration of a term. The teachers who took part were asked to bring case-studies of pupils for whose reading they had some concern. Thus Steve, who at this time was still choosing the pupil whose work he could present to our group, made the acquaintance of other teachers and their pupils. Here is how he saw his view of reading.

At the time the group was coming together, I was convinced above all that children can only learn to read by reading and not through games, kits, teaching machines or any other kind of supposedly related paraphernalia. It seemed to be a curious characteristic of the more 'systematic' or 'rigorous' remedial programmes devised for poor readers that the longer children fail at the central task of reading itself, the further they are removed from real reading of any kind. One scheme we heard of included, seemingly as an afterthought, 'supplementary materials'. These turned out to be books.

As she listened to the tapes of the lessons and discussions, Margaret found herself looking more and more closely at types of interaction between teacher and pupil, and between pupil and text, in one-to-one reading lessons. This is not something a teacher can easily do in the thick of a lesson, but is very clearly, even painfully, possible afterwards. Gradually Margaret learned to detect the effects of a teacher's intervention in the reading process and to begin to sort out some of the complexities. She began to wonder if the teachers' interventions (including her own), however well-intentioned, were unhelpful, even counter-productive. They often seemed to draw a reader's attention away from the very clues and sources of help that would have been of most use, towards explanations that were at best irrelevant and at worst confusing and misleading. Elizabeth succinctly articulated this growing suspicion by pointing out that an apparently 'logical way of making reading easy' was not 'necessarily logical to the child'.

While there is clearly great virtue in allowing a child 'to detect his own miscues and correct them' (Elizabeth's words again), carried to its logical conclusion, this principle (which owes much to Kenneth Goodman) implies a strategy of non-intervention. So why be there at all? Pupils who lack confidence (and what non-reader does not) feel they need the active support and practical assistance of their teachers, so obviously there is a reasonable expectation of timely support and some kind of active role on the part of the teacher. How could helpful intervention be characterized and this role be defined? How *do* teachers respond to what the child is trying to do?

This was a question for Margaret. Her teaching experience had been more varied than that of other members of the group and had to some extent reflected the fashions in the teaching of reading at each stage. Her strongest convictions were that, just as children developed language competences in the social contexts where they are 'learning how to mean',[36] so they developed reading and writing competences, *literary competences*, in the meaningful contexts for these activities. The difference between the teacher and the learner is the difference of the grasp of consciousness of what is involved in the activity. Thus understanding narrative, with its particular discourse, is not only reading stories, but understanding the way stories are told.[37] Another example of the obvious, this is also the confidence a young reader acquires. As the work continued, Margaret, like Judith and Elizabeth, wrote a piece for her colleagues that was eventually published as 'Handing down the magic'.[38]

We had all thought long and hard about our own practice and the pleasure of reading we enjoyed. Our coming together reinforced our best insights, however diverse were our beliefs in what we had to do to help a child to learn. We never lost sight of our freedom, the liberation of the mind that we felt reading had given us. As we worked with our pupils we were distressed, not so much by their lack of skill, for that we could help, but by their hopelessness, their feeling that they had been cheated because they had occasional glimpses of what made reading good for us. We came to understand more exactly, and to study in greater detail, the difference between our orientation to print, which we no longer took quite so much for granted, and our pupils' obvious familiarity with the conventions of television.

5
Early encounters

What is new is that the apprentice reader has to decide to withdraw
attention from the external world (including the book as an object)
and from his own internal world as a preliminary to an experience
which is unpredictable and in an important sense, unsharable.
The reader must agree to a surrender before fighting the battle.

G. Craig

When it was your turn, it was time to go home.

Andy

Opening moves

The assumptions most frequently made about teaching reading are
that the pupil *has* to learn and therefore is bound to be 'motivated'
so that a teacher with a good method and a good book will be successful in turning a beginner into an expert. Failure can then be attributed
to the pupil's lack of application or intelligence, to insufficient skill
or patience in the teacher, or to a poor supply of suitable reading
material. This is mostly unproven; we have too little evidence for what
we really need to know about early reading lessons. It is clear however,
that teachers make a difference, and, as Frank Smith says, if a child
is in difficulty it is wise to ask him if he likes his teacher.

Children in infant schools begin to read with enthusiasm and hope;
the teachers' expectations are matched by the pupils' eagerness to
undertake new processes as part of becoming more at home in a world
where language seems to open so many doors. Learning to read is learning that you can learn. Because the success rate is high, these early
interactions of pupil, teacher and text pass unrecorded and therefore
we have little evidence of what pupils and teachers do and say. The

best new studies are on videotape[1] and these reveal just how many negotiations are undertaken and how complicated is the task of mediating and understanding the rules of the game called 'a reading lesson'. One thing is clear, the successful teacher is the one whose instructions are a means to an end, whose rules are overruled by those the beginners make for themselves. Then the partnership changes and teacher and pupils collaborate to make reading an extension of experience.

Unsuccessful readers have known many beginnings; with a new teacher for 'extra lessons', with new methods, new books, new cards, new machines. Unaware that they share a poet's frustrations, their 'raids on the inarticulate' compound not only their failure but their distrust of teachers. To be selected for special attention is, for some, a hazard to be avoided at all costs. To show eagerness is to be open to exploitation. No wonder the 'motivation' of inexperienced readers is regarded as 'low'. Illiterate adults, driven by anger and despair and a knowledge that the world ignores them, make quite specific demands on those who offer to help them. But the pupil in secondary education, often ill-at-ease in school and with little status (where reading counts) outside it, is usually not clear about reading as such. He feels threatened by his incompetence and distrustful of adults who want to inquire into the state of his literacy, for that may mean yet another beginning and another failure.

It is as well to acknowledge the degree of risk that lies in the selection of pupils for special reading lessons. They may want to avoid being noticed because they have discovered that they can live their own kind of life in school as long as they are out of sight. Special lessons make teachers inquisitive as there is time to talk, so some pupils who need help never promote themselves to a teacher. Others want attention so badly that they not only see that they are noticed, but they also delay learning to read so that the lessons which ensure this singling out can continue. We shall show both of these situations in detail, and the different demands they impose on the teacher.

How a pupil gets help, the kind of help provided, how long it lasts and what happens all have their roots in the early stages of the relationship of the teacher and the pupil, these introductory sessions, when both partners, eager or guarded, negotiate what they will do and interpret the task that lies between them. One thing is certain, they both bring with them experiences and expectations that are the first trading counters. It is easier for the teacher to be enthusiastic. The pupil is bound, at this stage, to approach a new beginning with a certain degree of cynicism if not desperation. What the Newsons called 'the

tender leaves of hope' about reading have already been blasted.[2]
Generally, teachers select pupils for special lessons, although, as
we shall see, some pupils select themselves. Whoever initiates the
relationship retains some control over the conditions within which
it operates. We have already reported that, if the school is formal,
with fixed classroom routines, timetabled at all times, but the teacher
wants some degree of informality in reading lessons, the pupil has to
learn a new pattern of behaviour for the reading room. If the pupil
wants to keep a degree of freedom to choose whether or not he comes
to reading lessons, the teacher's plans for him have to include a prag-
matism even greater than she is used to operating in the everyday
situation in class. The more we look at the details of case studies,
the harder it becomes to make general statements about what happens.

There are, however, common themes. The choice of a pupil for
special lessons is never a random choice. Embedded in it are certain
unformulated assumptions that the teacher is making about 'pupils
of this kind'. Even when we say: 'This pupil ought to be able to read',
the nature of the 'ought' needs inspection. It may be coercive, i.e.
'should he be made to learn', or social, 'owes it to society', or self-
enhancing, 'owes it to himself', or reparative, 'has to be freed from
the bonds of not being able to', or even atoning, 'someone else has
failed him, I won't'. Our group asked themselves the question: 'How
did I choose my pupil?' The responses were almost immediate. We
chose the pupils we liked, those to whom a positive kind of response
was possible. It was a kind of authorized favouritism of the sort that
operates in classrooms everyday, that pupils know about even when
teachers think they do not. It is rarely regarded as 'fair'.

The obvious alternative is to choose the pupils with the lowest
score on the reading test. This has its own difficulties. Apart from the
poor reliability of most tests, 'wanting to learn' and an ability to
tolerate the isolation of special lessons play a large part in individualized instruction. The partnership of a pupil selected by a low test score
and a teacher who has only the numerical assessment of a pupil's failure
begins with other problems of 'motivation'. Neither feels committed
to more than the minimum obligations of their interaction. Then, the
rules of the game are drawn up so that the teacher produces material
which resembles the items of the test for the pupil to work on and the
pupil goes through actions of 'getting them right'. The consequent
test score may or may not change, but little else does, and certainly
not the pupil's nor the teacher's view of what is meant by learning to
read.

When pupils seek out a teacher and ask for help it means there is a possibility of mutual regard on which they can both build. Again, this may have its difficulties, notably the creation of a situation of dependence where the pupil may resist being detached from the teacher whose attention he has gained. Learning to 'go it alone' is delayed so that lessons can continue. Many children in 'remedial' classes make just enough progress to ensure that their teachers are pleased to have them there.

From this it will also be clear that, at the outset, we are hazarding a guess about the chances of success. It may be that the 'pupil I like' is the one who seems to have very little prospect of becoming a genuinely independent reader. The child with the odds heavily stacked against him, by home circumstances or other teachers, is always a challenge. An attractive personality, however defined, is more tolerable than the sullen silence of the non-trier. There is little chance of help for the pupil who does nothing to draw attention to himself, remains neutral to all school activity, is sufficiently literate, quiet, biddable or socially integrated to escape significant encounters. None of our chosen pupils falls into this category.

The closeness of the one-to-one teaching situation ensures that the teacher knows more about the pupil than is usual in the ordinary classroom. Steve, who organizes a large reading unit within the school yet teaches only one pupil in this way, separates out his special pupil differently from Elizabeth, who sees forty reading pupils in a week, and from Judith, who sees twelve. Vicky's situation puts her at the crossroads of her pupils' in-and-out contacts with school, so that her pupils swim into focus from a group which contains them, then they retreat after a period of being in the limelight.

Clearly, we have taken the trouble to know as much as can be discovered, without disturbing the relationship, about the pupil's social, community and linguistic background. We make judgments, implicit or explicit, about the relationships in their family, with teachers and with the peer group. We judge success and failure in our lessons and other teachers' responses. We also know something of our pupil's primary school experience, not only from the records, but also from the pupil's interpretation of that experience. It is interesting to note how, in our discussions, we often read to each other quotations from documents or reports that suggest negative aspects of the pupil's reading, and then we refer to incidents which belie these earlier judgments. Determination to make allowances for the chosen pupil is the strongest embedded attitude in the teachers whose cases are presented

here. The pupils begin with the advantage of being thought well of,
and, on the whole, they believe that they can be helped.

We gave our pupils the benefit of many doubts we may have had –
about the span of their attention and their staying power, for instance.
We were firm but not unkind. But our very acceptance of them, our
understanding of what made their poor reading more than a difficulty
with words on a page, may also have confused them. When they read
badly it was difficult to know whether we should show that we were
unwilling to accept work done half-heartedly, or to excuse it because
we knew the pupil had slept outside all night.

It was also difficult to discover at first what our pupils really thought
about their earlier failures. They had the usual alibis – too little time
in school, frequent moving, poor teachers who neglected them. We
accepted whatever excuse was offered as a sign of trust, although we
often doubted the explanations. We discovered in our early encounters
that the crucial moment in their learning to read was when they first
failed – in the early days in primary school. Then they saw the teachers
as a source of bamboozlement, not helping them to understand what to
do. Or what they did was not something they understood. Sometimes a
reading lesson asked for behaviour that bore no relationship to reading
done at home. The predominant feature of their condition was that
they had no view of what successful reading could be like. Only Trevor,
Judith's pupil, had a clear idea, and as this was in ill accord with what
he had hitherto been told to do, he put no trust in his best understandings, as we shall show.

As we listened to the tapes of the first lessons we understood how
we had chosen the pupils. We had intuitively felt that reading could
'nourish their enterprises'.[3] They had been conditioned into apathy
about reading, but something remained of a determination to try again,
even if it was only a grudge against teachers because of an unfulfilled
promise. Judith knew she was looking for a West Indian pupil as there
are many in her school who swell the statistics of 'low achievers'. Steve
spent some time looking for the ideal case-study pupil. Vicky's assertion 'I only teach children' showed her to be drawn to those with
special difficulties. Fiona and Elizabeth knew that their pupils were
threatened by the economic realities of the world outside school and
the views of them held by their peers. We confirmed that more boys
needed help than girls, but we were content to observe this rather than
to offer explanations. We judged, again by the instincts teachers understand but are rarely encouraged to inquire into, that each pupil had a
fair chance of success. We knew that the teaching and learning would be

singular, even idiosyncratic.

For our pupils, these new first encounters were bound to be accompanied by mixed expectations. They might see this as a last chance, a desperate try, another possible failure, or just a peaceful lesson. Perhaps we could bring more of this to light. In the meantime, however, it is best to regard these early sessions, hitherto disregarded, as examples of how teachers and pupils get on working terms with each other. They establish the base, the preliminary agreement about what is to be done. Here the rules of the game are negotiated, for the beginning at least.

Andy and Fiona

Andy and Fiona had many encounters before special lessons began. Fiona taught Andy's form English and, in a way, Andy was the pupil who selected himself. The information which now follows comes from tapes and Fiona's own writing.

Fiona's choice of Andy as a subject for study is easy to understand. He offers the challenge of the 'underachiever', the intelligent pupil who is at odds with the school system. He is fifteen; he dominates his class and is representative of it. Other teachers called it 'the sink'. All the boys in it see themselves as failures, except when they are troublemakers, football fans and bullies. They are typical of a wider group of older so-called slow learners who are so humiliated by their failure to read that their abject state is the greatest barrier between them and any attainment. They agree that they ought to be able to read; they do not see how they can change the way they are.

Andy has a low opinion of himself as a reader, but great determination and a strong character. Fiona's main concern at the outset is to help him to use his power and authority, his leadership and his undoubted intelligence to do himself some good, not only in evading the retributive actions of adults, but also in reducing his frustration and insecurity.

Andy's junior school record showed he was good at games, poor in class: 'a leader with no qualities of leadership', was the summary judgment – the very kind that sets up no great anticipatory pleasure or awareness in teachers. His difficult behaviour was attributed to the fact that he hated being unsuccessful, but could not succeed on the school's terms. His mother hit him when he misbehaved but his father's word was law.

In her early experience of Andy, Fiona wrote:

It's clear what these invisible qualities of leadership are. Every boy in his class knows that if he says he is going to throw a chair he will throw it. He is powerful for his age and he asserts his authority by a combination of physical threat and his hard-earned reputation of being afraid of no one, which is about all that he has to hang on to. Nobody challenges his leadership of the class, which is a pretty rugged one. The form teacher (a man with twenty-five years' experience) and their maths teacher (equally experienced) threatened to resign if the class were not given to someone else to teach. For these reasons and comparable responses from other teachers the class have an image of themselves as rock bottom in their year. Like Andy, who represents them, this is all they have to be proud of.

The file which is kept as a record of his progress reports swearing, (especially when he is made to feel inferior), disruption in lessons accompanied by threats, lateness, gambling and a court appearance on two charges of theft. Yet none of this rules out the possibility of friendly behaviour with teachers as individuals, provided they take no authoritarian role with him. In Fiona's English class his behaviour is usually either quietly subversive (gambling with a friend, stopping when asked, then starting again when Fiona is not looking, or starting off the others on a football song and then pretending to be busy), or seeking approval by isolating himself from the rest and copying beautifully neat work — never to be read in class.

But he did select himself. There was no first encounter in the sense that Fiona sat and waited for him. He kept nagging Fiona until she admitted him into her Room 42. Then he was *very* nervous. Fiona brought to the reading task the awareness of his record and the accounts of his behaviour and she added to these what her good relationship with Andy made available to her. For example, she discovered in Room 42 that he wanted to take home a book to his mother and to read to her correctly. She would be so proud she would probably give him some money as a reward. This was a new revelation, as in the ordinary class he said that Dad was the only person he cared about.

At about the same time as his special lessons began, Andy was tackled on another matter by his form master who casually mentioned his 'trouble with reading'. Andy grew red in the face, then sat down and cried. Thus, certain changes began in Andy after the first visits to Room 42. He was his old aggressive self. He looked at the Neale Analysis stories and said, 'Don't think I could read all them' and took a great deal of convincing that he wouldn't have to. When Fiona explained that a Breakthrough folder was for making sentences you wanted to write, he used it to produce: 'Mr S is a bastard', that is, he was testing the limits of her credibility and tolerance to see how far he could go. Fiona agreed that he could write this, but it would mean keeping his folder secret from people whom he might want to show it to later. Then he substituted: 'Today I come into school and I threw a brick through the window', which was true. (Note how he surmounted easily one of the surface difficulties of English spelling – *threw, through* – on his own.) He insisted that whatever went into the folder had to be in his own handwriting. He dictated for the Language Master: 'On Saturday I want to Chelsea to watch them play against Plymouth.' He had to be nursed out of his suspicion about the tape recorder which he rarely allowed Fiona to use.

In the early days Fiona thought it was touch and go as to whether he would continue to come for lessons. If he said at any point he didn't care, then he would feel he had to save his face and stay away. He always kept his word ('if he says he is going to throw a chair . . .'). But his moods were very varied: despairing, rejecting, enthusiastic in turn.

Observing his reading behaviour, Fiona decided that he could not be said to lack 'work attack skills'. If he was puzzled by phoneme-grapheme correspondence so that he gave up after attempts to identify initial letters, Fiona let him find his best strategy, which seemed to be an ability to recognize longer words as wholes. He was impatient of his slow speed; he wanted success in decoding to be regular, and constant.

From his earliest talk about himself on one of the rare tapes, we discovered how defensive his tone was, how humiliated he felt. ('My little brother can do it better than me' . . . 'I feel shown up.') This humiliation had deep roots. Speaking of reading in his primary school he said, 'When it was your turn, it was time to go home.' Fiona continued: 'If I try to talk to him about how he *feels* about reading, he is very reluctant to discuss it and only wants to get on with reading aloud. In class his attitude to me is very ambivalent. In front of his peers he is always struggling to keep control of events. He will form a group or play cards or sing, or announce his intention of working and settle down to copying from a book for a double period. If I set him any work requiring original thought or risk of spelling mistakes, he will either refuse it or get a more literate friend to go through it with him, so that it is perfect when it is handed in to me. He once made an excuse to tear up his exercise book after making a mistake.

In the special reading room, he was a good attender at first, then he became less conscientious if there was something more interesting elsewhere. Most of his antagonism to me drops away when out of his class. I am there to hear him read – as he often tells me in no uncertain terms. He will tolerate someone else reading for a short time, but cannot bear to discuss reading or anything else that will reveal anything about himself other than the tough image he projects for class consumption.

I see reading as his only chance of gaining the confidence to break away from his role of gangster and football fan, and to prove to himself that he can use his intelligence for other things besides the domination of his class. I haven't found out what prevents him reading fluently except that he has such a low opinion of himself that he must *think* he is a non-reader.

I feel so committed to getting him past this stage that I am wondering whether to give up teaching the class next year to avoid the conflict of roles between being his English teacher and his reading teacher. I have put this point to him and told him I am afraid we may fall out in class next year, but he refused to give any opinion on the matter. I don't know if I will ever get sufficiently through the shell he has built up to see him become a "safe" reader, and because of this shell my expectation of his success are lower than they were to start with. If anything, his determination and strength of character are working against him at the moment. He is so intense that sometimes I feel the paper will turn brown and burn.'

Now, long after this report was presented to the group, it is easy to see how Fiona feels something should have been done earlier for Andy. It is also clear that reading is only one presenting symptom in Andy's more general malaise. Fiona doesn't want to psychoanalyse him, only to give him a measure of success that she feels she can achieve and thus help him to break out of the circle of his failures. When children in other social situations are seen to make comparably high demands on themselves (see how Andy can't tolerate his failures) they are given praise for abilities and trying hard and they have their efforts matched by significant challenges. But Andy is being offered a baby game – reading; what kind of challenge is that for a fifteen-year-old group leader?

The discussion which followed this presentation is a good example of the group at work. No one said to Fiona, 'Why didn't you do . . .'; instead, they brought their experience of comparable teaching situations to bear on the problem.

Commenting on what we heard, Fiona said: 'There's a possibility that Andy's aggressive behaviour may get him suspended from school before I can finish the study. If he stays, he has to resign himself to the slow measure of his progress. On a bad nervous day he becomes so dispirited as to reject the lessons altogether . . . my best hope is that he'll try.'

The group said nothing at all about Andy's slow, deep-voiced reading through which his anger with himself, the task and the world can clearly be heard. When he became too fretted to continue, Fiona urged him on. When she heard herself again, she commented:

All this is very embarrassing for us. It's one of those sessions I feel I have to go through with kids — talking about 'you aren't stupid because you can't read' — that great thing you have to keep dinning in to them. I can't bear the sound of myself on the tape . . .
He won't do reading for any length of time without asking for corrections.

Michael: (who was present in the early stages):
How does he respond to the other kids in Room 42?

Fiona: He bosses them around a bit. To start with he was very hostile because he felt they were going to laugh at him — such a big boy; he's big and he sounds adult. He felt aggressive and was vulnerable — he's calmed down. If anyone else messes about in Room 42 he's very heavy-handed with them. He's a sort of . . . self-elected bruiser. He regards me as his best hope at the moment of being able to read before he leaves school . . . he regards me . . . well, it doesn't seem too clear . . .

As Fiona listens with the group to Andy's explanation of his primary school reading experience, she explains that when Andy says 'I feel shown up', she thinks he has taken a great gamble in saying it.

M: The next thing you said was important: you say 'it's not like that . . .'
Michael: If that had been me I'd have switched the tape off, before anyone else heard it . . . but what you're doing is just so human . . . we all have ways of encouraging people . . . which are hard in many ways . . .
V: Listening to the tape . . . we hear ourselves in contrast to the child . . . it makes one feel so remote: One's voice is so distant . . . and . . . we're struggling . . .
J: When I do that kind of encouraging, I don't actually know if I believe myself. If I was saying something like, 'Well, dear, it isn't

because you can't concentrate (is that what you said?) it's because
you don't know the sounds yet . . .'

Eliz: 'Yes . . .'

J: At the back of my mind, I may be thinking, well it really is just
because he *doesn't* concentrate . . . I do feel guilty.

V: That's why I think it's so embarrassing to listen to oneself afterwards: not only because it's bad, but also because one isn't sure
one's telling the truth.

E: That wasn't the case in that last bit, he's saying I'm no good and
she's saying, yes you are.

Michael: Or . . . you mustn't think of it like that . . . the bit about
riding a bicycle is good (Fiona had explained to Andy that you have
to take chances as you do when you can ride, this leads to a digres-
sion about Fiona's bike problems).

M: The point is a real one . . . the encouragement doesn't teach him;
it only makes it possible to teach him.

F: Yes, well, preparing the . . .

M: For what they need to learn, however they learn it . . .

E: Sometimes they know some of these things, sometimes encouragement makes it possible for them to do them, they want to hear
you saying it then . . . and every lesson.

F: It goes on to an awful histrionic thing about how some brilliant
people can't read, and you mustn't think you're hopeless.

M: The way the pupil sees himself as a learner is crucial. If they think
it isn't going to work even before we begin . . . it becomes part of
their lifestyle.

Steve: I was going to say . . . is there anything to be said for their
(i.e. the pupils') belief that you − the teacher − have a much clearer
idea of how it all works than you in fact have? You were saying,
well, you might be embarrassed about hearing yourself say − 'You
don't know the letter sounds' − because it wasn't too helpful a
comment . . . it might be good for the child to have an idea of you
really knowing what it's all about − what you really have to do . . .
by the time some progress has been made he may have forgotten
it all . . . the idea that there is something specific for him to do must
be an encouragement.

J: This tape was made early as . . . would it be damaging to you to
say . . . for him to be told by you . . . 'it's not because you can't
concentrate . . . it may be because you don't know the sounds of the
letters yet!' He may be happy to have you say it . . . maybe the child
needs to have you say − 'I'm going to watch what you're doing and

see if I can make out what's been going wrong: and not to – sort of – say, 'I'm *sure* you're bright enough to read.' The child must ask himself 'How does *she* know I'm bright?'

F: Yes, right from the start. But the thing that shines out about Andy – he's afraid he's *thick*.

E: But in fact you don't have to be very intelligent to read . . . I was told that usually anyone can learn to read . . .

M: You also want them to be reassured that we're not being easily dismissive, saying 'No, no, no, that can't be the case.' . . . You're saying the opposite of what everyone has been telling him for ages . . . they've been telling him he's thick . . . or that's how he construes it, and maybe he needed you to say, well, what shall we do to find out what goes on? [Judith's point.] This seems to be very good . . . halfway towards saying 'let's work out together what you need to know to do . . . the next move . . .'

J: It's the feeling that the child could be saying, Here we are again, face to face with glib reassurance, and they see through it . . .

Michael: If I think of the situations when I've needed it myself, as an adult, even though I sensed the words to be only a form of words I've absorbed the spirit in which they're offered . . . I do identify it in all its precarious state of genuineness and sincerity. I still take the tone of assurance.

V: I think it degrades who it comes from – not what we say so much . . . if he has confidence in you and knows you wouldn't say it unless you were serious . . . if a complete stranger came in and said it, it would be different . . . but he has known you over a period . . . you're predictable and comfortable . . . on the basis of that he'll accept you saying, you'll learn to read.

F: He's enormously touchy still. He wanted a friend to come up [to Room 42] and I was explaining to him as frankly as I could that the friend, who has severe reading difficulties, would need as much time as he needed, and to have them both up together would make him have less attention. At the moment when I said 'He needs as much attention as you need,' he said, *'Thanks very much'* – he was livid at the suggestion.

Michael: Holt[4] implies that constant over-encouragement may give the child a notion of what you expect of him which he then feels more and more anxious about failing to meet. I've never quite known what the breaking point was – where you can not *reward*, for that's a behaviourist term – without being overtly praising all the time . . . the suggestion is that when you get a good answer to a question the best confirming response is another question — that shows you're interested in what they have to say, but you've confirmed the value of it.

M: It's not just a case of encouragement. You have to see yourself *getting better*.

V: Supposing the child isn't working at making great strides and is conscious of it. What do you say?

M: The tape recorder helps: you can say, 'do you remember what you were like?' . . . Then play a bit that shows they have improved, even if only slightly — still they need to understand what they can't do and not be oppressed by thinking about what they ought to be able to do. People are upping the success rate all the time. . . . I find the balance tricky at every stage.

Michael: I'd be interested in the value of two people learning together — as when Labov[5] talks about the asymmetrical thing — the child can't escape . . . would it be better with a pair, so that the teacher can listen — or leave — or whatever?

The discussion continues on the topic of teaching two children together instead of one on his own. Fiona has found the group to be sympathetic listeners; they haven't given her orders. Instead they are exploring how to give the pupil enough insight into his position, the helpful blend of support, information and a hold on the future. Andy has had almost too much failure and wants to stand well in Fiona's eyes. So the group tries to help her to give him the encouragement he needs, but not too much as he will simply think he is bound to fail again — this time with someone he cares about. He needs both a new view of himself, *and* information about how reading works, *and* readership experience even beyond the kind of books he is prepared to handle at this stage.

Andy's anger has clearly subdued the group. They want to help Fiona but have too much tact to say 'Why don't you do . . .?' They know Andy needs better reading strategies, but they know too that he has to be prepared to see himself in a different light if anything is to make a difference. All of this may be second nature to anyone reading this; it seems fairly straightforward in a report. But Fiona's instinct, that if Andy is given another set of instructions that fail, he will be in a worse state, is a sound one. M said later in that session: 'If you're at Andy's stage you believe you will never be able to devise anything that will work. At the same time you don't want orders, because inside school and out you're being ordered all the time.'

Fiona chose to teach Andy because he was probably the toughest nut to crack, and also because she believed he had never really been taught. At this early stage we learned these things: the humiliation of hearing ourselves saying things we'd rather not have said; the difficulty of teaching a strategy for learning when the learner has no belief in his ability to succeed. Fiona helped us to be clearer about what we did. We became subtler in our self-awareness, and we came to understand that direct insistence, however sound ('do this and it will work'), is useless if the pupil cannot use the information he is offered.

Fiona's encounters with Andy made it quite clear that we could not have considered the problems of teaching a child to read as only reading problems. He comes to the task with his view of himself challenged by the teacher's view of him, his socio-cultural background and his total context of self-regard. Andy was the first pupil to say, 'You think I'm stupid', the remark echoed by every pupil we taught. What did he think Fiona wanted for him? All his behaviour suggested that he knew she wished him well, but sometimes that was also more than he could bear. His view of being a reader was equally muddled. He read aloud like a six-year-old, but he wanted to be good at it. He had some idea that he thought good readers wouldn't do what he was doing, yet he didn't know what else to do. Fiona's assurance that if he read more he'd get better was somehow not enough at this stage. When we listened to Andy we heard him do what teachers say they do when they teach sounding and blending, decoding, textual reproduction. He is slow, dull, plodding, angry at being subjected to the humiliation of it all, determined to get it right, but with no real intention to make the text part of his thinking, so that it remains an alien object.

Sharon and Vicky

Vicky put us all to shame. She recorded thirteen lessons in a row with a small group of girls which included one, Sharon, who was being singled out for special attention although the others were not to be made aware of this. Vicky explained what she did by saying that she just let the tape run in lessons, then she edited it so that we could hear the reading passages. All of this happened in the first term of our study. What you are to read now comes from Vicky's edited master tape of the lessons and the comments of the group on what they heard.

We have already explained the situation in Vicky's school whereby children in their first year can have reading lessons. Vicky chose Sharon because she seemed to be 'into' reading, although none of her other class teachers would have said so. Vicky saw her as 'difficult but interesting'; later she changed her mind. Her family is of Jamaican origin, but Sharon was born in London. She comes at the end of a line of three brothers and five sisters. Most of them have left home.

In all her reports about Sharon, Vicky mentions her moody hostility to the world around her. She is 'quick to express her feelings of whatever kind'; she shows 'anxiety when faced with reading'. Reports from all her teachers suggest instability, and Vicky is persuaded at the start that if Sharon could read well she would change the attitude of others towards her. Her easily distractable personality, volatile and aggressive, makes the task of teaching her to read and write an exercise for steady nerves.

Sharon came to Vicky's school with a reading report that said she was 'too impatient to think words out'. It included, 'will not look at initial sounds. Needs continual training to organize her thoughts and to be systematic. She knows the basic sounds but has difficulty in blending them together. Needs help with spelling and grammar when she writes'. Her primary school report gave her a reading age of 6.7 when she was eight. Vicky reports that she 'guesses wildly at words or waits to be told' and 'does not know the sounds'. She 'reads word by word'. When we listen to her, we are surprised by this view, she seems to be more fluent than we expected.

Vicky's estimation of Sharon's chances of success is based on the fact that despite her bravado, her noisy behaviour, the low view of her academic competence held by most of the teachers, Sharon likes stories and can retell a complicated story after hearing it once. She even relates the incident in one tale to another in a book she had had read to her. When she is being read to the quality of her attention is quite different from that in any other kind of activity she engages in. Yet her usual English teacher says she is 'very difficult'. Asked for her views on reading, Sharon says 'it's for tests or comics'.

Sharon had her lessons with Vicky in a stable group of girls all of whom were well-balanced and tolerant. None of their difficulties were so manifestly acute as Sharon's. She begged Vicky to let her take every book home, promising to bring it back the next day, but when no book was ever returned, Vicky would not let her take any more, despite protests and prayers. Sharon's favourite game was word bingo which she played with success but without any noticeable improvement in her reading.

From the thirteen recorded lessons, Vicky made a master tape from which we heard Sharon's insistent nagging, especially from the early session in which the *Take Part Book* version of *Flat Stanley* is read by the group. (These books contain plays made from well-known stories for children so that each character is given a part of the text graded in such a way that good readers and poorer readers may read together.) Sharon wanted the largest part and when that proved to be more than she bargained for, she argued for another one. We hear her read, *Flat Stanley, The Magic Finger, Are You My Mother, Mrs Pepperpot, Arthur.* She resents all writing and spelling tasks and refuses to compose a story for Vicky to write out for her.

We also hear Vicky wondering why she tries so hard with Sharon. 'What am I trying to get Sharon to read for? Why am I trying to get Sharon into books? Will there ever be books in her life? *Woman's Own* and TV more likely. Will she ever be able to read functionally (and better than she does already) in order not to be handicapped? But any more? To be able to help her own children when the time comes?' The crucial question for Vicky is, 'If she enjoys stories as she appears to, why is she not a reader?'

Sharon's reading is slow and laboured but fairly fluent. She groups about four words at a time. We felt that she might quite quickly get better because she has certainly 'got the hang of it'. Vicky's chief strategy is to keep Sharon going by suggesting that she reads ahead of a word that traps her. This is generally successful, as can be seen from Sharon's backtracking. But even when she is reading dialogue with a clear idea of who the characters are (e.g. in *Flat Stanley*) Sharon's voice still has the trace of the 'calling back' of early learners. She has some staying power and she can read to herself, but her irascible, unpredictable temper, her unease, and her manipulation of Vicky by covert threat of disruption make her a troublesome classroom character. Vicky treats her patiently, sometimes more reasonably than Sharon absolutely deserves. As long as she is at the centre of events, drawing attention to herself, Sharon is cheerful, enthusiastic and assertive.

Vicky's master tape and her field notes represent a considerable undertaking, not least in terms of the listening and writing time involved. From the tapes Vicky selected for us what she saw as 'characteristic Sharon utterances'.

'Miss, I'm always reading to you first. I'll be first but I'm not reading for long — ten minutes.'

'I don't like people sitting on the table when I'm reading.'

'My Dad used to read me bedtime stories. I read to my little sister.'

In some of them Vicky detects a kind of bluff, as when Sharon says she used to take home books from the school library but doesn't any more because her Mum and Dad buy books now.

Vicky's most sustained conversation with Sharon was initiated by Sharon to discuss Vicky's children. Sharon asked her how much pocket money they had and whether Vicky hit them when they were naughty. They discussed whether her children 'put it on' about not wanting to go to school, the time of going to bed, and whether or not they share a room. At one point, Sharon says, 'You know miss, white people, well, every time their grandmothers buy them a pram.' Later she asks: 'If your husband died, would you take the children to the funeral?' She added: 'You should take them, or how would they know he was dead?' There is no indication of how this idea arose.

The clearest sign of Sharon's competence comes when she is able to read for a long stretch. As she carries on the story, her intonation becomes more firmly linked to the meaning, her anticipations are more often confirmed and you can hear her behaving like a storyteller, differentiating the characters. There is every reason to believe that Sharon could make it, if her moods do not get the better of her.

The presentation of Vicky's summary tape at the last session of our first term was a special occasion. This was really our expression of pleasure in getting what Elizabeth called, 'the whole child'. We were still tentative about discussing the teacher's strategies in lessons, anxious to approve of each other rather than to suggest alternative ways of behaving.

V: While you're actually doing it you can't stop (i.e. to ask yourself what you're doing). They get very irritated if you interrupt. You must keep going . . .

M: We're now working it backwards . . .

V: You can pick up some things afterwards, but not a lot; they're not interested in their mistakes after you've got on with the story . . . it's gone, it's happened, it's not relevant any more . . .

M: Could we make a collection of the kind of things that make them falter? . . . (the example discussed was an adjective clause).

Judith: She falters at 'underneath'.

S: Not at under . . .

V: I gave her *underneath*.

S: 'Under' would do . . . I thought she got as far as *under* . . .

V: No, no, well . . .

S: *Under*, rather than *underneath* might be the word she would use.

M: Can we be sure about that? Why are we picking on this, d'you think?

At this point two kinds of discussion are progressing. We are focusing on Sharon's strategies, and we are trying to find a way of working together where disagreement is not threatening. Within the sub-text of our talk is an exploration of what constitutes evidence. We are also trying out tentative ways of challenging each other. The discussion of the first encounter with the child is our way of coming to know her and Vicky better; it is also the proving ground for the first encounters within the group itself. Vicky is still thinking about a question from Judith as to whether *Flat Stanley* was new text for that group of children, or known text. The question is important, because we have already agreed that children's performance is better if they have some idea of the totality of the narrative they are reading. Vicky then makes a significant point about a book as an object, which brings us to another landing stage.

V: In general . . . when . . . if . . . they choose a book from the bookshelves to read on their own, I try to make sure very child has a book they're reading, they read to me sometimes . . . I don't . . . um . . . sometimes I just let them read without any preliminary talk . . . that might happen frequently . . . um. . . . I don't have a policy of talking about every book before they read it.

M: In the end they have to find their own way in . . . I think it helps sometimes.

V: But some of them seem able to choose a book and find their way in . . . look at the title, the pictures, the size of the print, the distribution of the print . . . so, um . . . there's a lot of preliminary looking before they actually read, and they seem to have very clear cut ideas of what they will read and what they won't read.

M: I'm keen to record that as something we all know and never mention. It's never a case of choosing a book (whoever chooses) and starting. Even if they cannot read much.

V: They know what they can read.

M: They have firm ideas about what they can read . . .

V: Yes, absolutely; it may be the shape of the book, the colour; at this

stage pictures are very relevant and the size of the print is crucial
. . . you can produce any number of books and you think this is
just right for them, just what they're interested in . . . the right
vocabulary . . . and they just say 'no'.

I think it's better for them to run around and find their own
books. . . . If they're really stuck and don't want to try or to read
anything . . . it's useful to tidy the shelves . . . so then they have a
real look at them.

M: They share this with good readers who also talk about what first
strikes them and what they look at, there is a 'getting into' problem at any stage . . .

V: Some just won't do what you want. . . . I always feel anxious about
not having enough books. They should be able to reject a lot and
still find something.

Michael: In playreading, how important is the relief that comes from
not having to read constantly . . . they read a line, follow one . . .

M: What are they doing when they are not reading . . . are they looking
and listening to the story as it comes out, or preparing their next
line . . .?

E: They are often preparing their next bit . . . in a good group they
support each other.

F: And don't you find that when it's not their turn they can read it
much better.

E: Enormously so. . .

V: Yes, you're getting her to read through the performance . . . it's
important to her . . .

M: You can't separate the reading you do from your vision of yourself
as a reader . . .

V: That's it you see. My problem is to keep some kind of a belief that
she has in herself as a reader while actually bringing her performance
up to her estimation of her competence . . . not, perhaps, belief in
herself as a reader even . . . just belief in herself . . .

Michael: How does she stand with the other kids . . .?

V: They let her get away with a lot . . . she's been a lot of trouble . .

A discussion of this kind deserves a very 'thick' analysis to unravel
all the layers of implications for teachers, pupils, publishers, curriculum
makers, remedial specialists and reading theorists. It is too glib to say,
as many essayists have done, that Vicky's concern is to improve Sharon's
'self-image' so that she may read better. Vicky is arguing that teaching
Sharon cannot be separated from the realities of her cultural and social

context, the way language and learning serve her needs, the chances of success for both when the limit of Vicky's tolerance is great and Sharon's is very little. In sharing their thoughts and experiences, both teacher and taught make more possible what one wants to do and the other has very little vision of. By means of books and personal encouragement, Vicky offers Sharon a change of role, values, opportunities and experiences. The next step has to be Sharon's. But she is not persuaded that she needs to learn to be literate. Reading has no embedded function in her life. Stories are largely part of an oral culture that she may also find in a book, but she is not sure where to look for them out of school.

Before the end of our first term together we discussed Vicky's view of Sharon and her chances of success. Tentatively, knowing that to criticize the amount of work Vicky had done would be to alienate her from the operation, Margaret tried to raise the question of how the selection was made from all the raw tapes of lessons to make the master tape. In order to decide what she would leave out, Vicky must have operated a view of what constituted *evidence*, what it was important to keep. But the raw tape had been wiped and used again. It was clear, however, that, like Fiona, Vicky rejected the exercises and games – word bingo and the like – as diversions from the real task of making readers who interact with texts. If Sharon was to learn to read, then reading would have to become part of her as well as something she could do.

For all that she regretted the loss of the raw tape as evidence of how Vicky made her selection, Margaret was persuaded that this significant contribution to the group's work showed just how complicated the evidence was to become. The group as a whole was very appreciative:

J: I think you've set up an amazing model for us.
V: I didn't realize . . . for I was a guinea pig. . . . I didn't know what I was letting myself in for. . . . I gaily left the tape on the table and acquired yards of tape for which I . . . sort of . . . picked the odd pearl . . . you know, actually finding that odd pearl . . .
Eliz: Did you listen to it all again.
F: I'm surprised you got as far as picking . . .
V: Yes.
F: Pearls.
J: I don't know how you found the time to do it . . .
V: I think this is something to learn from, in a way. . . . I wouldn't wish it on anybody else.

E: Do you know when you hear it . . . 'that is a pearl?' or do you
only know when you hear it again.

V: It's like editing a film . . . you select this short and that . . . the one
you look prettiest in.

E: Do you know during the lesson . . .?

V: During the lesson, no. I've got five kids and there are all different
things happening at the same time . . . I just let it run.

Michael: What did you feel as you listened? What is the experience of
being the participant and the listener?

V: Pretty traumatic: certainly for me, possibly in that I was conscious
of all sorts of things . . . I didn't enjoy it because I didn't enjoy hearing my own voice so continuously. It was quite revealing . . . about
all sorts of things I do . . .

J: Do you think you've learned?

V: Yes, I've learned quite a lot myself which . . .

J: You now know.

V: I wouldn't want to go through all that again . . . you see, what I'm
trying to get at is whether we should . . . if it would be more practical and realistic just to have the reading passages of what we do and
not . . . you know, the comments on the child as a whole, because I
think that's just too much . . .

M: I think we needed it all: the data is what you've got . . . the selection
is how you look at it . . . what you did was to distill it out for us. I
suppose that if we were really being 'scientific' we should hear every
single word on the raw tape and to put several kinds of 'search
editings' on it — as they did at Harvard in the early language acquisi-
tion studies. But we're working teachers finding out the worth of
our practical wisdom . . . we can monitor your selection, even, to
look at what you are looking at . . . and we can say, 'you have
given us a picture of the characteristic difficulties encountered by
this child' . . . whatever happens I don't think we can make a good
selection from a small amount of tape, we can only work with long
stretches of it . . . none of it is wasted . . . if we want to say 'what
was she like doing this?' then we listen to it.

V: There's going to be a great deal if everyone's going to do it.

M: We'll have to do a lot of editing when we've decided what we want
to keep . . . but we'll certainly want to know 'that's what this child
was like when we began!'

F: I very much endorse this: out of the mass of tape that I've got I've
created for myself a whole lot of lovely material. The things I've
missed during the lesson I can now go back over when I've got the

time. I haven't worked out my distillation process yet, but here it all is.

M: Supposing, in the light of listening to all of this we had to ask ourselves, 'In what terms can we now discuss a pupil who has reading
problems?' . . . In the books the descriptions are all the same . . .
the terms are set up for us . . . sounding and blending . . . word
attacks . . . poor intonation. . . . Supposing we wanted to say . . .
something like . . . 'You think a non-reader has reading problems.
But our inquiry shows that reading is, in a way, the least of their
problems . . .' If we're trying to be pretty fundamental to ask 'what
are children with reading difficulties *like*? . . . you can only come
up with saying, 'well, they're like Sharon or Andy, like this and
this' . . . They've got so little in common that it's useless talking
about them as if they were a group. That might be something to
say. I don't think there's hard evidence like this about. . . . So I'm
asking you to be patient . . .

V: Before I start with another pupil I'd like to define more closely
what I'm doing . . . and whether it's for me or someone else.

M: Do it the way for you, I think.

V: I'll do less of this free running or I'd leave out about writing or
chatting to a friend . . .

M: It's having it there that counts. . . . That could have meant leaving
out all these views Sharon has about class and white people.

V: I'd make the tapes, but I wouldn't be able to edit them in the same
way.

We now knew the full extent of what we had set ourselves to do, and
we decided we should only be able to do what we could. Vicky had
clearly pointed out that involvement in the group was costly in time
and commitment, but so far the results in terms of awareness of ourselves, and a new consciousness of our interaction with our pupils had
been worthwhile. Perhaps part of her disappointment came from the
fact that Sharon's story breaks off here; she was removed to a special
school as her needs seemed to warrant it. This, too, is the reality of
much of this kind of teaching. The group sympathized with Vicky
but were also persuaded that her efforts to make Sharon feel more
of a person could not have been in vain.

As the result of these first term discussions, we felt more at ease
with each other. Some sensitive areas remained and we had not yet
put together Vicky's passionate belief that reading is to enjoy stories
and her trained response, 'You have to read exactly what's there.' We

were now agreed that some aspects of remedial provision did more harm than good, and that reading needed to be purposive and part of the child's intentions for himself or herself. We had survived the early traumatic listening to tapes where we heard ourselves saying things to children that made us blush with embarrassment. We had also done a fair amount of reading for ourselves.

At this point, we also began to realize our limitations. As the taped evidence mounted, we realized we could not deal with all of it equally in the course of our ordinary working lives. Yet what we had collected was already changing our views of our teaching. We decided, therefore that we should press on to do all we could, and not settle for less than we had to.

Chris and Elizabeth

At one point we discussed whether Margaret should go on a round of visits to see the pupils and their teachers together. We decided that, as consultant and scribe, her task was to see the pupil through the teacher's eyes, to construe the teacher's construing of the pupil rather than to interject an alternative vision. Margaret learned quickly just how sensitive each teacher was to the pupil's needs, and in the early days everyone hesitated to offer comments about the pupils' reading behaviour lest it should appear to be a criticism of a teacher. To begin with, the reports of lessons were made up of narrative incidents and circumstantial detail of the special conditions of the lesson itself. Gradually, we began to offer each other suggestions and intuitions. We coined for Chris, Elizabeth's pupil, the idea of 'the evader', taking care, however, not to let this condition our view of his progress.

From the first encounter Elizabeth made it clear that if Chris was to get better, he would have to bring his eyes to the print — a feat that he avoided more successfully than any of the others. Yet, even when she saw that this was Chris's first problem, Elizabeth knew she could not simply take a straight line through it in case she found herself with a pupil whose only determination was to resist her best efforts to help him. It was Elizabeth who said, 'I find I can't plan lessons. I can only go back over them and learn from them, but I still can't plan the next one.' Yet she can generalize from her experience, and at all times she asked the most penetrating questions.

Elizabeth told the group about her early encounters with Chris when we had already begun an inquiry into what progress would be like. We had quickly become aware of one of the most difficult tangles of longitudinal studies, the need to look at three stages at once: the one we had just completed and were writing about, the current one in the class with the pupil, and the necessary planning for the next stage. We found that we concentrated on the present and the past, but even so, our meetings were now too short for us to cover all the ground or to collect all that became evidence when we had sifted the tapes. Consequently, we agreed that we should let Elizabeth, Judith and Steve put us into the picture without too much time being spent on commentary, except where it was necessary for elucidation. So Elizabeth and Judith now give us the bare bones of their early encounters with Chris and Trevor, but we shall meet them again.

'Chris had been at the school one term when I started to teach there. It was then the spring term of his first year (1974). At that time the withdrawal groups for reading consisted of 12–15 pupils, and most of those who were to teach reading had themselves arrived at the school the previous September and found themselves with a few periods of reading on their timetables. The school had bought the *Step Up and Read* materials,[6] and most of the teachers, including Chris's were using this. She told me at the time that, although he was very backward in reading, she thought he was very intelligent, and she wanted to find extra time to help him as he seemed lost in the big group. His reading age on entry was 7.6 on the Schonell Silent Reading Test and at the end of the first year it was 6.4 on the Schonell Graded Word Reading Test.

I took him on at the beginning of the second year. He was in a group of four: one boy from his own class, another second year boy, who was a chronic truant, and another boy, also given to periodic truanting, from the third year. Chris's attendance, however, has always been exemplary, and so it happened that there were long periods through the year when he was the only pupil present. One of the things I rapidly learned about Chris was his love of talking, and a great deal of our time was spent in conversation. One of the things that he told me was that his father was mentally ill, that he suffered from schizophrenia [his word] and was unable to work.

When Chris came to me he used phonics almost exclusively to find his way through a text. He never seemed to predict or guess a word. He did seem to be paying attention to what he was reading, though he rarely commented on it. When asked, he said that he didn't like reading, that he found it hard work. One might have guessed this from the way he read, and the way he occasionally contorted his face with effort in the process. He very much enjoyed being read to, and showed considerable powers of concentration when listening. He also liked dictating stories to me or on to tape.

He has more than once commented on his primary school experience. The following quotation is from a taped interview which Chris and Clairmont, another boy in the group, made:

Clair: What did the teachers treat you like at your primary school?
Chris: They treated me like if I was a thick little idiot. They put me on the side. They give me drawings to do. They didn't make me do work.
Clair: Did they put you at the back of the class?
Chris: No, not that, but they made it really feel obvious that I was a dunce by giving me drawings to do and that.

He also said that he was nearly sent to a special school, only his parents intervened. The school psychologist made a report on him just before transfer to secondary school. On the WISC scale his verbal score was 104 and his performance score 80. The psychologist records difficulties in motor areas and says, "he will need a detailed remedial approach at senior school and at the same time will need to be encouraged to dispel his anxious inhibited attitude to written work . . . the senior school may find it appropriate to contact the psychologist again should the remedial programme fail to show results". She reports Chris's mother as saying that they nearly lost Chris at the age of three from a severe feverish illness, and concludes "the question of mild brain damage must be left open".

The primary school profile shows a reading age of 6.06 on Holborn, and sums him up as "intelligent, articulate, but a non-reader". The profile also says that he had no grasp of sounds, despite considerable help. This is a little odd in view of the fact that a year later phonics appeared to be his sole strategy.

He talked about explanations for being unable to read in a discussion with his third year reading group.

Me [Eliz] : Why do you think you had difficulties in reading?
Chris: Because when I was three I went into hospital. . . . I had scarlet fever . . . and about five other diseases all at one time . . . I had to go in hospital. They reckoned that . . . if it wasn't my . . . er . . . my own strength I would've died already. I just can't grasp it anyway. I think it's something in my head, something happened to me then,

I think Miss, when I was . . .
Me: What sort of thing do you think?
Chris: Like when, you know, when you can't do something or other
because you're so ill you can't do nothing to –
Fay: Yeah, I know what you mean.
Chris: You sort of lose a gap in your mind . . . you lose some of your
mind 'cos, er . . .
Fay: You think of one thing next minute, then you lost it one minute.
Chris: Yeah, you can't grasp things like, miss, 'cos you forget it.
Me: Is that how you feel about reading?
Chris: I'm always forgetting things at home as well, Miss.'

Elizabeth's account of the early encounters take for granted that Chris
is teachable in her eyes. He behaves like an adult, at least in conversation. He gives reading a fair chance in terms of attendance and concentration, but he successfully evades contact with troublesome text as
often as he can, as it is 'hard work'. Most reading teachers recognize
the beads of sweat, the tense hands and furrowed brow of the struggling
reader. Like others, Chris is not fighting only with the text, but with
all his past failure to make print yield meaning. Elizabeth sees him as
the victim of his earlier teaching, which she also has to struggle against.
She is hampered in that the strategy Chris uses (phonic sounding)
gives him no help, while the psychologist who tested him says he can't
use that very strategy. There is a let-out clause for them all: Chris,
the psychologist and Elizabeth. Only Elizabeth does not accept the
excuse of Chris's early illness (the psychologist's hint of brain damage)
and proceeds to treat him as a possible learner. She has solid evidence
that Chris's view of himself 'as a non-reader' is well and truly ground in.
   Here again is evidence of the importance of the very earliest primary
school encounters in the reading process. Being ignored, being told to
'draw', or exclusion from the principal reading activities in the class are
poor substitutes for taking the process actively in hand. 'They treated
me like if I was a thick little idiot' – is behind every effort that Chris
makes. That is the burden he is trying to shift with his attendance and
concentration. Elizabeth's problem is to make the bridge between his
enjoyment at being read to and these agonizing efforts. Chris thinks
there is a gap in his head that is a lack of memory – a lost trace of 'how
to do it'. He has several options open to him: should he let Elizabeth
tell him what the words say until he can tell himself what to do to get
the meaning? Should he keep looking at what he knows? He can recognize words and thus dispel his fears about his memory. By knowing in

in advance what is written down, he can lose the anguish of tackling new sentences especially if he has composed them. All of these things will help; the phonic strategy does not.

But the problem of the evaders — and Chris is clearly one — is not solved by exercises and 'skill' practice because these simply confirm reading as the kind of thing phonics were invented to explain — a tangling with the words, not an engagement with the discourse and its meaning. In the early stages Elizabeth could not make Chris discuss what he read. Reading wasn't for that purpose; talking did not need print, print was not talk. Again we see the pupil looking at the task not at the reward which, with another part of him, he fully understands. To become a reader, Chris has to negate his earlier experience in ways he finds intolerable. He has to take chances, to find out that he tells himself the story in the book. He must learn to expect to be successful. And because nothing in his experience has led him hitherto to try any of these things, he is unwilling to risk even one of them. Elizabeth's quiet tolerance is both reassuring, in that she is clearly out to help him, and threatening, because she is not strongly insistent on drill and therefore might not be supportive enough, in Chris's eyes. She knows what she wants to do; she expresses it as '*to bring the experience of being a reader closer to him*'. Chris's problem is to be confident enough to let her try.

Trevor and Judith

The first encounter of Judith and Trevor has to be seen in the context of the conflict in the school between the remedial department and the English department. Judith chose Trevor because he was the classic underachiever. He should have learned to read, but had mysteriously failed. Judith had taught him in his first year mixed ability English class, so that his reading lessons were, in fact, a tutorial extension of their work together.

Trevor was now 12.6. Born in London of Jamaican parents, he did not know that the couple he called mother and father were, in fact, his grandparents. In his early days in primary school his reports said he was 'confident, reliable, enthusiastic' and he had settled in well. But by the end of his two years in the infant school he was reported to be 'backward'. By the time he reached secondary school his record said, 'nervous and shy but popular'; 'pleasant', 'affable' and 'gentle' are other words used. His vocabulary was said to be 'poor' and it was recorded that he 'gave up easily'. Judith's view will emerge, but when she first met him she registered that he carried with him the rigidities of a strict home which had priorities of cleanliness and godliness.

Trevor selected himself for reading lessons when he knew that Judith was helping pupils individually. In many ways Judith found in Trevor an ideal pupil. He is keen on school, never truants and is always possessively loyal to his teachers. In class he reproves other pupils for eccentric behaviour and he is even strict with Judith. Far from hiding his lack of skill, he is proud of his special lessons and he comes to Judith's room even when he is not due for a lesson. He dislikes any interruption and he 'tuts' loudly if anyone comes in, even another member of staff. Judith says he is 'a lovable child' and 'very young for his years'. He greatly enjoys listening to stories, and on this Judith bases her hopes for his success, just as Vicky did with Sharon.

He has one tutorial session each week. He begins by putting up a token resistance to being taught — a kind of ritual, as if he expects Judith to overcome his reluctance and so enhance his chance of standing well in her estimation of him. In some ways he controls the session, especially when he rejects what Judith has brought for him to read and substitutes his own choice of material. He likes some new thing each time and he says, always, that he has a bad memory for what has gone before. He prefers to read 'baby' books, and when he finds anything difficult he sighs and regards reading as a chore or a memory game. He slides out of all strenuous effort.

Trevor's attitude to Judith is certainly ambivalent. He looks to her for help, resents interruption of his lessons, but at the same time he wants to prove Judith inefficient. For instance, he once wanted to memorize sounds from a word game. Judith found it difficult to get him to see that this activity was not helpful. When he was exasperated with his failure to do what he thought had to be done in the business of remembering sounds, he said, 'Next year when I can't read what will I do? Then I'll leave and go to the adult illiteracy centre.' He wouldn't let Judith tape-record his responses to the questions about why he couldn't read. He even wiped the tapes.

Above all, Trevor wants to drive Judith to the limit then ask to be reassured that he will still learn — that is, when he has refused to do what he is asked he still wants to know if Judith supports him. He sees his reading as something that he once had then lost. The prospect of taking the process in hand for himself is a daunting one, so he needs the assurance that he will not be blamed if he fails. For this reason in particular he finds it difficult to do more than just start. His crucial alibi is a thirty-day return voyage from Jamaica where he had been staying for nine months. He says he learned to read in the West Indies, but on the boat coming back he simply forgot it all. 'It was that journey, you see,' he says.

It is fairly clear that Trevor construes the reading task as important, hates himself for not being able to do it, clings to this alibi and sometimes blames Judith for failing to teach him. He still sees reading as something that will happen to him rather than a process he has to undertake to further his own intentions. Trevor sees himself as someone who has to learn to read by putting himself into the right position, the right attitude and frame of mind — even the right desire. He is persuaded that learning is reinforcement by someone outside himself. Judith's continuing presence is his guarantee of success. But reading, for Trevor, is a chore, like washing up, making things tidy, coming to lessons on time, all the things that a persistent mother has ritualized as 'good' and bringing reward. Judith says, 'He thinks that reading hasn't been "granted" to him. It's a brink situation all the time. He twitches like a hamster.'

Looking back at their early encounters, Judith says of her interaction with Trevor, 'I came out of these tapes so badly, emotional, blatant, brainwashing him into doing it my way.' Before she could concentrate on helping Trevor, Judith had to excise the dominance of Trevor's mother who had insisted that 'memorizing sounds' was the key to 'literacy', influenced by the BBC's programme for adults. When the early sessions became wholly unpleasant because Trevor insisted on learning phoneme-grapheme correspondences and did it so badly, Judith tried to persuade him that his reading would get better as a result of reading something he wanted to read. They also played Scrabble; Trevor was good at that, but Judith knew it was another diversionary tactic. Perhaps she felt she had been over-optimistic in expecting him to collaborate wholeheartedly on *her* terms when it was clear that to do so Trevor would have to change his expectations of what a reading teacher actually *did*.

So, there was a battle of wits. For instance, Judith asked Trevor what he wanted to be when he grew up. He said he'd be a footballer. By way of reassurance Judith said that she thought this was possible, and Trevor retorted, 'Ever heard of a footballer who can't read and write?' Judith construed Trevor's resilient persistence as his next best hope of success. When they are reading together and Judith seems about to help him, Trevor calls out, 'Wait, don't tell me; don't tell me', when he sticks. As the result of some of the early encounters Trevor now goes over what he has read with confidence. He has learned to scan ahead. But even when he has refused help, he waits for the word or the meaning to 'surface', even when he has been encouraged to try other strategies than 'sounding out'.

In common with Vicky, Fiona and Elizabeth, Judith sees Trevor's view of his task as the legacy of earlier teaching. He wants to be given as few clues as possible. He treats reading as a guessing game, not in the linguistic sense described by Goodman, but as an extension of the classroom ritual of the teacher asking questions of the 'guess what's in my head' variety that teachers ask so often. The story, the thrust of the meaning, the cohesion of the text, are all part of a process that Trevor cannot yet relate to the language that he uses every day.

Judith suggests that Trevor is in a quandary about his reading because he does not know whom to trust. With Judith he makes slow progress because he wants to throw at her all his failure and what other people (especially his mother) say *should* be happening in reading lessons. He genuinely believes that there is a 'key' to reading that Judith is not giving him. Judith sees his determination to prove that he could read as keeping him going, even when it is overlaid by a deeper belief that he will never do it. Her instinct is to give Trevor enough success to let him see himself taking the process in hand; to understand that he *has* the key. She also knows that this will lay on him a burden of precisely the kind he moved away from. She says, 'I need doses of Frank Smith every now and then to restore my faith in what I'm doing when Trevor wants a work sheet.'

There is an early tape-recording of Trevor on his own. He did not want his sessions recorded, but on one occasion when he 'couldn't face going to maths', Judith asked him to read into the machine. Instead of reading he made up a story about a haunted house, full of sound effects and simulated fury, made louder by interventions on his clarinet. It was the sound of a very angry little boy.

Perhaps Judith's anxiety for Trevor, her self-criticism and frustration arise as much from her concern to see him escape from being the victim of his classmates as well as his overall situation. Her attempts to understand his thought processes, his world picture, his construing of himself were always, in her judgment, only partially successful. All her sympathetic attempts to understand what it was like to be Trevor also shook some of her dearest held beliefs about reading. Judith wants reading to be part of Trevor's life. *He* wants it to be some kind of skill, like football, that he has in addition to everything else.

Trevor had one great advantage. Right from the start, however

stilted and recital-like was his reading aloud, he would *interrogate* the
texts, keeping up a running commentary of his own views set against
those of the author. Judith's problem was to get him to see that this
was readerly behaviour, however 'babyish' the book.
Quite often Trevor refused even to attempt to read the book Judith
offered him. Then she would let him return to some more simple text
just to confirm his feeling of success. Trevor's great luck was Judith's
book supply.

Judith: This morning I chose something obviously too difficult. *The
Magician who Lost his Magic*. He wanted to read it – he knows the
story, I think . . . he floundered hopelessly and gave up. I said he
could choose another, so he chose *Big Dog, Little Dog*, which is in-
credibly easy. He ran through it and loved it. It brought him back
to knowing he was a reader. . . . I do definitely think that every now
and then he needs to be thoroughly at home in a book that reminds
him that he is getting on . . .
Vicky: I find this with Ladybird books. I may bring some in and my
pupils say they like them, they're the ones they can read . . . they go
back to them . . although they're awful to read. They feel they are
on familiar ground.
Steve: But I know well that what one child finds difficult another finds
easy, so there's no point in all those stars and circles that grade the
books. They're really just grading the children again. At least I
thought so until I went to visit a school last week where the children
had done the grading. That was interesting because it had been done
very thoughtfully. I don't like labelling things but . . . it's all very
well to say 'go and choose a book'. If there are book cases full of
books you sometimes haven't a clue. But if you think that 90 per
cent of the books you are looking at have been chosen by your
friends as good to read at your stage, you're likely to stick at
choosing for longer . . .

Judith sums up the end of her first stage with Trevor:

'At the beginning he thought that reading was only to do with letters
and sounds, and if I abandoned him to a text he would mumble
through without making any sense at all. My initial view of my task
was to give him support so that he could pretend to be a reader. That's
where I got those lovely early tapes from, *Mr Rabbit and the Lovely
Present*, and so on. He was reciting as much as reading, but he began to

know what it felt like to read. . . . I was also convinced that if I hadn't
gone on reading to him, he would have lost sight of the fun of reading,
the fun of stories . . . it was the only way I could give him enough
support to read back to me. . I read a lot of books several times and he
read them back. *Jim and the Beanstalk*, for instance, lends itself to
dramatization. I suppose I had to persuade him that it was all worth the
effort. The way I actually did that was to sit back without the book
and let him see that he could have my attention. . . The crunch comes
when you start withdrawing support, which he hates, because he still
goes back to letters and sounds and they don't let him feel he is reading.'

John and Steve

At this point it is good to recall the kind of patience the members of
the group had to show towards each other. We listened to whole lessons
with all of their indecisions and the accompanying explanations. There
were the normal group supports too. We gave each other book titles
and accounts of success; we mourned over our shortcomings. All of
this took time and can be of little interest now outside the group whose
concerns they fed, although you have only our word for what we have
left out. Our sessions now occupied whole evenings. The collaborative
pattern was developing strongly and we were becoming more patient.
Of us all, Steve listened longest as his early encounters were presented
last, but when he came to talk about John he elicited from the group
some of the best insights in that first six months. Steve told the group
that the head of English had said, 'Here's one who can hardly begin.'
Someone had done a Daniels and Diack test that gave him a reading age
of 6+. He arrived for his first lesson with Steve with a piece of writing
he had done about aeroplanes. The group agreed that the writing was
about six- or seven-year-old level. Steve reported that his new pupil
was physically, emotionally and in behaviour, very young for his age
(11+). He told anecdotes in the graphic way of younger children,
making aeroplane noises and lots of interjections. We heard him on
the tape of their first meeting when Steve asked him to read his written
piece. He read it word by word, hesitantly but accurately for the most
part, and with only a little help.

Margaret asks the group: 'What crosses your mind when you hear
him reading like that?'

Steve: As it's the very first time I've ever heard him I'm saying to

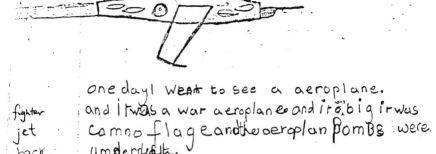

fighter

jet

back.

engines

One day I went to see a aeroplane.
and I was a war aeroplanes and it o̎big it was
Camnoflag eandthe oeroplan Bombs were.
Um derntedt.
and it was a jec fighter and it was a jet—
engines with the engines at the back.

myself: he's relying so heavily on memory and it's something he's
interested in . . . I think there are a lot of words he wouldn't be able
to read out of the context of what he's written. I'm encouraged that
he does that, and he reads it more competently the second time.
Vicky: I wonder if it's a kind of formula he uses if he's asked to write
something . . .
Steve: You mean, perhaps he's done it all before?
Judith: He said he went to see an aeroplane . . .

Steve then explains that they had discussed the aeroplane incident with
the tape-recorder running. John spoke very quickly, telling of a visit
to a war museum where a particular incident occurred. Steve later
listened to John on the tape and wrote up the incident as he told it.
Here is Steve's version, completed by John who filled in the gaps left
in the transcript. The title was added in the second lesson:

My Holiday

When I was away in a children's home we went on holiday and we
went to see [a kind of museum]. And there was tanks and there was
aeroplanes and helicopters. I sat in a tank. And no one knew it was
open and nor did I. I was just walking along and I fell in. I was
climbing over the top of it, because you weren't allowed to climb
over that one you had to pay 10p. And I was walking along and I
go AAAAH!! and I fell inside and the door shut on the top and
everybody else was walking past and when [my uncle] was looking
for me I pop my head out of the thing and I had a big bruise right

there and I had stitches all the way along and I had stitches on my lip.

Steve had left a space at the end of the second line. John added 'a kind of museum', pronouncing the words clearly and carefully. With this text between them, Steve and John discussed the tank incident. This allowed Steve to learn more details about John's life in the children's home. As we listened to the tape of the lesson we heard John, unprompted by Steve, reading the lists of words on the classroom wall. He has no difficulty in doing this. Then he turned over the pages of *Asterix the Gaul* which was lying nearby and said, 'It's not in our country's words, is it?' Steve hovered between asking general questions and asking him to read aloud – a difficult thing to do with a comic. (Hence the usefulness of this kind of material.)

Later in the lesson, Steve asked John to read his composition again, and in the group discussion of this tape he said he thought the reading was better because it had 'more momentum'. Margaret asked if John had any idea about the way in which what he said had become what he read, how his anecdote became a text, but Steve wasn't sure.

Vicky: I wonder how much he was understanding?

Steve: I think his style of reading would lead you to believe he doesn't know. . . . He talks so much and so fast . . .

V: It's part of his stream of consciousness thing . . . he's so fluent in speech. . . . I wonder if you talked about it again . . . brought it back to him . . . his reading would have been better . . .

Judith: I've got the feeling that you could have given him a totally unseen piece and he would have done it no worse.

V: A lot of it sounds like a first encounter – he was struggling with the words.

J: Was this the first time anyone has typed out his speech? He must have been quite stunned . . .

S: Yes, he was quite surprised by it all . . . I thought I'd just try . . . see how much better he is on the second line . . .

M: Is he better? How is he better?

We listen again and hear him say '*Mewzealand*' for *museum*.

S: Isn't that what much younger children do – get words confused on sound . . . when there isn't much semantic connection . . . then we go through a terrible palaver when I try to make him break it down: *mu-se-um* – there is a tremendous problem . . . it keeps coming out as Mew-see-land.

J: It's an *idée fixe* . . .

M: There's an association between what he knows (NZ) and what he doesn't yet hold as a word (museum). I wonder what kind of an idea he has for *New Zealand*?

We discuss this, but do not resolve it, so we shelve this problem as a 'collector's item' after fifteen minutes of listening and puzzling. Later on, John says; 'across' for 'along' every time and we disagree about whether or not John is reading better. Steve says he'd like to do a miscue analysis on both the first and second readings to see if there are strategies operating in the second reading that were not present in the first. The difficulty is that Steve is helping on both occasions. But John does, in fact, get more words 'right' on his own at the second reading. Steve is persuaded that in the second reading John is using reading strategies not remembering ones. Margaret thinks that when he reads he is cueing from initial consonants.

J: Did he say *f-ell*?

M: He was going to say left but he then said f-ell [we listen again].

S: He has no hesitation about *helicopters*: but *sat* always poses a problem. Both times he read *s-at*.

V: *Across* is all right for *along*, isn't it, in meaning at least?

J: How many times did you read this small piece?

S: Three times. I wouldn't normally press anything so much. It was just an exploratory stage with him – seeing what he'd do. Ten days later, although he said 'I don't have to read this *again*, do I?' he got *across* and *along* quite right until the last line when he said *across* again.

M: Did you ask him how he thought he might remember the difference between them?

S: I probably said – wait . . . I'll find it . . .

M: If you did tell him, he'll try to remember what you tell him. If you ask him, 'if you had to say what was the difference between *across* and *along*, what would you say?' either he takes on your exaplanation for himself, or he makes his own.

Steve is uncertain what to do next so Margaret asks the group to help.

V: I'd be tempted to open the situation up a little . . . leave books around him . . . see if he'll suggest something . . .

S: What he'll do is . . . he'll use the typewriter to copy out the first pages of books he wants to read, like *Where's Charlie.*

J: Do you think he's successful in avoiding work?

S: If you mean his looking around and reading what's on the wall, or looking at the tape-recorder or the typewriter, I don't think it's avoiding . . . he flits around.

J: He talks of his children's home quite openly.

E: It looks like no external hang ups. . . . 'My social worker' . . . in the tones of someone who thinks he's got it all sorted out . . .

J: But he's not *involved*, he's not *there*: he's just *doing* it for Steve, but not *caught* when he reads . . .

V: I think the writing was the same . . .

J: Yes, now that you mention it again . . .

Already the group discussions are taking on a different colour. We are not offering Steve things to do, we are trying to see what John is doing. The frustration of Judith's 'He's not *there*' is all too familiar. Performing reading rituals does not make readers at this stage.

M. suggests that the group's early encounters involve them in a double stance: the first, towards understanding what is happening in the lesson; the second, towards formulating the insights that evolve from the practical situation, the incipient hypothesis. Here an important distinction is emerging. If a pupil 'takes on' or accepts what he thinks is the teacher's view of the task (John does what Steve asks), then the teacher will be satisfied when the pupil does what he expects. (Steve says the reading is better the second time, but the others do not agree.) We move to the point that it may be more important for the pupil to work on his own view, or to come to a view, of what he has to do, even if he reads a little less well, provided the task is somehow part of him. Then the teacher will discover intention and strength. Steve, by offering John his own words to read, thought he was doing that. But John, wanting to please Steve, evaded the real involvement of understanding that *his* writing had *his* meaning. Instead, he read his own words as if they were unfamiliar. He read them as he had been taught to read – word by word. Now the group helps.

Judith: How much schooling has he missed?

Eliz: I have this feeling that his schooling hasn't impinged itself on him . . .

J: See if he can dictate a real story instead of transcribing his speech . . . even type it . . .

S: How do I get it set up so that he tells me something worth telling?

J: I'd shift the emphasis to stories you read to him. He's got to experience the excitment of being taken through a story . . . give up
   getting things out of him.

V: What's his experience of being read to?

J: I wonder if he has been read to.

E: I'd read fairy stories unashamedly, then he could read the bits of
   repetition. Everyone listens to fairy stories – especially boys – *The
   Gingerbread Man*. He could read, 'Run, run as fast as you can' and
   get some sense and some rhythm . . .

At this point we remember the project called *Make a Story* and *Explore
a Story* which might help. We agree that John's view of what reading is
needs to be expanded. Luckily the situation we described in Steve's
school provides extra help from a number of interested adults, so when
John's evasions of the tasks Steve proposed looked as if they would lead
to a breakdown of their good relations, a school governor took over. She
came to a discussion of John's reading, and wrote this afterwards:

We have reading lessons for thirty-five minutes only on Wednesdays
and Thursdays. We started in February this year (1976) and have
between us read some ten or twelve books. John is often away from
school. Until last week, all our sessions started with resistance: 'I
can't read, I can't read *that!*', and went on with 'can I finish my
picture for history,' etc. I have always countered this with, 'yes you
can read . . . you will see . . . let's try it before you say 'I can't read
that'. No you can't finish your picture now because this is a reading
lesson and because I come here specially just to see you for reading.
At which point he will slide rather reluctantly into his chair and will
go from resistance tactics to distraction tactics. You know – something that is happening in the playground, counting the pens (of
which he has many) in his inside pocket. But I feel a sense of
urgency. All I know is that this kid will be able to read if I can make
him concentrate on reading, and I tell him so often. He also says his
eyes go funny when he reads. His eyes have been tested and they say
there is nothing wrong with them. So I induce concentration – a
three-way force between John and the book – what he deduces
from the words and pictures – and myself as a prop, supplying
words he cannot get, answering questions about the story, urging
him to read on to find out the answers himself. I keep a pointer over
the line he is reading moving steadily along the line. He often moves
his finger below the line in the same way. I think it makes it easier

for him to home in on the sentences. He is very sharp if the picture doesn't relate to the story; he wants to know why . . . 'There is such and such . . . that picture is wrong'. . . . He also guesses what is going to happen on the next page and passes some shrewd comments on the characters . . .

Steve had clearly taken care to see that the suggestions made by the group were carried on by his successor. But Judith's awareness of John's immaturity, his determination to keep school and all its works at arm's length is borne out by subsequent events. John is full of unease, and adults in school make uneasy demands. With his other helper he was much more relaxed and talked about himself more. The turning point came when they read together a book in which a boy's father escaped from prison. John pressed on his helper the information that his father too was in prison. When this was accepted, but not explored, his earlier resistance decreased, there were no further confrontations with Steve and his reading improved considerably.

What the teachers learned

The details of these early lessons showed us some of the complexities that arise when teachers attempt to create a new learning context. When we began our work we had no examples to follow, no hard data of what counted. We think we have produced the kind of evidence that is usually neglected or passed over. For all the advances in the study of classroom interaction and the unremitting growth in reading research, the two have rarely been brought together. Sara Delamont's work[7] relates to ours, but her assertion that it would be easier to do research into initial encounters because the investigator is in the same knowledge state as the participants needs modifying. We believe that we have offered something more than 'the autobiography or non-fiction novel popularized by Blishen'. Better still, we ourselves have acquired a grasp of consciousness of the pupil's view of the teacher's view of the task.

These encounters demonstrate how the opening 'moves' of interactions both reveal and conceal the intentions and understandings of the pupil and the teacher. For instance, the pupil may expect to be told what to do in order to read a passage. If, after he has read a line or two, the teacher asks a question about the events of the story or the nature of the information given, the pupil may try to relate this to the reading he is doing, rather than call on experience outside the text. Then he is not sure how to construe the question, or what his teacher *means*. When the pupil looks at the book he is not always aware that the meaning he brings to the text is part of what the teacher expects him to get *from* the text. In all of the encounters we have reported, you see us, with our pupils or in the group itself making and remaking the interactive context and formulating the conventions of our future exchanges. At the same time we try to hold this web steady in order to understand its pattern.

When we began to look at the kind of evidence that these opening sequences offered, we saw ourselves establishing a co-operative principle in Grice's terms.[8] For all their apparent straying, the conversations are topical, related to the reading text, or to the view of the task that each teacher holds. We also see the teacher establishing routines of turn-taking, inviting the pupil to take equal responsibility for what is happening. But the pupils are not equal partners, and they know it, so they keep conversations going, not always to avoid reading, but simply to discover what kind of reading behaviour is acceptable. You have seen us trying to make our intentions clear and to keep success to the fore. You can also see the pupils hedging their bets about what to do to please their teachers and thereby they co-operate in their own domination. The pupil escapes if he does what John did – perform the actions of reading without understanding. If the lesson is not a success, the pupil can still claim that he did what was asked of him.

From the first encounters we learned, painfully, how easy it is to block the pupil's way forward, to make reading seem simple if we don't make the reader responsible. We identified in ourselves common features of repressive discourse which we all try to avoid. We have to tell our pupils when they are wrong, but to redirect them without giving them negative views of themselves is not easy.

In so far as these early lessons are about pupils 'getting on terms' with their teachers, they show us how we negotiated, at top speed, contracts of operation that were rarely premeditated except in the context of acceptable human behaviour. It would not occur to us, for example, to discuss a pupil's failure with someone else while he was present, as we have often seen happen. We would never say about a book: 'Of course, you can't read *that*.' Nevertheless we often hung our heads as we listened to what we did say in the heat of the moment.

In the beginning teachers usually tend to look at the complexity of social relations and cognitive processes. Yet this is not only what we hear when we examine the lesson details. We know that both teacher and pupil have to *deconstruct* certain expectations of what will happen and replace these with new ones. No pupil found these lessons exactly what they had expected from earlier experiences of 'remedial' teaching. Nevertheless, they were unwilling to believe some 'special' lessons could be different from others. So Chris held back, Sharon made extra demands, John and Trevor lay low in their different ways, until the negotiations for interaction were further advanced.

The situational variables, the moves made by each pupil and teacher, were highly specific to each pair. Both were teaching and both were learning; 'going beyond the information given' by each to other was different for all. Only later could we determine what progress would look like.

6

Two sources of evidence

Any sort of fiction is as much an abstraction of reality as any other
mode of discourse – and a high level one at that.

James Moffett

The tape transcribed

The problem posed by Vicky's editing of her master tape is the one
constantly encountered by the readers of these pages. We want to
show you the evidence, but you have only what we select. Here are two
extended pieces from Judith's lessons with Jamie, the pupil who replaced Trevor when the latter went back to the West Indies for an
indefinite period. The first is a transcription of an early encounter in
which Judith encourages Jamie to talk about reading so that she can
choose books for him. Judith added the comments after she made
the transcript.

Judith:	Jamie:	Comments
Would you say, Jamie, that you thought your reading was quite good, quite bad, or needed help . . . or how do you feel about your reading?	I don't know, Miss, it's not brilliant.	Defensive about his standard.
It's not brilliant. What would you call brilliant reading? How would you like to read if you could read brilliantly? What would it be like?	It would be good, Miss.	Fairly ignorant of advantages of reading well.
How would it sound?	It would sound like when you go to work and that, you read . . good.	Stock reply
Yes, and what does that mean to read good, what does it mean to you to read well?	Helps you more.	
Yes, and what's the difference between the way you read now and reading well?	I'm not bad Miss at reading.	Again, defensive. Indeed, has quite a high opinion of himself (+ potential).
So, how would you like to be better?	I wouldn't mind being better though.	
What would make it better? What would make your reading better?	If I read and read all the time, if I read more.	Has he been told this? Or is this a very important answer.

Judith:	Jamie:	Comments
If you read more? Do you not read very much — what was the last thing you read then?	In school?	
In school or at home.	Um that poem that . . .	
That book called *Mind Your Own Business?*	Mmm, not M.Y.O.B. uu - Spike Milligan.	
S.M. What did you think of those poems?	They was good, Miss.	
Which one can you remember? Any one.	Ning, nang, nong.	
And had you read that one before — in your primary school?	No, not in my primary school.	
Where had you come across it before?	We've got it — we've got a book like that in our house.	I wonder.
In your house, have you? So you almost knew that one off by heart did you? Yes. Now before that book, what was another book that you read?	There was that one what you told me to read.	

Judith:	Jamie:	Comments
The story, *Mr Miacca* wasn't it?	Yes, that story.	
Can you remember any of that story?	I can't remember it. No Miss.	
No, do you find it difficult to remember what you've read?	Yes.	
Difficult to tell the story again?	Mmmm.	
Why do you think that could be?	I can't remember it all.	
Can you remember bits of it?	Yes, um – er, when the mum tells him not to go round the corner of the man'll get him.	
That's right. So if you wait a minute, the story does come back to your mind doesn't it? Good. She said that the bogey man will get him didn't she?	Yes.	
When you were in primary school – which primary school were you at, Jamie?	William Patten	

Judith:	Jamie:	Comments
W.P. Did your teacher listen to you read a lot?	Not in the fourth year.	
Not in the fourth year. So do you think that in the fourth year your reading didn't make much progress?	Oh yes, I was – did – yes, we went – used to go downstairs for reading.	
You went downstairs to somebody else? What was that person – what sort of things did you do with that person?	We read things over and over again.	
What sort of things?	Like – um- in any (indistinguishable) sort of – not the same but like the same – sort of – like word.	
I see. So you had to practise did you with certain words? How did you find that?	Miss, the book was easy.	Again quite confident re ability.
What about the story?	The ball goes in the water and things.	
Things like that. Were the stories not very good – was it really just a practice, was it?	Yes.	

Judith:	Jamie:	Comments
Did you enjoy going down there?	No, it wasn't. I didn't like it, Miss.	
Do you feel it did any good?	Yes, it did some a lot of good.	
What was it that the teacher told you that did good? What did she tell you that helped?	She said your work was getting much better.	Praise worked
So she said nice things to you and that made you feel good did it? Did she ever say things like 'do you know the sounds that the letters make?	Oh yes, she did – when you have to write a thing on the board and sort of sounding.	
You had to sound the word?	Letters.	
What sort of letters did she write up? Can you remember? Would she write two letters together?	Yes – um – like one letter we had to sound it like 'b' – b b.	
Did you find that easy?	Yes.	
Do you think that that helped you with your reading?	Yes, it did a lot.	Maybe because it was easy.

Judith:	Jamie:	Comments
It did. And had anyone given you help like that before? No. So what sort of help had you been given before the fourth year in the ordinary classroom? What sort of things did teachers tell you then? Cast your mind back – it's too far away is it? Can you remember the first story that you really thought was a great story – that anyone told you?	Miss, I didn't read a lot of stories.	Does this mean I don't know what stories have got for me?
No – that somebody read to you? The best story you've ever heard.	Oh yes, in the fourth year we did read *Charlie and the Choc. Factory* – they read us that and about Australia.	
A book about Australians?	No – um – it – um – about when people liked in the	
Ah, I know Maoris, Aborigines.	Aborigines and (indecipherable).	
Hmm and you found that interesting?	Yes.	
Because it was about another country or because the story was good. Can you remember?	Oh – about another country.	Again, the story did not interest him.

Judith:	Jamie:	Comments
About another country. So what sort of things would you like to be able to read if you were a really very good reader?	I don't know, Miss.	
What sort of stories?	I'd like to read *Charlie and the Choc. Factory*.	
To yourself. Yes, have you tried to read any of it to yourself. No? When Mr Bevan or I are reading it to you in class do you listen — sit back — or look at the page and try and follow?	Look at the page and follow.	I must check up on that.
And do you find that it's easy to do that?	Yes.	
And you can still take in what it means?	It helps you to read more.	
You think it does? Yes. Who told you that or did you decide that for yourself?	No, the teacher said if you look you'll find a new word that you haven't seen before.	Remembers instructions.
Yes and do you think that's true?	Yes.	

Judith:	Jamie:	Comments
Yes, OK, well look, I'm going to ask you to read just something. Is there any book that you particularly want to read?	No, Miss, give me any book.	Confident.
You'd like me to choose?	I'll try to read it.	
All right – and you'll try to read it – and if you find that there's a word you don't understand or can't work out try and tell me what it is that's difficult so that I know how to help you. OK? I'm going to start you with a terribly easy book so that there are no problems at all. Have you ever seen these before? Yes. Did you have them in your Primary School?	Yes – we did – I-I don't think I read them.	
You don't think you read them. This one is a story about a crocodile. OK? Mm.	Shall I read this?	
	Crocodile lived on the river bank. Then li-liks-lie in the mum, mub, mud.	Dialect problem.
Right, read the last sentence again.	They lea, lied – it's not 'lied', Miss.	

Judith:	Jamie:	Comments
It's not what?	Lied.	
No, it's not lied. What is it?	Lead.	
Well if it was 'they lead in the mud'. . . . I think you've got the right idea — 'they lie in the mud'. Did you want to say they lied in the mud?	Mmmm.	
Well in fact we say 'they lie'.	They lie in the mud.	
Yes, good.	Sometimes crocodiles play. Crocodile(s) have sharp teeth. Oh yes. Crocodile have long tails. Crocodile have little legs. Crocodile are dangerous.	Why does he leave out the 's'?
Good.	Once a crocodile was laying in the mud.	
Now you looked up at me when you read that word there. Why did you look up at me?	I didn't think it was right, Miss.	Dialect again (or does he say: 'I just thought it was right'?)

Judith:	Jamie:	Comments
Got got an 'a' in it – mm-well can you guess what it is? What did it tell us about his legs before. 'Crocodiles have . . .	Little legs.	
Right. What's another word for little?	Small.	
Yes, does that say small?	No.	
No. What sound does 'sh' make? Do you know?	sh.	Knows some phonics.
Right any chance of getting it now? His . . .	Straight.	But can't apply them.
No, all right. I'll let you know what it is – his short legs.	Oh, his short legs didn't not move.	
Yes, before you go on a minute – how are you going to remember that word now, Jamie, that word there.	The sh – no – yes.	Does he realize that although he knew the sound it wasn't that which worked for him that time?
What would help you remember it now, so that if you come across it again, you'll be able to read it?	Little.	

Judith:	Jamie:	Comments
You'll remember that it's another word that means little?	Mmm.	Has got several strategies going for him (see below).
Yes that's a good way – good. OK.	He-he was very still. But crocodiles are dangerous.	
Good, it's funny how long words are easier to read than short words isn't it. Like children who are learning to read – you know those books like Janet and John or something and they have the word aeroplane in them. Nearly always the children can read the word aeroplane and they can't read the little words like 'and' and 'the'. Why do you think that could be?	Maybe they saw the picture.	Knows to use picture clues.
Yes, the picture would give them a clue and when they see . . .	A and Oh – the long word.	Initial letter length of word.
Yes.	They think aeroplane.	
Yes, good, well done, I think that's just what does happen. OK.	A boat s-um slipped – sailed.	

Judith:	Jamie:	Comments
Good.	Look Miss — I thought 't' as in tailed' and put an 's' on it and it's sailed.	Another strategy.
Good. Thank you for telling me — that makes — I can really understand how you worked it out now — Good.	Sailed up the river. The crocodile did not move. A fly sat on the crocodile's head. He opened one eye and winked.	
Good, the fly has disturbed the crocodile hasn't it?	Mmm. The fly flew off. It flew over the water — A large shining fish saw the fly and wanted to eat it.	
Good.	The fish jumped out of the water with a splash. It c . . . catched . . . no.	
Well, read the rest of the sentence.	Caught.	
Good, well done. It means almost the same doesn't it but you worked it out that although 'catched the fly' makes sense in fact that word says 'caught'. Well done.	Caught the fly and gobbled it gobbled it up.	

Judith:	Jamie:	Comments
You know what gobbled means do you?	Mm-it means swallowed it.	
Yes that's right – eat it greedily. . . . Go on.	It goes right through your mouth and (indecipherable)	
That's right.	The crocodile opened bo, but.	Phonics not working for him. What can he do? Apply another strategy which I will give him.
Now, how can I help you with that word. . I think I could help you by telling you not to look so hard at that word but to look at this one.	Eyes.	
Right. Now read from the beginning again.	The crocodile opened both eyes.	It worked!
Right. Did it help you? Now what could you tell me about what I've just told you. I've given you a sort of rule to follow. What is that rule Jamie?	If a word came – you don't know you go on to the next one and then start again.	Able to formulate rule. . . .

Judith:	Jamie:	Comments
Good — well done. So if you come to a difficult word, look on a bit, look at the words that follow it and maybe you can guess it. Good, well done. Now you worked that out for yourself and that's very intelligent. Right. On you go.		
	He saw the fish. His short legs moved. His long tail moved. He . . . s.s. . . .	
Can you use that rule again now — that rule that we've just learnt?	He slid — into the water.	And apply it.
Brilliant. Now you see how it worked for you. Good Jamie.	Yes.	
	and swum . . . after the fish.	
	The fish swum fast but the crocodile swum faster.	
What's going to happen?	The crocodile's going to eat it. The crocodile's jaws opened wide. When they shut the fish was inside. Then the crocodile floated back to the river bank.	Able to predict story.

Judith:	Jamie:	Comments
		Look and say?
Yes, how did you know that word 'floated'. You're quite right and you read it beautifully. How did you know that was floated? You just	I knew the 'float'.	
That's a word that you can recognize easily;		
	Yes – floated back to the river bank slowly he climbed out of the water and went to sleep in the mud.	
In the where?		Voluntary comment on picture.
	Mud. Don't you go near him or he'll gobble you all up – he's big, Miss.	
Yes, why is he so big compared with the men?		
	'Cos, he's nearer than them.	
That's right.		
	Crocodiles are dangerous.	
That's right.		
	Miss – that's been in that book about three times.	Observant, reflective.
It's a sort of warning isn't it every now and again. Can you find the other places where it says crocodiles are dangerous?		
	Yes, it's down there somewhere.	Verifies.

Judith:	Jamie:	Comments
Good.	Here, here and here.	
Right. You're quite right. It comes three times. It's a sort of warning. Look at the last picture and who do you think is saying 'crocs are d'? Who do you think is saying 'don't go near him?'	He's saying that.	
To him. Yes.		He's pointing to him
It's almost as if he's wagging his finger at him and warning him. Right. So that's quite – although it's a very easy little book it's got quite a nice little story hasn't it – the whole business of the crocodile going after the fish and its obvious how very powerful he is and how very strong and how easily he could gobble up a man as well as a fish – people have their legs bitten off by crocodiles. Right – well what did you think of that little book Jamie?	It was good, Miss.	
It was good? Do you think it's the sort of book you would like to read or would you like to read something different?	I'd like to read something different, Miss.	

Judith:	Jamie:	Comments
And how – in what way would it be different?	Er – um – I like reading comics.	Ah, is this a way of entry?
You like reading comics. Do you read comics yourself?	Sometimes, yes.	
What comics to you buy?	*Beano* and *Dandy*.	
And you don't find those difficult to read at all?	Some words are like 'smashed' and things like that.	
Those are easy to read are they or difficult?	Or something like, 'kill, kill, kill' and they've got some of it lines.	
I see. What do you do when you come across a difficult word in a comic? Do you ask somebody or leave it out?	I leave it out.	
Does it make much difference if you leave it out?	Not really – it does sometimes but sometimes it don't.	Another strategy.
Do you sometimes think that if only I understood what that word meant I would understand more of the story?	Mmm.	
Yes, well that was smashing.		

Two things are striking in this lesson: the pupil's acceptance of the teacher's questions, even when, as here, the answers involve a stringent self-examination, and the extent to which the teacher puts pressure on the pupil. Jamie puts up a spirited defence against what he takes to be Judith's judgment of his reading, that it isn't very good. He is caught between a chance to criticize his primary school lessons and a genuine belief that they were helpful 'for some'. He is convinced that he got better when he was praised, that sounding letters was helpful, but he also acknowledges that he didn't read a lot of stories. The story he now reads with difficulty is meant for younger children, but he can both use and explain a new strategy for tackling words he doesn't know. As he is gradually drawn into the story he looks for picture cues and words he recognizes. He offers to try harder and responds to Judith's help. Yet, when he has finished, it is clear that he wants to be known as a reader of books other than *Crocodiles are Dangerous*.

Here Judith is trying to get a purchase on a number of things (too many, she thought later): Jamie's attitude to reading, his previous experience of stories, books and lessons, and his view of the task ahead. She is looking for his most secure strategies, and she wonders if she ought to pay attention to his dialect. Her greatest satisfaction is in Jamie's ability to respond to her encouragement to take risks, to discuss the meaning of the piece, and to point out what he notices. She confirms the kind of awareness that she thinks will prove helpful. Whatever phonic skills Jamie has, they fail with a word like *short*. Judith accepts his assurance that he will 'remember it next time' because it's another word that means 'little'! The prospect is an unlikely one, but if Judith tells Jamie that his tactic will not work, she will deprive him of the confidence that comes with predicting. You can see how Jamie picks up enough security to offer a suggestion as to how children tackle what they don't know, ('maybe they saw the picture'), how a long word may be more easily recognized, and how he worked out 'sailed'.

In the group discussion that followed we talked about dialect. We had enough confidence in our own experience and what we had read[1] to be sure that, whatever they actually saw on the page, some readers turned prose text into dialect utterance because words come to them most naturally in that form when they speak. Jamie is thrown by 'lie' not only because it is part of a variable English verb, but also because the writer uses the bookish present tense to indicate habit.

Later we understood how dense Judith's explanations were, and Jamie's great anxiety to please. But as Jamie's reading grows more fluent and his share of the conversation more spontaneous, Judith relinquishes her leadership. Jamie puts the incidents together and begins to see the narrative pattern ('that's been in that book three times'), and how he can verify his guesses.

You see here the inexperienced reader at work. He still doesn't know what escapes him; he wants to believe he can get better, but he is not sure what is to be trusted: the first lessons, the sounding out, or Judith's confident assertion that if you read past the word you don't recognize 'you go on to the next one and start again'. We asked each other if his greater conviction lies in his saying 'if I read and read all the time, if I read more'. Is this a repetition of what his teachers have told him? Judith says he is fairly ignorant of the advantages of reading well, but he must know that successful readers are spared the intensity of this particular kind of interaction. Jamie has Judith's kindness to sustain him, but he has to work very hard.

Although this takes a long time to read, it is only part of the lesson. Judith and Jamie went on to a new story about a boy who had recently arrived from the West Indies and was homesick. Jamie responded instantly to the story and Judith gave him all the help he needed to start quickly. He understood the incidents and the motives of the characters, but somehow the hero's name, Donovan, gave him great trouble and he broke it into three syllables each time he said it. All his other pauses seemed to indicate a checking back and forwards in the text. He also discovers the author's use of 'flashback' to recall earlier incidents in the life of the character. Jamie seemed to understand the technique after he had questioned Judith's explanation of how it works in films. His pleasure increased when Judith told him he understood what the writer of the story was doing.

There have been many discussions about the virtues and value of hearing pupils read aloud,[2] but a lesson in which the learner discovers a workable strategy for dealing with new text, and is invited to behave as a reader with a valued response to the matter of the narrative, and is helped to understand how the author does it, is an hour and a half well spent. Judith's last words in her notes are: 'very keen to come again. Concentration 100 per cent throughout.' She now says she would not try to cover so much ground on so little acquaintance. We wondered if this would satisfy those experts who ask for more systematic instruction of poor readers.

What the video reveals

The virtue of the video recording is that it makes even the most straightforward lesson anthropologically strange so that we can see what we take for granted. Our awarenesses were enlivened by our most successful tape, a later lesson of Judith with Jamie which we all agree is as typical a 'special' lesson as we are likely to find. First we see Jamie helping Judith to set up the camera and then they sit down, side by side.

They are reading Roald Dahl's *The Magic Finger*. The lesson begins with the usual negotiations: finding the place and looking at the pictures, recapitulating the story so far. Judith takes time to discuss an early episode in which the heroine discovered her power to transform into animals the people she doesn't like. Jamie begins to read at the part in the story when the heroine's neighbours return from shooting wild duck. The magic finger is about to work again. The story is written in the first person, a convention that gives Jamie no trouble. Jamie's reading posture is alert, but not anxious; he is now at ease with Judith.

He settles to read the page they agree has been reached. Then he suddenly offers to read *Donovan* instead. This sudden prolonging of the negotiation may be to delay the hazards of beginning, to bargain for something easier or familiar, or just to cut down the reading time. Judith gently urges him to choose the text he really wants to read, and Jamie agrees to share his reading time between the two texts. Thirty minutes later, after a highly sustained effort, he has forgotten about this intention.

Judith keeps the narrative drift in Jamie's sight throughout, after an early tangling with the confusion of 'b' and 'd'. At one point the heroine says she 'saw red' as the result of the massacre of the wild ducks. Jamie reads the words correctly, but a subsequent discussion made it clear that he had no idea of the meaning of the phrase as such, but he did understand that the heroine was angry. He follows the sequence of events, and as he warms to the story his early two-word chunking and the calling back tone of his reading give way to longer uninterrupted passages of meaningful, secure oral production. When there is a pause it is a natural break which Judith extends into a rest as Jamie's concentration is fierce. You can tell at once when he is out of his depth; the words are right but the sense has gone. After another pause to sort out what is likely to happen, he picks up again, first of all in the calling back tone and then with greater naturalness and security. When Judith leans back in her chair, Jamie's shoulders relax. He seems under much less pressure than in the tape-recorded lesson. Judith encourages him to use gestures to explain what he understands. At one point a character shouts: 'Hey' which Jamie has clearly never met before in print so Judith dramatizes the scene. Later the text has 'Be off', which Jamie reads as 'before', and then falters. Judith asks him what he'd say to drive away an unwanted person and he replies 'get lost', which Judith accepts, knowing full well that Jamie's version is instead of what he doesn't expect to hear in school, even if he sees it in a book. Then comes another surprise.

Jamie discovers that the boys in the story are carrying real rifles. There is a perceptible increase in his involvement at this point, an increase in speed and bodily tension, so that when Judith unexpectedly asks, 'Do you approve of shooting wild birds?' Jamie is confused, first because he is genuinely being asked for his opinion about something in the text, and then because he senses that the expected answer is *not* 'yes'. Here is a new situation connected with reading: the excitement of the prospect of real shooting – common enough on television – linked to the responsibility of making a judgment. He agrees that shooting wild duck is cruel. Then he returns to the text with greater speed and his miscues decrease as he races to find out what happens.

Later experience with teachers to whom we showed the tape helped us to understand that many things which experienced readers seem to do naturally are never actually *taught* in reading lessons. Jamie needed help to relate the earlier incident in which the heroine transformed her teacher into a cat to this sequence where the hunters are turned into birds. A practised reader knows that expectations are laid down in an incident at the beginning of a novel and called on as the narrative unfolds, but this was not part of Jamie's reading experience. He also discovered in this lesson that the views he held about incidents and habits in real life are relevant to what he read, sometimes as parallel instances and sometimes as contrasts. When Jamie is invited to express an opinion about a wild duck hunter, his natural inclination is to say that shooting is exciting. But the unfolding of the story depends on his agreeing that those who shoot may also be shot, that events in fiction are value-laden, that the reader has to have a view not only about certain kinds of people in the story but also whether or not he agrees with the way the author construes events and characters. This is Jamie learning how readers respond. As we watch him, we see how he braces himself to offer Judith his view, as if he were bound to be rejected, although there is absolutely no sign that this is likely.

Teachers outside our group who saw the tape said much less about Jamie than about Judith. They discussed at length her invitation to Jamie to pause, reflect and consider what the story suggests besides what the words actually say. By now Jamie is using the rule he learned in the lesson Judith transcribed in the previous chapter. He now scans ahead or takes a second run up to the word he does not recognize and is usually successful. But there is still a belief amongst observers who have had little experience of working in this way that more attention to Jamie's confusion of 'b' and 'd', which he admitted at the beginning of the lesson, would have guaranteed some other success. We had, by now, abandoned this idea so that it always came as a shock to us to realize that if Jamie's increased fluency and confidence and understanding seemed to us to be important ways of judging his progress, we still had a lot to do to make this conviction available to others who could watch a video recording of a lesson and still not see these things.

Then, as we wrote this report, we looked at the film again. Here is Judith's commentary on what happened.

The session we filmed would have been informative if only an audio tape existed. We would still have been able to measure such things as the balance of talk and reading, the number of questions fired at Jamie, the volume of his sighs, the extent of his miscues. We would still have been able to note his struggle to recall the story, to link the episodes, to consider the characters' motivation. What we would miss and what in fact I only fully perceived *when watching the video with the sound turned off* are aspects of the physical inter-action between teacher and taught and how, cumulatively, those aspects transmit as powerful a message as anything spoken and may critically impede or dramatically advance progress towards the goal of independent and meaningful reading.

Let me describe the scene. The table before us is mostly stacked with Jamie's books, the two books he has chosen to read, his writing notebooks, my record book, pen and paper. A second copy of *The Magic Finger* is also there. We sit beside each other, which seems friendly. Whilst Jamie initially turns over the pages himself and presses down the centre of the book, I relieve him of this chore later and hold down the corner of the page as well. When I ask him to write, I thoughtfully produce a pen which I later discreetly remove when he uses it to point at words he reads.

None of this would be evident on an audio tape. Even on the video tape with the sound on one is primarily focusing on the spoken interchanges. But look again at the scene as I have described it. The orderly table in front of us may in fact exclude and intimidate Jamie. Certainly the idea of choice becomes notional as you perceive me 'tidying away' the options I appear so generously to have offered. And my extra copy of *The Magic Finger* — I never open it, seeming to need to follow the same print as Jamie. Is the message one of comforting cosiness or calculated control? The sitting alongside where I can oversee the book at all times could also be construed as less trusting than sitting opposite where I could be an audience. Jamie's reading aloud would then have a real purpose. And leaning back in my chair so that I am slightly out of Jamie's range of vision — does this indicate a wish to minimize the intensity or am I in fact controlling from behind? Does Jamie feel the unseen pressure behind him? My arm resting along the back of his chair may further confuse the message.

Jamie's behaviour with the pages of the book looks promising. We see him flicking through, attempting to piece a story together, using the pictures. As he starts to read he holds the top right hand corner in readiness to turn the page and he enthusiastically rubs along the centre fold. Once the page is turned his reading speed increases noticeably as he senses the progress he is making. Why then do I deprive him later of this aspect of becoming a reader? By the end of the lesson I am doing it all for him thereby increasing his dependence, robbing him of simple competences that may make all the difference to how he feels about himself as a reader. And as an aspiring writer, Jamie surely has his own pen. By pressing mine on him and later withdrawing it, albeit discreetly, I again reduce his autonomy and maintain him in the position of a child who submits but who probably does not ignore.

So the mismatch between the declared aim of helping Jamie become a reader and the 'hidden curriculum' which effectively removes the means is the first, troubling evidence the video releases.

However there is a second and much more heartening element which emerges as I watch. I started to analyse the eye contact between us as far as was possible. Jamie appears to look at me for three separate reasons. Firstly, he commonly seeks approval for words he realizes he has guessed (guessing may still have connotations of cheating for him) or which still seem unlikely to him. Secondly, he will search my face as I question him, hoping, as so often happens, to 'read off' a possible answer. And thirdly, he will look at me obediently when I am explaining something to him — or as frequently happens — dramatizing something in a more or less convincing way.

It is this aspect of dramatization that I suddenly realized had a direct and observable connection with the development of Jamie's understanding and involvement in the text. When one matches the incidents or concepts I choose physically to demonstrate — whether it be the tingling of the magic finger, the size of robins, the beating of wings, the thinness of the crescent moon, the height the transformed Gregg's reach from the ground — with the spontaneous comments, real questions and 'correct' answers to questions that Jamie offers there seems to be no doubt that the visual stimuli, the 'acting out', the hearing of the voice which exclaims 'Hey' or 'be off', bring to life to the text in a way that the flat words on the page cannot generate for Jamie on their own at this stage in his reading life. It cannot be incidental that his question, 'How do they get as small as that?' can be asked because the tininess of the robins, indicated by my cupped hands, has for the first time really signified something to him. His only spontaneous reading between the lines occurs when he says, 'Mr Gregg gives a yell because he realizes he's grown wings.' This is spectacular compared with the passive way in which he has received most of the text and may have been possible, not only because of my dramatic presentation but because he joined me in physically recreating the sensation and sound of flapping wings. Actually, Jamie gestures and acts rather less than most children and this may be something he needs to be encouraged in if, as seems so likely from the video, it is an important link between the cold print on the page and the lively, re-created recognizable story that one tells oneself when reading is going well.

Every viewing of the video reveals more and more. If much of its evidence is sobering, much also is encouraging and exciting. The Jamie we see sighing, wiping his brow, concealing a yawn suggests that reading is becoming physical torture inflicted by teacher. The Jamie we see fidgeting remarkably little, concentrating dedicated to the task in hand, suggests a determination that, given the right sort of help, should result in successful reading. What the video and the analyses we have arrived at over the years since it was made have made possible is a slightly clearer picture of what that 'right sort of help' could be.

7

What progress looks like

As an event calling forth the critical reflection of both the learners and the educators, the literary process must relate *speaking the word* to *transforming reality*, and to man's role in this transformation. Such a perception will lead the learners to recognise a much greater right than that of being literate. They will ultimately realise that, as men, they have the right to have a voice.

Paulo Freire

As we taught and talked about our pupils, so our work with them changed. We counted that as progress, for us at least. But what chances had those who survived the early encounters of becoming independently literate? After our first four terms together we took stock.

We knew we had learned different kinds of patience; to wait longer for the pupil to make his own attempt to make sense, for instance. Kenneth and Yetta Goodman visited us and heard some of our early tapes. While we were flattered by their appreciation of our care, we were brought up short by their observation that we were still doing most of the work. Unless we could transfer the responsibility for reading more firmly to the readers we should simply be promoting another form of the kind of remediation we were anxious to avoid.

By this time we had also decided that if the readers are to develop their own strategies for interacting with texts, then the interpolation of clues which distract from the meaning of what is being read is less than useful. When Judith included a discussion of Jamie's 'b' and 'd' confusion in his reading of *The Magic Finger* it was clear from the videotape that Jamie's attention wandered because the discussion offered him only more attention to his confusion, not a way out of it.

While we agreed that to deprive our phonic-fixated pupils of every vestige of faith in the strategy of 'sounding out' would make them more insecure, we compromised with our belief in its inefficacy by promoting the use of the first letter of a word as a clue to guessing it, while still emphasizing that meaning is paramount in the reading process for the inexperienced. More and more, however, it became clear that when a word should be easy to sound out yet the pupil cannot 'make it mean', the reason lies in the fact that the word is unfamiliar, not in the pupil's lack of skill. The word *brink* on the first page of Ted Hughes's *The Iron Man* is the classic example. Conversely, we were confident that our pupils could read words they knew but had never seen before in print even when these were outside the scope of phonic divination; *ought*, for example. We had come to understand how most of the features of the written language caused problems, especially embedded clauses, left-branching sentences, the anticipation of a question after *when*, *why*, *what*, *who*, and so on. But we were also surprised to discover how the high particularity of literary text, especially when the images or metaphors had the concreteness of objects, offered very little difficulty. In *The Iron Man* again, no inexperienced reader stuck at 'his head was as big as a bedroom'. By now we understood, from a multitude of examples, why Paul Kohlers is emphatic that 'text can be comprehended only if it is read for meaning in the first place; reading to identify words is both unnecessary and inefficient.'[1]

As we listened to our second year tapes we discovered that our tolerance of each other was both greater and less. We were still patient but more demanding. We forced explanations from each other where once we had been content with sympathetic understanding. Our greatest regret was that we lost Fiona. We went too slowly for her. Andy's needs were urgent as his schooldays were drawing to a close, so Fiona rightly abandoned the group in order to help him. We missed her as she challenged us sooner than we were ready to challenge ourselves. We heard, indirectly, that she had continued to teach Andy after he left school until he was successful. This reminded us, again, that progress may lie in shaking off the school's view of reading in order to find a more convincing one.

What of our pupils; how did they see their progress? If they adopted the view generally held, that advance means a higher test score or a demonstrable ability to cope with the class texts in book-laden curriculum subjects they might have been disappointed. But we could point to the fact that our pupils came willingly to lessons where once they had had to be fetched. They now read more for themselves and talked about what had engaged them in their reading. The most difficult thing to explain to others about the problems of inexperienced readers is their inability to acknowledge that they need help. This is what they demonstrate when they stay away from school on examination days or develop mysterious illnesses when confronted with unexpected difficulties. We counted as progress the fact that our pupils no longer did these things quite so much.

We could also point to an increase in readerly behaviour of the sort that everyone takes for granted; the length of time spent with the same book, the desire to finish a story, some genuine engagement with the theme or the action. All this we shall show in what follows. We still longed for the kind of commitment that we knew in ourselves, but in understanding that better, we also understood the conditions of its operation. We hoped for demonstrable fluency, more appropriate intonation in reading aloud. Above all, we wanted to be sure that our pupils intended what reading intends, so that we could produce evidence of all of these things. One day we hoped to find the tolerance of uncertainty that characterizes, not general bamboozlement, but the confidence of the expert reader who makes his bond with the author and lets the text teach him or her how it is to be read.

So we agreed that we would examine four successive lessons from each pupil for evidence of what progress might be like. We shall show you how we looked for it.

Vicky and Tracy — confirming the role of the reader

Tracy, you remember, is Vicky's pupil after Sharon. Her initial stage is even further back than Sharon's and her idea of what readers do is vestigial. For her, progress would be to feel what being a reader is like, especially in recognizing on the page what she already knows. Here is Vicky's report of early lessons:

I had two sessions with Tracy, then she was away for three weeks. We were both still at the exploratory stage, Tracy trying to feel which way I would jump and what I expected of her, and me trying to find out more about Tracy and endlessly turning over strategies and approaches to reading. I already felt three things fairly strongly. One was that as all Tracy's encounters with reading appeared to have been long and dreary (books are 'long'; looking apprehensively at a book she says, 'does it go right through, Miss?') and almost wholly negative. She patently hadn't learned much about reading. I felt that her reading matter should be enjoyable and short; that we should share poems, with Tracy reading the refrains and repeated lines, and that the stories should often be bizarre with intriguing illustrations. Secondly, and perhaps this was the hardest to achieve, I felt that Tracy should read successfully, that she should not flounder and struggle but that by being given the right back-up and by my introducing the book thoroughly, even imperceptibly 'feeding' her a page before she read it, she should find herself reading. One way of doing this, I thought, would be to bring in stories and nursery rhymes with which she was already familiar so that she had a powerful echo in her head which matched the words on the page. I also thought she could make her own book, dictating the text to me and then reading it back. Thirdly, I quickly found that through long periods of absence from school and for whatever reasons at home, Tracy was not familiar with a lot of poems and stories which are thought to be part of our cultural background; 'Jack and Jill', 'Polly put the kettle on' and many others appeared unfamiliar. So while looking for chords and echoes I was also trying to let her have some of our shared experiences. To some extent therefore, I had to tailor my second aim of providing Tracy with familiar material, but I did find that when we, by chance, came across a poem or story she had some recollection of ('Old Mother Hubbard' and 'Goldilocks and the Three Bears'), the rewards were great.

Lesson one

During the previous encounter we had finished with Jan Pienkowski's *Meg and Mog* which I had offered in my attempts to provide enjoyable and well-illustrated books which are fun to read. This was a failure; partly, I think because the book is too distracting visually, with the text woven in and out of the gaudy illustrations. So for the following session I thought I would give her something where she would find herself on sure ground; her own dictated account and a book that was less stimulating visually and which had an easier text.

When Tracy comes in I try to make connections with the previous session.

Me: We wrote a book. Do you remember it, about your shopping? I'll read it first, you see if you can follow and then you read it to me.

Here is the text:

On Saturday I went shopping with my Mum. It was her birthday.

We went to Chiswick. We went in this shop where they made their own bread and cakes. My Mum bought some rolls and doughnuts and bread. I got a new polo neck for school. My Mum had had a party on Saturday night for her birthday.

Tracy had been able to read it back immediately after dictating it to me, but that had been three weeks before. It was the first piece in her own book and much was invested in it. I was nervous that she might have forgotten it and feel she was failing, so I read it myself to run her in. Tracy chimes in and reads the last line. Then Tracy volunteers the following anecdotes neither of which had a lot to do with reading and certainly not to do with the passage just read. In both of these she presents herself in a successful light. The enthusiastic and confiding way she tells me about these events makes me wonder if she was thinking about them while we were reading, whether I should have had a fallow period when she came in to tell me things, or whether success in reading, however minor, prompted her to provide further evidence of success elsewhere. Here is part of her talk:

Tracy: Miss, you know yesterday, in our class, English, our teacher
    told us to do, write a picture down and I done it. It was really good.
    The top part I did but then it went silly at the bottom. But it was
    really good at the top part.
Me: What was it of?
Tracy: The mices had to follow the man or something.
Me: The Pied Piper?
Tracy: Miss, it was really good. My Mum liked it. I done it good.

I show appreciation, then Tracy continues:

Tracy: Well, last week, Miss, I was boring in my house so my Mum
    brought me this colouring book. On the back of it I made up a
    poem. It doesn't make sense though, my Mum said. It was about the
    army. She said it was good to get 'army' though.

Afraid that to ask questions about this would take us away from the task in hand, I then ask Tracy to read the dictated story from her own book which she does much better than she had done three weeks previously, losing it only once at the beginning. This seems to have been fairly successful in that Tracy actually had the experience of reading fluently. The disadvantage of this sort of reading is that it is stale news by the second reading and not very interesting in itself to read about. To move on I ask Tracy if she would like to tell me about something else and she quickly volunteers a description of a Christmas shopping expedition.

Tracy: When I was off school I went out and got a pair of shoes and my Christmas stuff. I got my birthday present and my Christmas present. Shall we write that down?

As I write to Tracy's dictation I try to engage her in what is going down on the page. As I write the words I say each word aloud:

Me: Watch me write the words, Tracy, and you'll see how they take shape.

When I get to 'Christmas' I say:

Me: Christmas is a nice long word with a big C.
Tracy: I always know – notice 'Christmas'. I don't know why.
Me: Where do you see 'Christmas'?
Tracy: I see it in cards. In shop windows when they say 'Come in and buy your Christmas cards'. And you see it on wrapping paper.

This talking about Christmas is not directly helping Tracy in her search for meaning but could, I suppose, be helping her to see that some long words wherever you meet them, are constant friends and nothing to be afraid of. When, I write the word 'blade', Tracy notices that it looks like 'black'.

Tracy: Miss, that looks like 'blue' or 'black' that word, don't it?
Me: Yes, its got the 'bl'.

After dictating, Tracy reads what I have written. The lesson ends.

Lesson two

I start with another Dr Seuss Beginner Book, *Sam and the Firefly*, which other children with similar reading difficulties had found within their grasp. It is easy to assume it will be too difficult for Tracy. She cannot identify the animals in the pictures and seems not to be thinking about the book at all.

Tracy: Miss, I like the other book better, where he lost his hat. Can I
read it again? I like it.
Me: Which one was that now?
Tracy: And they went looking for it.
Me: Was it *Cat in the Hat*? One of those?
Tracy: Every time he turned it over, it weren't in there.
Me: Oh, *Ant and Bee*. Shall we read *Ant and Bee* instead? Go and find
another Ant and Bee book then.

We had read *Ant and Bee* two months before and Christmas had come
in between so it must have been a strong and enjoyable experience for
Tracy to have remembered it over such a long period. I suppose it also
contrasted with the book we had just abandoned which she had failed
to engage with.
Tracy goes over to the shelf.

Me: *Ant and Bee and the Doctor* is quite fun.
Tracy (holds up *Ant and Bee and the ABC*): That was it, weren't it,
Miss? Can I read it again? I like it.

I persuade Tracy to read a different *Ant and Bee*. This one is called
'*Around the World with Ant and Bee*'. The first '*Ant and Bee*' book
she had read had twenty-five pages, each one with the same text for
each letter of the alphabet and I move Tracy on to another book in
the same series. If I were seeing Tracy every day to hear her read, I
think I would have followed her lead back to the book she remembered
enjoying and would have let her enjoy it again. As it is, the weekly
session when I see Tracy on her own we think and talk reading and it is
something private between us. This has meant that Tracy is not keen
to read to me when she comes with five others in a 'Withdrawal Group':
'No, Miss, I read to you on Tuesday', she will say if I suggest she might
read when I see her with the group. (Partly she is inhibited by the other
girls and partly she feels reading to me is safely channelled into the time
when I see her on her own.) Sometimes she is happy, though, on these
other occasions to look at the pictures, or even read to herself some
of the books we have read together in our one-to-one sessions. Holidays
and absences, combined with the fact that Tracy does not read to me in
the group, mean that Tracy does not read to me a great deal at all. I
did feel at this stage a certain urgency, a need to move on.
    I start reading *Round the World with Ant and Bee*, talking about
the picture a little:

Me: You turn the pages for me.
Tracy: Miss, who's Bee, him?
Me: How can you remember which is which?
Tracy: Cos of their 'ats'.

Tracy reads but finds it difficult and gives up, so I continue reading. In this book a drawing of an umbrella is substituted for the word. I ask Tracy to say the word 'umbrella' when we get to the symbol. She does this successfully.

Me (after Tracy has read 'umbrella' several times): It's easy to read when the words aren't there, isn't it, Tracy?
Tracy: Yes.
Tracy reads.
Tracy: Rain, rain go to Spain. So they . . . (pause)
Me (reading): decided to go.
Tracy (reading): decided to go and look for Bee's lovely (text: lost) umbrella in Spain.
Me: Have you ever been to Spain?
Tracy: I'm going to Tenerife with my sisters. My Mum's going with my other sisters and their husbands. I don't want to go with them as they make me look after their children.

I go on reading.

Me: While they were flying to Spain they sang . . .
Tracy: 'Rain, rain, go to Spain' over and over again. Bee hoped he would find his lost umbrella in Spain.
Me: So why do you think they sing, 'Rain rain, go to Spain?'
Tracy: Because it starts raining and you put your umbrella up.
Me (laughing): Exactly.
(Which is not, in fact, the reason at all.)

Round the World with Ant and Bee is less repetitive and has more text than *Ant and Bee and the ABC* which Tracy had read and enjoyed. She has occasional 'runs' as when, after labouring, the thing comes together and she read, 'Someone in Spain told Bee to look for his lost umbrella in a country next to Spain . . .'. But then she meets two words which had foxed her before: 'called' and 'France' and she stops. All the features of 'called' only remind her of her previous failure. Because she still thinks reading is about getting the word right, something like this sequence of internal reactions might underlie that unfruitful pause. Tracy sees the word 'called', recognizes it to the extent that she thinks, 'Ooh, that's the one I couldn't get before', a familiar sense of failure follows. Then she wonders perhaps if I'm going to give it to her or not. If I don't, then the sense of failure may be compounded by fear and a feeling of helplessness, a not knowing what to do next. She freezes and is unable to think about meaning. Tracy is still not sure what reading is all about, and it is going to take longer than the few sessions I have had so far for her to behave like a reader. I feel that if she did, she would have delivered an adequate version of the tale, once over the initial textual hurdles. For the most part she is still trying to read the words and the words get in the way of the meaning.

A miscue analysis, done later, revealed that she had very little going for her here. She expects the book to be like the previous one, but here the word-play has changed. The text has a low predictability for Tracy, who does not know the rules of this particular reading game and finds them difficult to learn.

I then choose a Dr Seuss Beginner Book, *Are you my mother?*, for Tracy to read. This is a story with a limited vocabulary, a lot of repetition and low-tone illustrations. A number of children I had taught before had read it relatively easily. I was also looking for something low-key in visual impact after the failure of *Meg and Mog*.

Me: I thought you might read one of my favourite books called 'Are
     [and here I point to the title] . . .
Tracy: . . . you my friend?
Me: Well, it might be friend, but in this one it's 'mother'.

I then proceed to give Tracy a synopsis of the story.

Me: It's about a little bird who hatches out of an egg and his mother
     knows he's going to hatch so she rushes off to find some food so
     he'll have something to eat when he hatches out, and he comes out
     while she's away and because he's never seen his mother, he doesn't
     know what she looks like so he has to go on looking all over the
     place to find out who's his mother.

Tracy makes no comment after this rather lengthy introduction. I wonder how much she took in and how much it helps her. I was trying to get her to take on the book even before she began reading it, but I get very little feedback to show what sort of ground my words had fallen on. Perhaps I should simply have talked more about birds and nests and eggs.

When Tracy starts reading I prop her up with explanations, clues and hints, but for several pages she is in a fog. Tracy starts 'I find . .', a miscue stemming from the previous page, where the text is 'My baby will be here! He will want to eat!' I think, logically though not grammatically, she anticipates the mother bird saying 'I (will) find something for my baby to eat!' I knew Tracy would not read 'must'; it was not one of 'her' words (she always gets 'away', 'she', 'play' and others). The breakthrough is when she reads words she doesn't know just because they fit. Unless she is into the story, I can spot the 'unknown' minefield looming ahead.

Me: Now, she says, 'I must get something for my baby bird to eat!'
    You read it.
Tracy: I must get something for my baby bird to eat! she said. I will
    [she did not get *will* on the previous page] be black!

Here I give the wrong clue to which Tracy, in the context, gives the right answer.

Me: Nearly. It's rather like 'black'.
Tracy: Blue (!).

My suggestion has diverted Tracy from the sense to the graphics and she loses the meaning.

Me: 'Back.' She's going away but she will be back.
Tracy: How long does it go on for?

Later on in the book Tracy gathers steam and reads more easily. Then, at about half-way through, the story becomes more far-fetched as the baby bird becomes desperate and starts wondering if the broken-down old car, the boat or the plane are his mother, the vocabulary expands and I can feel Tracy is flagging. I suggest I read to give her a rest. Tracy, right until the end when I ask her to read the summary, intones with me as I read. I am surprised at this as I felt she needed a rest and I was prepared to finish it off for her. I don't stop her, not knowing whether she enjoyed chiming in with me as I read or whether she had misunderstood me when I said I would read the rest and thought I meant her to read with me. She reads the last page by a feat of memory, recalling the order in which the baby bird had queried first animals, then things.

It had been a struggle but there had been moments when she was reading: occasions when the words and phrases were repeated rhythmically. At the time I felt the experience had been fairly successful for Tracy. Later on I felt it had been only partially successful. I was more conscious of the incredible effort she was putting into it. When Tracy got to know me better and I found shorter books with more rhythm and repetition, she did feed back her enjoyment by saying, 'I like this' or by asking what happened in the end.

Lesson three

At this session I decide to try a different tack. I bring in a pile of Picture Puffins among which are *Angus and the Ducks, The Giant Jam Sandwich, Old Mother Hubbard and Her Dog, Harry the Dirty Dog, May I Bring a Friend.* I put them on the table and ask Tracy if she would like to read one now and take one home. She says she would like to read *The Giant Jam Sandwich* and take *Old Mother Hubbard and the Dog* home. I start with OMH, showing her how much easier the text is and that she might take GJS home to read with her mum.

I feel this session is a fairly crucial one for Tracy and for me. It was the first time when reading to me, at any rate, from a printed book that the text came off the page and Tracy found herself reading. It was not without a lot of effort but this time it worked. The echoes of the rhyme she knew long ago matched the words on the page, and even when they didn't match, she says something that fits the rhythm of the verse and makes sense. For 'she took a clean dish' Tracy substitutes, using the picture, 'she took a cake down'. She puts a bit of herself in too at one point. She says, 'She went to the bakers, to buy him a loaf of bread' instead of 'to buy him some bread'. In her world she goes to the baker's 'to buy a loaf of bread'.

Tracy still tries some things that don't work. She describes the dog as 'playing a ploon' for 'smoking a pipe'. She thinks the long pipe in the illustration is a musical instrument, but there are obsolete words in the rhyme like 'hosier's' and 'tavern' and one cannot know what instruction she may have had on the different instruments of the orchestra. The pipe looks not unlike a bassoon. But Tracy does not flounder and struggle this time; she adjusts, self-corrects and charges on.

I intervene, but I feel this is more because we are sharing the text and because there are the obsolete words referred to above, than because I need to help her out of hopeless positions. Here are samples of our working together.

The book itself has low-key two-tone illustrations with a double page for each verse:

Tracy: Old Mother Hubbard
      Went to the cupboard
      to get her [poor] dog a bone.

She does not know or remember the word 'poor' so leaves it out and carries on to the end of the line. I know the word 'poor' will appear before 'dog' on every page, so I get Tracy to try and think of it.

Me: What sort of dog was he? Do you remember how she used to say?

Tracy thinks I am referring to the last word 'bone' and tries 'boneo'.

Me: Her poor dog a bone.
Tracy: Bat [self-corrects] But when she got there
      The cupboard was bare
      And so the poor dog . . .
Me: Had.
Tracy: Had none.
Me: None. Now what sort of shop does one go to here?
Tracy: She went . . .
Me: Tracy, what sort of shop is this?
Tracy: Bakers.
Me: That's it.
Tracy: She went to the bakers
      To buy him a loaf of bread
      But when she come back
      The poor dog was dead
Me: Is he really dead do you think?
Tracy: No.
Me: Just pretending. Isn't he?   ·
Tracy: She went to the . . .
Me: Now this is rather a funny sort of place. It's called a joiners.
Tracy: Joiners.
Me· It's really where they do carpentry.

Tracy: She went to the Joiner's
      To buy him a collar [coffin].
Me: Coffin.
Tracy: But when she got there
      The poor dog was a . . .
Me: Laughing.
Tracy: Laughing. She . . .
Me: Now, it doesn't say 'she went to the . . .' so can you think what she does here? She's doing to get him something to eat and she's taking something off the shelf?
Tracy: She took a cake down.
Me: Well, that doesn't quite work. She took a clean dish . . .
Tracy: Dish
      To get him some . . .
Me: Tripe.
Tracy: But when she come back he was . . .
Me: What's he doing?
Tracy: He was playing a . . . ploon.
Me: He could be. He's smoking something. What could he be smoking? It's a very funny kind. What else do people smoke? It's not a cigarette, it's a stick with a round thing at the end.
Tracy: Oh, yeah, I know, a pipe.
Me: Well done. That's exactly what he was smoking.
Tracy: She went to the fish shop
      To buy him some meat . . . fish
      But when she come back
      He was licking the plate.
Me: It could be. What rhymes with fish?
Tracy: Dish.
Me: That's it.

The reading goes on, with Tracy stumbling and me supplying the clues to the rhymes. When the tape runs out and I turn it over, Tracy says: 'I like this.' But you can see her problems from this verse:

Tracy: She went to the tailor's
      To buy him a coat
      But when she came back
      He was riding a horse.
Me: What's he riding?
Tracy: Pony.

Me: And what rhymes with 'coat'? The word is like coat but it's an
   animal with horns. I'll read it and see if you can get the last word.

I then read the verse and Tracy supplies 'goat'.
   The last verse, where the rhythm and sequence change, floors Tracy.
She gets through it with a lot of prompting. This is not surprising as
there are words like 'curtsey' and 'bow'.

Me: Now, what were all the things he could do?
Tracy: He could sing. He could dance. He could write. [She omits 'He
   could read.']
Me: What's the other one?
Tracy: He could bite. (At last, a real dog!)
Me: Well, let's look at these two. He could? Remember? He could do
   something with the news?
Tracy: He could write.
Me: The other one. He could . . .
Tracy: Read. He could write.
Me: Read the last line.
Tracy: He could sing. He could dance. He could read, he could write.
Me: You enjoyed that, didn't you. I think it would be an idea if you
   took that home and read it to your mum. She'd have to help you
   with the words for the funny shops they use.
Tracy (turns to title page): Miss, we didn't read that bit. Oh yes, 'Old
   Mother Hubbard and her Dog'.
Me: You're quite right, we didn't, did we? Did you ever hear that
   story before?
Tracy recites the whole poem.

I feel she could not have recited it before reading it this time. Tracy
subsequently read this book a great many times and took it home. It
became a friend, a confirmation that she could read. The book and the
poem stood for what people do when they read what they can take
pleasure in. For the first time Tracy intends what reading of this kind
intends. It could be argued that Tracy will never read for literary
pleasure but only for reasons of basic literacy. Whole programmes have
been built on this assumption. But here, beginning to behave like a
reader, she is also learning how readers share enjoyment, and retell
stories that everyone knows.

Lesson four

When with her withdrawal group, Tracy told me that she had read *Old Mother Hubbard* at home and she reads it again to me. Attempting to follow this lead and find more nursery rhymes that she can read and enjoy, I bring in *Lollipops* (Longman) and a very battered *Giant Golden Mother Goose* (Hamlyn) which has plenty of clear, simple colour illustrations of the kind enjoyed by very young children.

During this session we look at a lot of nursery rhymes while I try to sense Tracy's familiarity with each one. I am looking for any rhymes which can repeat the success of *Old Mother Hubbard*, where the sounds in her head match the words on the page, and especially for ones where there are refrains and repetitions so that Tracy can experience reading. Without the echoes from the past, nursery rhymes are difficult to read: Their interest lies in their being unpredictable and absurd. They present an upside down world. What mice *run after* the farmer's wife? Vinegar and brown paper to mend a head? I would not like to predict my way through another culture's nursery rhymes if I was not too sure of the language. On the other hand it is the jokes and the strong rhythms that make them remembered as well as the fact that they are 'children's first poetic memory'.[2]

Me: Right Tracy. I've got this book of poems [*Lollipops*].
Tracy: Miss, do I go at 3:00? [The bell is at 3.5. Tracy had to miss half a double period of science by coming to me and she slightly resented this. It may be that she liked science because she was able to do the practical work.]
Me: Yes, I'll let you go at 3:00. Alright? I'll keep an eye on my watch which is right today. Now, there's some poems in here. Do you know one called 'Bobby Shaftoe'?

I read the first verse. Tracy looks at me shaking her head and saying nothing.

Me: Let's go and look at some others.

I try 'What are little girls made of?', 'Little girl, little girl where have you been?' and 'Simple Simon' without much success.

Me: Do you know 'John had great big waterproof boots on?
Tracy: How does it go, Miss?

I read it.

Tracy: Oh yeah, I've heard of that.
Me: Do you remember when we had that rain thing up on the board?
     Do you remember? Were you there?
Tracy: I saw it up there when I come, but I wasn't there then.
Me: And someone wrote this one on one of the boots.

Tracy attempts to read the first part but with difficulty. The second
part I read while she chimes in and then finishes on her own with 'and
that said John is that'.

Me: Do you know about this? Rain, rain go away?
Tracy: Yes, Rain, Rain , , , , , here, Miss [she checks with me that she
     has started in the right place].
Me: Yes.
Tracy: Go away . . . come . . .
Me: Again . . .
Tracy: Another day. All the . . .
Me: All the . . . children.
Tracy: All the children
       Went out to play
Me: What about this one? 'It's raining, it's pouring' It's a good one for
     this afternoon isn't it?
Tracy: It's raining, it's pouring. The old man snoring. He went to bed
     and bumped his head, and he couldn't get up in the morning.
Me: That's it. It's all written down there. You know those raining ones
     [turning to 'Mother Goose']. I think we'll try this one. It's very
     old but it's got all the favourite ones in it. Let's have a look. See
     what we can find in here. Do you know, 'Three little kittens?'
     Not very well? Do you know 'Polly put the kettle on'?
Tracy: Yeah.
Me: All right, you read this one then.

This is a good one for Tracy as the first line of each verse is repeated
twice. In the final line of the first verse I have to help her with 'we'll'
and in the second verse with 'gone'. We try 'Three blind mice' which
Tracy makes heavy weather of and we read the last verse with Tracy
saying it with/after me. I suggest we try 'London Bridge' as it has a lot
of things the same in it. Tracy reads three verses with me supplying the
words for the materials and the reasons for their being unsuitable to

build the bridge with. She appears to be enjoying this tour of familiar rhythms and words from the past.

Tracy: Miss, can't you get these in school?

I think she means a collection of nursery rhymes to take home. The one she is reading is not in a state fit to be lent.

Me: I haven't got a book of these in school. Maybe they've got one in the library. They might. I don't know. Try 'Hey diddle diddle'. Don't you know that one? I'll read it to you and see if you can remember it. Then you could read it back if you do.

I read it with questions and references to the illustrations but Tracy says that although she knows it, she doesn't know it very well. We turn to 'Jack and Jill'. Tracy reads the first verse perfectly. She doesn't know the second verse and I carry her through it.

Me: I expect you heard these a long time ago, Tracy.

We then try, 'Hickory, Dickory, Dock' which Tracy reads without much help. 'The Queen of Hearts' does not get much reaction from Tracy. Then suddenly we find we are on familiar ground.

Me: Oh, look what we've got here.
Tracy: Old Mother Hubbard.

Tracy starts reading the first line and then goes back and reads the title, showing her confidence and her determination to do the whole thing properly. She comments on the rhyme of 'coffin' and 'laughing'; she is safe with 'smoking his pipe' and when she is uncertain she scans the illustrations for clues. She is as appreciative of the 'wig-jig' rhyme as she is scornful of the earlier one, and confident enough to express this view.

Tracy: I was telling my sister [grown up] 'Old Mother Hubbard' and she was telling it back to me. And some others her teachers used to tell her about in school.
Me: That's a nice thing to do.
Tracy: And her husband makes sorts of rhymes like that, like. This girl, my cousin, called Debra Ann, well, her Dad says to her, her

name's Debra Ann. Well, her Dad says to her:
> Debra Ann
> Bread and jam
> Marmalade and treacle
> A bit for you
> A bit for me
> A bit for the people.

Me: That's lovely. Do you remember any others your sister told you?

Tracy: She told me a lot, Miss. And I was telling her back what I learned in here.

Me: Who taught them to her? Did she tell you?

Tracy: Sometimes my Mum did and in school the teachers, and she used to read them out of a book like this.

In our discussion we asked if Vicky should have found something more like written speech, less linguistically demanding in one way and more in another. You can see that we would also have concerned ourselves with: is she reading or remembering? Why doesn't she 'get' words like 'goat'? Why does Vicky let her guess so much and yet tell her so quickly? But our concern here is with the nature of progress. Here is the relevant part of the discussion. Margaret has just summarized Tracy's case as 'in a touch and go stage'. Then:

Judith: Why were you nervous?

Vicky: Good readers just roll on and make sense of it somehow. But until they've got to that stage I just *know* what's going to happen.

Judith: But for many teachers of reading the notion that you could be nervous on behalf of a child is perhaps quite discouraging.

M: When you say, Vicky, that you just know, what does that knowledge consist of?

V: It's mostly arrived at from your limited experience of hearing them read . . . I don't know how I arrive at it. . . . I don't know what the process is. Give me any piece of writing for Tracy to read and I know that she will halt there, there, there. What she was able to read at that stage was so limited.

J: I don't think I could be as confident as that. It's so dependent on the mood of the child as she comes in, or on remote things like the feeling of being on top of things.

E. I think it's easier to be sure with kids who are very poor readers. As they get better it is more difficult to judge what they will do one day and not the next. If it's a real beginner, you see those pitfalls looming ahead.

J: Your anxiety really was that she was making no progress?

Vicky explained about the gap of three weeks since their last meeting. She was nervous for Tracy, because at their last lesson she had done less well than before and Vicky wondered if she would have fallen back even further. Vicky admitted that by reading Tracy's own piece to her again she was not only trying to diminish Tracy's possibility of failure but also to reassure herself.

E: Why should you worry? The first time she read it was just after
   she'd dictated it. Those are two fairly comparable situations anyway.
V: So now she's dictated it, read it back once, heard it from me once,
   although there has been this three-week interval.
J: You don't think that your nervousness could have been at your own
   contemplation of pushing the passage at her without reading it to
   her first?
M: Vicky understands this; she says that the disadvantage of the second
   reading is it's stale news and not very interesting itself to read
   about — not the most gripping stuff.
V: I do think about that. Why should she want to read it in the first
   place.
J: You have to be careful about that. People could turn round and say,
   'You lot claim you believe in reading for meaning. There could be no
   point in reading this because you've already got your meaning out
   of it.
M: But if it's good you don't mind reading it again.
E: Yes, she'll mean to say 'the pleasure is not so much to find out what
   it's about', but to say 'it was me who made it up'.
M: Savouring, enjoying, bringing back the experience. All the things that
   Jimmy Britton says are language in the spectator role.[3]
V: It's not only reading for meaning, but reading for reading, partly
   because I wanted her to have an experience of behaving like a reader.
J: Your justification for doing this repetition is that she gets a taste of
   what reading successfully *feels* like.
V: Yes.
M: Getting the meaning doesn't only involve discovering what the text
   means.
J: It could mean a delight in the fact that the words are coming off the
   end of your tongue because you actually half remember them and
   actually coinciding with the black marks on the page.

V: Children when they start reading read books they know, don't
   they? They read well-known stories.
M: If they're lucky. Is that what you wanted to do?
V: I was feeling after that − it's difficult with Tracy to find things she
   might be familiar with. I'd like to have known which stories she'd
   had read to her or what she really knows, but somehow that's just
   not accessible. She can't reach back to find stories, poems or whatever she has stored from her early experience!

The discussion then moved to Vicky writing 'Christmas' and Tracy's
recognition of it. Vicky says, 'Here I'm taking an isolated word. I don't
often do that', rather defensively, as if to defend some outmoded practice. 'A lot of people could say that's not reading. You've just told her
what it says'.

M: You have to do this on the run. When you reflect afterwards you
   say 'Was it a flop or wasn't it?' The important thing is the later
   speculation as well as the decision at the time. To some extent we
   want to know how to seize opportunities rather than to prescribe
   'what to do'. So you tell Tracy about Christmas and how you write
   it.
J: I think that's what makes people like us interested in reading. When
   I first started listening to children reading I thought it was the most
   boring thing in the world.
V: I didn't know what I ought to be listening for, that was the thing.
E: Chance comes into it a lot.
J: The whole speculation about whether your path is actually getting
   there, or whether it's just really zig-zagging hopelessly . . .
V: It's a difficult thing to get over − it takes a long time.

The next point to emerge dealt with choosing material for Tracy, a
theme implicit in all of the lessons in this series. Tracy responds very
violently to what she does not like. Vicky's experience with a book
called *Sam and the Firefly* has always been good because the story has
lots of action and movement and the reader is impelled to carry on. The
main character also does skywriting which is part of the fun. Vicky
takes up the account of Tracy's response.

V: But right away Tracy took one look and it was an absolute disaster.
   She didn't seem to know what a cow was, in a picture. I didn't seem
   to make the thing exist for her. She looked right at the start as if

this just wasn't for her. It was a shock to me, another of those constant surprises.

E: Prediction wrong again.

M: The problem wasn't the readability of the text, but Tracy's response?

J: Do you think it has nasty recollections for her as a book that had been pushed at her in primary school? Or is speculation of this kind pointless? We'll never discover what makes one book work and another not. I tend not to give them books they reject out of hand before they've even started. I don't know if it's fruitful to go on trying to find out why.

V We could just accept that there are books they reject and not get steamed up about it.

J: You've said in your comment that it appears to be too difficult. It may not be. It may just be that your second comment, 'She seems not to be thinking about it at all' may be much more accurate. She just doesn't want to know and therefore if you did force her to read it she would read it badly. Then you would again come to the conclusion that the book was too difficult.

V: I think I tried to get her to start. It was terrible. I tried to make the book into something by talking about the animals and so on, and she just wasn't there. I've seldom encountered her resisting with such force as I did with this book.

J: You contenanced her change . . .

V: Anybody in their senses would.

J: I don't know . . .

M: Others might say 'she needs more phonic exercises. She isn't ready for it.'

V: Nobody who has any experience of reading would have kept her at it.

J: They might. By saying you 'just switched' the book you are giving encouragement to people who feel guilty when they don't push things through. You're saying that's OK. That's being flexible, that's responding to what the child is trying to do. That's where you make progress, so you're right to be emphatic here. Your comment that the book 'had failed to engage her' is absolutely right. That's just what happens.

But to Vicky's confusion Tracy now picks a book that she has read before, which represents no real advance. What was Vicky to do?

J: We're back to this instinct thing again. You feel it's time to move her on.

V: I think what I did is open to other explanations. What do you think?

M: Again, we're working on it afterwards. That isn't what it's like at the time. You have to make instant decisions. When you reflect on them you decide there are other ways to decide and you may make another choice next time. We're able to see what we're doing in ways that aren't available to others. The most important way is that we're checking the teacher. It's Vicky we're looking at as well as Tracy.

V: I felt guilty when I played back the tape. She'd gone to the shelf, chosen a book that's perfect, then I said: no, in fact we'll do this other one.

M: You were actually saying, 'We've read that. We're going to read the next one that's like it.' It's a good instinct to say, 'We've been over that bit of writing.' Remember your earlier comment about Tracy's piece, 'it was stale news by now'. So you want something new for Tracy even though she wants to stay with the security of a story she knows. You are confirming your belief that she's ready for the next step.

V: That's very charitable. I worried about that a bit.

Later in our discussion we asked ourselves: What makes a reading experience successful? Vicky saw that, at the time, she had assumed that Tracy had been successful. Then, on reflection she had not been so sure. Remember that Vicky's chief concern had been to make Tracy feel that she was reading as a reader does.

M: Are there ways of examining how you actually make judgments about whether or not a reading encounter is a success?

V: I brought this point − that I'd had two different responses to the same experience of Tracy reading *Are You My Mother?* Tracy hadn't been able to read very much and we'd got through the whole book in various ways: with me reading some of it, a lot of talking, her reading some of the repetitive bits, and so I felt fairly confident that this had been some sort of progress. But when I came to listen to it afterwards, I listened to Tracy reading and I was more conscious of the *effort* when I heard her again.

E: I nearly always have that experience, actually.

V: It worried me that one could have two such different experiences (or see the same experience in a different light) and I wondered whether one should listen to lessons on tape much more often.

M: What gave you an impression at the time that there had been some sort of progress?

V: I think I'd felt at moments, not through the whole book, that the thing had come together at certain stages, and then I describe how the plot got more complicated, and she was losing it. Then I said I'd read, and then this thing at the end where she chimes in with me, quite unexpectedly. When I said I'd read, and she reads it with me when I hadn't asked her to. She must have been following and she must have wanted to do that.

E: Aren't you looking at it in different ways? The first time you're comparing it with what you know she's done before, and it seems to be better than that. Then you listen to it again. You're listening to someone read, and you think that she just reads badly. That's what you do when you listen to somebody read. If you distance yourself from the actual process of that person whom you know reading something a bit better than they have done before, and you suddenly stop and think - - God, they're still reading word by word!

V: The first time you hear it maybe you hear a little bit more what you want to hear: you don't hear so much of the evasions, hesitations, her breathing, because . . .

E: You're almost doing it with her . . . being her.

V: Willing her. You're more tuned to the positive things that are coming out of it, whereas when you sit back in a sort of detached way . . .

E: . . . it's a more active process the first time.

V: . . . it's passive afterwards. You're more conscious of her doing it.

E: It's almost as if you're doing it when you're doing it the first time with her. You're so tuned to what she's trying to do, the good things she's trying to do.

V: You're trying to make the thing proceed . . .

E: You're picking on the good things and encouraging those.

M: I was thinking of the teachers who listen to children reading every day. How much of this is part of their awareness?

E: You need a certain amount of peace and quiet to do the first kind of listening: to enter into it you have to concentrate hard. I find it difficult to listen to someone read unless I can fully concentrate.

J: The normal classroom situation, e.g. in a primary school, the teacher's priority is to hear everyone read. I've watched teachers stop children in the middle of a sentence. It's a formal exercise. They're not involved in the way that we're discussing.

V: When you hear someone read you aren't criticizing in the way that you are later when you're also examining your efforts and the effect you're having on the reader. You're monitoring yourself . . .

E: You are to some extent. You stop yourself from jumping in and you are aware that's what you've done.

V: The thing I'm not sure of, that comes out of this, is which was it? Was the reading experience what I first thought it was for Tracy, at the time, or was it what I thought it was subsequently?

M: I can imagine you saying at the time: 'She's better than she was before', and later you say, 'What a long way she's still to go.' Looking back you say one; looking forward you say the other. You need to say both. If you don't hear yourself and the kid in the second situation you don't know what there's still to do.

E: But someone else can hear your reader and say how bad he is, but you know that progress has been made. We need both perceptions so that we don't look at them as failures.

V: Are you listening more perceptively the second time?

J: Maybe life would be like that if we heard ourselves over and over again.

Here we are looking at our reactions to the delicate business of hearing children read aloud, the sensitive perceptions we need to make at the time, the finality or non-finality of judgments, and gradually the difficulty of estimating progress begins to emerge. Tracy is clearly better than she was, but still a beginner in every sense. Yet Vicky has persisted in her desire to make reading attractive, to let Tracy feel the swing of success.

Whatever else these lessons show, they make us wonder: what happened in all the years before? Tracy isn't in need of remedial teaching; she has never been taught at all, and is a prime example of what Bruner taught us to call 'conditioned helplessness'.

Judith and Trevor — what happens to the pupil's view of himself as a reader?

The text is Judith's.

Trevor had been coming to special reading lessons with two or three others once a week for a year when this series of four lessons took place. You will remember that he selected himself for extra help. In the first year he was a complete beginner and under pressure from his authoritarian home to learn to read now that he was at secondary school. He was originally in my mixed-ability English class, so immediately assumed a proprietary air towards me in the small withdrawal

group. He set the tone by being always punctual, conscientious, atten-
tive, receptive.

Throughout that first year he convinced me that his chances of
success lay in his obvious love of stories. Right from the beginning he
listened critically to stories and was able to anticipate twists of plot or
volunteer possible endings. He liked listening to the same story again and
so he eventually took on the reading of these stories, surprising and
delighting himself by discovering that the marks on the page actually
bore some relation to the sounds he was making and the story he was
unfolding in his head. It was tempting, from my point of view, to
prolong this honeymoon period of 'remember' story-reading, but
Trevor's puritanism and my anxiety dictated that we engage with
more demanding tasks. I began to offer him unseen material to read.
Although I gave him much support by outlining the story first, it was
then, I think, that his old anxieties and convictions that he would never
learn to read became reactivated. His attitude towards the task became
negative, he employed numerous delaying tactics, he allowed his
resentment towards me to be voiced. Equally, my quiet conviction that
Trevor would learn to read took a battering, and I became didactic,
urgent, proselytizing. It was at this stage that the following four lessons
were taped.

I cannot say that my instincts to push Trevor towards independent
reading were wholly mistaken. After all, spending the best part of a
year on traditional pre-reading activities seems a long time when the
pupil is already in the secondary school. During the period of these
tapes, and afterwards, there were occasional positive gains made and we
never lost our joint delight in relating what we were reading to our own
lives. But to hear Trevor's increasing rejection of my invitation to him
to read is discouraging in view of the high hopes I held for him at the
start of the year. I think for me the hardest thing at this time was to
avoid colluding with Trevor's defeatist view of himself as a reader.

Lesson one

Much of the previous lesson had been spent in a misguided and time-
wasting effort to get Trevor to compose a list of words starting with a
'sh' sound. In fact Trevor had picked up a great deal of phonic/graphic
information from his exposure to print over the last year, and my
yielding to feelings of panic because Trevor was unable to *verbalize*
this information was, I think, indicative of my loss of a sure sense of

direction about this time. I was determined not to spend time on so demoralizing and fruitless a task in this lesson.

I begin by reading *Spit Nolan* by Bill Naughton. Trevor interrupts to describe, at considerable length, his first-hand experience of go-carting. He becomes more and more eloquent and exuberant. 'I used a drill not a red-hot poker like Spit did to make my hole.' 'I mashed up my Dad's drill and he made me pay £2.50 for it.' He regales me with anecdotes about the school workshop's accidents and losses. I ask him if he would like to read. 'At 5 to, I will read.' 'I will read from here to here.' 'I'll read if you turn the tape-recorder off.' Eventually, he begins in a muted, resentful voice, but I quickly perceive that the task is too demanding and abandon the venture, assuring Trevor that he will find *Spit Nolan* much easier to read when he's older.

I next choose *Paul, Hero of the Fire* by Edward Ardizzone, which I know Trevor has had read to him at his primary school. I rely on that faint memory to support him through this reading.

The section of the text tackled by Trevor in the following transcript is this:

> Once upon a time there was a small boy called Paul who lived with his mother and father in a pretty house with a large garden.
>
> He had a dog called Fido and a cat called Blacky, and, as it was holiday time, he should have been happy, but instead of being happy he was bored and worried.
>
> He was bored because he was tired of playing by himself and worried because his mother seemed so sad and his father so cross.

Me: I think you'll like this.

Trevor: You start first.

Me: No, I want you to start straight off.

Trevor: No, I want you to start first.

Me: Where shall I read to then?

Trevor (good-naturedly): Oh all right. I'll start first. I'll read to here. [reads] One upon a time.

Me: What was the first word?

Trevor (clearly, at good speed, phrasing correctly): Once uponce [!] a time, they [there] was a lonely [small] boy called Paul who lived with his mother and father in a palace [pretty] house with a little [large] grandfather [garden]. What is this? [points to word 'large'].

Me: Large.

Trevor: Large, great, . . . Miss?

Me: Garden.

Trevor: Garden.

Me: It's not a palace house actually. It's a pretty house.

Trevor: He had a dog called F . . .

Me: Fido.

Trevor: Fido and a cat called B . . .

Me: Blacky.

Trevor: and as it went, was holiday [s] time he set . . .

Me: Should.

Trevor: Should have been playing [happy] but it . . .

Me: What's that word?

Trevor: Playing.

Me: Why do you think it's 'playing'?

Trevor (quickly): not playing, happy.

Me: Good. Now how did you decide that it was 'happy' and not playing?

Trevor: Somebody told me.

Me: You told yourself. I didn't tell you.

Trevor (cheekily): Somebody told me from next door.

Me: If you can tell me how you worked it out, then I could begin to understand what was going on in your mind.

Trevor (perky): I just knew it was 'happy'.

Me: Why did you decide that 'playing' was wrong?

Trevor: There ain't a 'p' at the beginning.

Me: Mmmm.

Trevor: Instead of being happy he was sad [bored] and worried.

Me: Do you think that's 'sad'? Why do you think it's probably not 'sad' although it makes sense?

Trevor: What is it Miss?

Me: Tell me first why it can't be 'sad'?

Trevor: It aint got an 's'.

Me: It hasn't got an 's' at the beginning. What has it got at the beginning?

Trevor (yawning): 'b'.

Me: And do you know what sound a 'b' might make?

Trevor: 'Bu'.

Me: 'Bu' it says 'bored'.

Trevor: Bored.

Me: He looks bored in the picture, doesn't he?

Trevor (delighted): He looks happy to me.

Me: He doesn't.

(Heated debate follows.)
Me: I wonder why he's bored. Why might you be bored in the holidays?
Trevor: Nothing to do.
Me: Yes, well maybe that's the same for him.
Trevor: He wants to go to the fair and he can't go.
Me: Let's read on and see.
Trevor: He was bored stiff, no, because he was telling [tired] of
     playing. What's this?
Me: Tired.
Trevor: And wouldn't [worried], Miss?
Me: Worried.
Trevor: Because his mother said [seemed] . . .
Me: Seemed. .
Trevor: Seemed so . . .
Me: That's not a difficult word, is it?
Trevor: 'Tis to me, Miss.
Me: Well, do you remember how the other day we were looking at
     rhyming words?
Trevor (protesting): Oh Miss, Come on, Miss!
Me: No, I want you to think. What does that say [I write bad]?
Trevor (sullen): don't know. [Pauses] 'bed!'
Me: Bad. Now change the first letter. What sound does an 's' make?
Trevor: Sss.
Me: Bad and . . . ?
Trevor: Said.
Me: Well, sad actually.
Trevor: Sad.
Me: Yes, he was worried 'cos his mother seemed so sad.
Trevor (quickly): And his father so cross.
Me: Good.
Trevor: Finished! Hurrah!
Me: So he's got problems with his parents 'cos they don't seem very
     happy and he's bored 'cos he's got no one to play with. On we go.

Trevor put up great resistance claiming that he's reached his initial
goal, that 'it ain't fair' on him. He repeats several times how tired he is,
how his foot hurts, his belly hurts. I protest that we want to find out
why Paul's mother is so sad. This spurs Trevor on for a moment, but
he collapses again, pleading weariness.

I suggest that he is 'giving up' which stings Trevor into the accusation, 'It's a year now, Nothing's happened'. I am stunned into momentary

silence and then I start the long haul of re-establishing Trevor's image of himself. I refer back to how little he could read when he first came to me, how long it takes to learn such a complicated task, how my son is still learning after two years. Trevor totally rejects the picture of himself as illiterate a year ago ('I could write my first name, my second name and my surname'), but looks into a future where he gloomily predicts that he won't be able to read in the third form, the fourth form, the fifth form.

The session ends on a muted note with Trevor reading flatly, needing me to provide nearly every word and then leaping up as soon as the pips go. It is difficult to salvage the good things from a session like this and too easy to chastize oneself for proceeding officiously and blindly.

It is perhaps important to look at the dynamics of the whole lesson. My reading of *Spit Nolan* and the discussion around that took the first three quarters of an hour. Throughout the time Trevor was ebullient and committed. The section of the lesson covered by the above transcript lasted five minutes and the protests and accusations summarized above took up the remaining ten minutes of the lesson. I have tried to give some indication of the spirit of his approach to reading as well as his achievement. A lot of his responsiveness disappears as he struggles to decode the text and there is only one indication ('He wants to go to the fair and he can't go') that he is attending to the message. (In fact he jumps to the wrong conclusion, but at least he's thinking.)

The text is approximately eighty words long. Trevor reads sixty of those eighty words correctly first time. Of the remaining twenty which present problems, he spontaneously corrects one word, at my suggestion corrects two words, asks for help with six words, two words remain uncorrected, three words are omitted. I provide unasked two words, and I correct four words.

This would seem to be reading at frustration level. Is the text too difficult? There are certainly some structural difficulties in the central paragraph: 'he should have been happy' is complex for a beginning reader (though not beyond Trevor's spoken range) and the accumulation of words like, 'happy, bored, worried, sad, cross' may leave a very muddled impression in the reader's mind. But I don't think the text can be held to blame for this very unsatisfactory end to the lesson.

I think two organizational changes might have helped. Firstly, the first part of a lesson is probably a better time to ask a child to read, while he is still feeling fresh. Trevor's excuse that he was tired is probably only too true. Secondly, I think I could have read Trevor into the story more and made it less of a test situation. I knew he had heard the story before, but in the event that was not sufficient support.

The demands I make on Trevor to be explicit about his difficulties with certain words are met with phonic/graphic explanations which is disappointing in view of the fact that much of my aim during the previous year had been to train Trevor's eyes away from the features of words and to convince him that he could predict his way through a story. But Trevor seems only able to offer explanations on that level at the moment, and I accept them though I am not able to make much use of them.

The questions left uppermost in my mind after this session are: have I provided Trevor with enough opportunity to practise reading in this session? To falter your way through a mere eighty words in one lesson seems a wholly inadequate experience. Have I confirmed in Trevor his belief that reading is fun only if somebody else is doing it? It seems to become a painful, slow, and totally different experience for Trevor when he's doing it. By taking on so seriously – even somewhat emotionally – the task of building up Trevor's confidence, do I betray my own fear that I will not be able to teach him to read? The next lesson mercifully redeemed the situation.

Lesson two – three days later

Our previous lesson had been an intimate, somewhat intense, ultimately rather fraught one-to-one session. Today Oliver joined us and I invited Trevor to begin reading *Paul, Hero of the Fire* to Oliver and me as audience. He enters into the spirit of the occasion, clearing his throat self-importantly and setting off confidently.

Trevor: Once upon a time they [there] was a sad [small] boy called
    Paul who lived with his mother and father in a tall, beautiful
    [pretty] house with a large gate [garden] . He had a dog called F . . .
Me: Fido.
Trevor: Fido and a cat called Black and as it was holidays time he . . .
    [long pause] .
Me: Should have been.
Trevor: happy but inside [instead] of . . .
Me: Instead.
Trevor: instead of being happy he was [pause] bored and worried. He
    was [pauses] bored [pauses] because he was . . .
Me: Read on a bit.

Trevor (pauses): tired of playing by himself and would [worried]
Me: You've had it before. Look back.
Trevor (eventually): Worried.
Me: Good.
Trevor: Because his mother said . . .
Me: Does that fit in? His mother something so sad? Would 'looked' fit it?
Trevor: No, there's no 'l' at the beginning.
Me: But this word means much the same as 'looked'. I'll tell you – it's seemed.
Trevor: . . . seemed so sad and his father so cross.
Me: Good.

Trevor has reduced his mistakes by half and some of the miscues ('sad' for 'small', 'beautiful' for 'pretty', 'gate' for 'garden', 'Black' for 'blackie') are semantically acceptable whilst others ('inside' for 'instead', 'would' for 'worried', 'said' for 'seemed') show his effort to make some sort of phonic/graphic matching. The construction 'should have been' is still beyond him and so possibly is the concept of 'seeming'. It is interesting to note that the words 'bored', 'worried', 'because', and 'tired' which gave him difficulty before, are this time retrieved by him, if only after long pauses. The reading takes the same length of time as in the previous session (five minutes) because of these pauses, but the story seems to survive rather better.

Oliver then takes over the reading with Trevor acting as audience, suggesting alternative words. He is very involved in the story, commenting on the picture ('even his cat looks miserable') and the vocabulary ('who says "darling" these days?'). The text covered by the boys is as follows:

One day when Paul was sitting as quiet as a mouse trying to read a book, he heard his father say to his mother, 'Darling, it's no use. We can't go on as before. The market has gone all to pieces. We have hardly any money left. I am afraid we must sell the house.' Then he heard his mother sobbing and sobbing.

This made Paul feel sad. He loved the house and hated the idea of having to leave it and go to some smaller place.

'Oh Blacky and Fido, what shall we do?' said Paul. 'We must make some money or we shall have to go away.' But Blacky only miaowed and Fido only wagged his tail, which did not help very much.

Then Paul went out and met his friends, Alf the Coalman and

Tom the butcher's boy, and asked them for their advice. They both said, 'You must get a job.'

On the way home Paul had a wonderful idea. He would get a job at the Fair.

Next morning he got up very early while his parents were still asleep. He dressed quickly and put into a small suitcase a shirt, two vests, one pair of pyjamas, two pairs of socks, a spare pair of shoes, face-cloth, soap, toothbrush and toothpaste. Then he wrote a letter to his mother and father and said goodbye to Blacky and Fido.

Darling Mummy and Daddy, I have gone to get a job and make some money so please dont cell the howse. love and kissis from paul.

By hard walking Paul soon arrived at the Fair. 'Your money to come in', said the man at the gate. 'Please Sir, said Paul, 'I have come to get a job. Must I pay?'. 'Ho, that's a nice story, that is! Trying to get in for nothing are you, you young rascal?' said the man. 'Pay your money, or outside you stay!'

So poor Paul had to give him all the money he had.

We are interrupted by the head of the remedial department collecting information about withdrawal groups. Trevor proudly enumerates the number of times he sees me, but Oliver would like to dissociate himself from me ('I've got better things to do').

Oliver asks why I don't correct him on every word (I allowed 'dear' instead of 'darling'). I explain my methodology and Trevor adds his advice, 'If anybody's listening, you must make it make good sense, even if you say some of the words wrong.' Oliver then substitutes 'We will have to' for 'must', classically illustrating the point. Trevor says 'He puts extra words in but it means the same.' He actually gets quite excited when he glimpses the possibilities that the idea opens up and we discuss how to substitute 'horse' for 'house' would be unfortunate in this text, whereas to substitute 'crying' for 'sobbing' would leave the text unaffected. Trevor is intrigued by the word 'sobbing', demonstrating the difference between a sob and a cry, and then dismissing 'sobbing' as an old-fashioned word. Trevor takes up the reading:

Trevor: 'Oh Blacky and Fido. What shall we do?' said Paul. 'We must make some money or we shall have to go away.' But Blacky only . . .
Me: Miaowed.
Trevor: Miaowed and Fido only barked [wagged]
Me: That would make sense except for the words coming afterwards —
his tail.

Trevor: Wagged his tail which did not happen [help] very much.

Me: Now where's the word you've made a mistake with?

Trevor (pauses): help, help very much.

Me: Good, Trevor. Don't you feel when you correct yourself like that that you can do it? You must be very pleased with yourself. I didn't tell you that word. You're quite clever enough to work it out. You've got it all up there.

Trevor (challengingly): And it won't come out!

Me: It will come out. We don't have to rush things. It'll come on its own when you're ready for it.

Trevor: I'm ready now!

Me: Come on then, let's go.

Trevor: Then Paul, wait, went out and made his fortune.

Me (laughing): I like that — 'went out and met his . . .

Trevor: Friend.

Me: Good. These are his friends, Alf the . . .

Trevor: Cobbler.

Me: Coalman, actually.

Trevor (very excited): Wait, wait, wait. I'll find it, don't read no more.

Me: Sorry.

Trevor's mounting enthusiasm and confidence encourage him to insist on his independence of me. He is reading at a good rate, and making very plausible predictions, which indicate his involvement with the story. Later, in this spirit of optimism and inquiry, he volunteers an explanation of why the word 'butcher' is difficult.

Trevor: the 'c' is blocking me. 'But' and 'her' I can read. The 'c' is blocking me.

Later he examines the word 'asked'.

Trevor: 'Ask' is half the word, then you add-ed. But it sounds like a 't' — 'askt'.

Later he focuses on the word 'their'.

Trevor: There is a different way of writing 'their'. This one's got an 'i' and that's blocking me. Take away the 'i' add an 'e' and you've got the other 'there'.

Oliver then joins in a long discussion about the difficulties of written English. Trevor seems elated, on the verge of new discoveries all the time.

We arrive at the word 'idea' in the text, which neither boy can guess. As it had occurred earlier, I flick back through the book to find it, but Trevor says there was no point looking on page 1, because Paul was far too sad and bored at that stage of the story to have anything approaching an idea.

Paul's misspelt letter in the text is eagerly read by both boys in unison. The handwriting and irregular spelling prove no problem. Trevor reflects that Paul's parents are going to be worried when they receive the letter.

Unlike the previous session when Trevor had to be pushed to go on reading, this session is characterized by enormous energy, optimism, concentration and reflection. When I suggest they worked hard enough, they deny that they are tired, and Trevor takes up the reading again.

Me: By hard walking . . .
Trevor: Paul soon reached at the Fair
Me: Do we say 'reached at'?
Trevor: Got. No.
Me: Arrived.
Trevor: You must, your mother [your money] . . .
Me: This is the man at the gate talking now.
Trevor: Your money to come in [inside] said the man at the gate.
    'Please sir', said Paul, 'I have some, come to get a job, Must I pay?'
    'Who' That's a nine stories, no fine story, nice story that is. Trying
    to get in for nothing are you, you yours young hooligan – no.
Me: Hooligan's lovely – a better word than they've got there.
Trevor: Rebel?
Me: Rebel would be good as well, and you know it begins with 'r' –
    rascal.
Trevor: Said the man. Pay your money or go outside your [you]
    stay. So pay, no, poor Paul had to go he all him [give him all the]
Me: Which word have you slipped up on?
Trevor (pointing to 'all'): This one here.
Me: No, you've got that right.
Trevor: So poor Paul had to give him all. But you don't give all. Who is
    all?
Me: Read on a bit.
Trevor: . all the money he had.

Me: Now read the whole sentence again.

Trevor: So poor Paul had to give him all the money he had.

Me: That makes sense now, doesn't it? Good Trevor.

Oliver takes over until the end of the lesson, with Trevor maintaining interest to the end, describing how a coconut shy operates, and offering suitable words when Oliver pauses, even though he is not actually following the text.

This session was cheerful and lively throughout, with each boy conscious of his audience and keeping the story line alive in his mind. There seemed to be many promising moments. The repeated section stood more firmly on its feet with half as many errors as on the first reading. There were several examples of where Trevor was able to self-correct after I had suggested he read on a little ('barked', 'wagged his tail'), ('you must, your mother, your money' said the man at the gate); much inspired guessing in context (even with some graphic matching) — 'made his fortune' for 'met his friends'; 'hooligan' and 'rebel' for rascal. Much analysis of what is 'blocking' him — (but*c*her, ask*ed*, the*i*r) and some spontaneous self-correcting where maybe he was doing his own looking ahead: 'Then Paul, wait, went out . . .' and 'I have some, come to get a job.'

The amount read by Trevor in this session is almost exactly double that of the previous session, and he listens to and shares a similar volume of reading from Oliver. More significantly, there is much less dependence on me and the beginnings of a very real excitemeent as he steps into the world of the reader.

The discussion point in the group was about 'new text'. This opened up the question of whether or not you could call it 'reading' if the reader already knew what the story was about. The ability to read is nowadays understood to be the ability to get the message from new text.

S: No more *Hymns Ancient and Modern*, you mean?

M: That, the Psalms and the bits of the Bible you knew before you read it. Even in Vicky's attempts to get Tracy to remember 'Old Mother Hubbard' as a starting point. When people talk about literacy in 'the old days' they also mean something like that.

S: You're talking about the jump from reading what you already know to what you don't already know. What's not clear is, to what extent he knew it. Was it something completely new, or something Trevor had learned by heart, something he knew the drift of, something

he'd heard you read, something he'd actually looked at while you
were reading it, there are different levels.

J: I suppose I mean all of them . . .

S: You've actually used the phrase 'remembered' and 'story reading' –
a nice way of putting it, but to what extent is it remembered?

J: He never knew the story off by heart in the way that Tracy could
have known 'Old Mother Hubbard' . . . I don't think she did . . .

E: One could know a nursery rhyme . . .

J: Certainly none of the books could Trevor have recited without the
book . . .

S: I find exactly this the problem right at the hub of it, moving from
the known to the unknown and the independence of being able to
pick up a book and just reading it without knowing about it . . . all
the time you come back and say, how can I ease that transition . . .
how can you, instead of suddenly whipping away a whole chunk of
support from underneath, 'now we're going to try something new',
how do you gradually take it away brick by brick. I've said this
before and never completely resolved it. We are looking for practical
ways to make the jump from something you've read to him so that
he has heard it word for word, knows it very well, maybe you have
to say quite a lot about it, or read him the first part, because that's
the hard part, when you're getting into it. Then, not the later part.
I'm just juggling in my mind. . . . How do you make that withdrawal
of support gradual? The way this reads sounds as if you said, 'right
now, we're plunging into the great unknown'. And the response
from someone not in our group reading this is 'Oh well, that's what
she did. She suddenly left him too much on his own . . .

E: But the next bit is interesting too. I found with Chris that it's the
lack of confidence as much as not knowing what it's about that
makes him unable to read it. If he's listening to someone else read he
can put in the words even if he isn't looking at the book 'cos he's
using all those strategies that he's using when he's reading something
he knows. He's not panicking because of the print, and so it's partly
making them (the readers) go on doing what they were able to do
before and apply it to something a bit different.

J: It's like children who can swim when you've got your hand underneath them, not touching or holding them up . . . running alongside
the bike.

M: Is there a running alongside phase in reading? Is this something we
have to think about in reading terms?

J: I'm convinced one can make the withdrawing of support a really graded process of withdrawing support. I'm quite sure we make mistakes because we are under so many pressures, have so many doubts and anxieties about what's happening. But maybe the more one does it, the more the personal anxieties come under control, and we know when to exploit the moment, I'm sure its not impossible.

S: It never works out as a steady growth of withdrawal; its five bricks ahead, six bricks back.

M: Is it successful when the reader knows what's on and begins to say don't tell me, don't tell me . . .

Now we're putting things together better from what we said in bits at the start. The group then agrees that Judith's point in her introduction 'to avoid colluding with Trevor's defeatist view of himself' is what she should concentrate on. (Something we couldn't have said in the early days.)

The discussion continues with a recapitulation of the group's discovery that the most difficult thing to decide was what would make a difference to the reader's competence; we agreed that the teacher experienced a 'feeling of panic' in case she/he could not make this decision. Books about teaching reading suggest that this is easy.

E: They tell you what to do and you are expected to just get on and do it. That's why you get panicky; it's the over-confidence of the other people. Perhaps they're right.

M: At what stage would it have been reasonable to ask Trevor to tell you what it would have been helpful to know? You remember how I kept on saying, 'See if you can find out what it would have been helpful to know'? Could he verbalize that? Frank Smith and the Goodmans are always saying 'Give them helpful feedback!'

J and S: They can't really tell you.

S: The most disappointing thing I ever had with Tom was when I tried to wheedle out of him what it would be helpful to know, and I realized that there was no intelligible way of forming the question.

J: I wonder what we'd like to hear? I say to Trevor. 'How did you decide that it was "happy" not "fame"?' I wonder what I hoped to hear?

S: You hope to hear 'because that would have made very good sense in the context'.

J: Yes.

E: It's not too bad in the context . . .

S: It makes sense, doesn't it, Miss?

M: We see him in the first bit taking his eyes off the page, the great resentment.

E: The typical bargaining thing, I'll read from here to here.

J: I've got a bit on tape in the third lesson when he says ten times he's not going to read. *Ten times.* I wonder if I should transcribe that so that people will know what resistance really is.

M: If you could bear to it would help . . . and Vicky's thing about 'is it *long*, Miss'.

S: Does it go right through?

E: And the heart dropping. . . You've really caught all this evasion and bargain, excuses and pains he's got. Kids must do that when they're being given those phonic exercises. Don't they say 'my foot hurts' when the teacher says, 'get plugged into the wordmaster'?

M: Well, with a machine you're still in charge. But this bargaining is also about your relationship with your teacher. 'Is your concern for me based on how well I do this', is what they're saying.

E: It's such a responsibility for doing the work. If you don't do the work, there is often another chance later on. But with reading, you may feel that if you try this time, and it doesn't work, then you've had it.

J: I was reading about anorexia the other day, about not wanting to eat. It seemed just like Trevor. Basically he doesn't want to be a reader. I think anorexics don't want to be adults; they want the dependence of being fed.

M: Anorexics are always being tempted with food, like little ones. Responsibility for doing the work. Is that what we're concerned with?

J: It is interesting that Trevor on this occasion came in just as *I* gave in. It's as if he's been playing a game, and as we've reached a stage in the game he becomes workmanlike again. 'Oh well, OK'. A ritual we go through.

M: Another trading ritual.

A pause while we all consider this. We then proceeded to talk about interruptions by the teacher. Elizabeth points out that Frank Smith says it would be unnecessary to interrupt a pupil when he 'got it right'.

J: They'd be confused if you asked them 'how do you know that says "mother"?'

S: I don't think it's any more wrong than interrupting them when they're wrong.

J: It's interesting isn't it?

(Pause.)

M: You have a different focus.

S: To which Goodman says (I'm not sure that I would say) 'if its wrong they'll have to come back to it; if its right they'll go on; you shouldn't stop them'.

E: I feel as Vicky does that if they're wrong they'll plough themselves into the ground. They'll be in such a tangle that they won't have the confidence to say, 'Oh well, that was wrong. I'll go back and do this again.' They'll say, 'I've drowned.'

J: That's right.

M: If that's the case, we still haven't given them enough confidence . . .

S: If that's the case you have to go back to where they would be relaxed enough for this task . . .

M: Which is what Vicky had to do.

E: Yes.

J: The big advantage of stopping them and saying 'Why did you think that word was "mother" when it *is* "mother"?' and they read it correctly, is that they would then have to defend their choice and you might then find out quite a lot about what is going on. They'd be worried initially and think, 'Oh' . . .

E: They'd say something else . . .

S: It would be incidentally productive or interesting to us as a research group. It could be counter-productive from a teaching point of view.

J: The advantage wouldn't be that they should be explicit about their process. The advantage would be that they know they could be stopped and asked to defend their choice, whether right or wrong, and they would sometimes . . .

S: Seems to me to be bringing their focus down to individual words again, which might be a very big price to pay . . . you go back and say 'that word was', and you're back at the old business of word perfect reading in the future rather than reading for meaning. On this riding a bike thing, again, you don't say 'why did you wobble the handlebars left to right' because the one thing you won't want them to do is to think about keeping their balance. Pursuing this analogy, the 'Why did you do that?' has to go out of the window . . . I'm not necessarily saying that we should. If we say it's not so much like riding a bike as driving a car, there *are* certain things that you do make explicit. You don't operate random combinations of the pedals. You do have to know which is which.

J: I think the child's morale would be kept up if sometimes you asked them and they found they were actually quite confident to state 'yes, it's "mother"', and 'I know it's "mother".' It would change the balance between teacher and pupil and give the pupil the feeling that sometimes he was right, whereas if you only stop them when they're wrong they're always wrong. I don't know if this would be psychologically boosting or if in fact you lost what little advantage you had. This could be a novel idea. The Goodmans would suggest not, but stopping the child after he's *right* . . .

M: There are bits on your videotape where you do just that, for encouragement . . .

S: But it's in relation to something that's been done wrong . . .

J: It's slightly different. What I said in the video is, 'How did you get the word "yesterday"? That was really clever because I didn't expect you to get it', or something like that. It isn't something like, 'Are you sure that the word is yesterday?' which is different . . .

M: Ah yes . . .

J: It is giving him the feeling that he could have been wrong, and he would have to find out if he had been right or wrong [I've changed the pronouns here to keep the cohesion. M]

S: It's touch and go, pointing out to someone, 'You might not have been right there . . . that was a tricky one' . . .

J: It has an element of playing a game.

M: It fits into the overall pattern of the trust situation.

J: I suppose you could say to the child, 'I'm going to stop you from time to time about words you've read. Sometimes you'll have read them correctly, and sometimes incorrectly . . .

S: With the type of children we're working with it's too testing really, particularly the fact that it's focusing on individual words – that I don't like, the one thing we're trying to pull them away from. I'd actually like to hear the tape here because the transcript doesn't tell you everything. I think that where you speak it's following a pause from Trevor – not indicated on the transcript.

J: The next lesson indicates the pauses because there were many pauses in the next lesson.

S: The way this reads suggests that you were jumping in where you needn't.

J: Yes, I was. I think that will come over.

S: I think you should make that criticism of yourself more explicit because it's something we would have said to you at the time when we discussed it.

J: I could have gone on for page after page criticizing myself. I don't know if this is what we want to do . . .

M: We've decided that we're up for judgment, but only to the same extent as the child is. Where it becomes clear that we can make a point by being self-critical.

J: I do think we can make a point here. It's important to make it. I'm sure I don't jump in as fast now as I did then. I would like to have my slate cleaned in this respect . . .

E: I think Trevor . . . we said the character in the book looked bored in the picture and Trevor said he looked happy. That's classic of certain kids.

J: It's a refusal to be cowed on a level where they know they can operate. He can't operate on a reading level and I beat him at it every time, in repartee he can talk me out and that's why he argues with me. I've had the most amazing debates and discussions with Trevor, and I'm quite sure it's because he has to hang on to his identity in the areas where he's strong.

E: Chris says, 'this picture isn't at all like what I've just read. There are fourteen little wolves in this story and I've counted them in the picture and there are only thirteen.'

J: I've got a marvellous tape of Trevor pulling these *Mr Men* books to pieces . . . so good, not only the pictures but the language people use, the plot, which is feeble and predictable.

M: Trevor's lit. crit. a year from now would be good. What about the bit where you got the the accusation that nothing had happened in a year.

J: I was stunned into silence. You can hear the pause on the tape whilst I gulp. It was so close to what I was thinking. I was thinking, 'it's a year now that I've been teaching Trevor and he ought to be able to read'. That's what he's saying.

M: Is it an accusation, or an agreement with you that he ought to be getting better?

J: I took it to mean that I haven't yet taught him to read. An accusation − not self-abasement.

S: It's what one says to one's doctor after the medicine hasn't worked.

J: I can tell you from the doctor's point of view that it is a very hurtful thing to have to hear. Even if you know it isn't your fault that the pills haven't worked, you still take it very personally.

We then turned to the third lesson which occurred three days later. Judith takes up the tale again.

Lesson three

If I had made time to listen to the tapes of the two lessons just described before I saw Trevor again, could I have identified and re-created
the conditions that made the second lesson so much more positive than
the first? Would I, for instance, have ensured that Oliver was there
again? Would it have been obvious that Trevor should be reading within
seconds of entering the room? Would it have been important to find
out how much Trevor wanted to go on with the story? Would it have
been crucial to let him start off with familiar material?

It seems obvious that a teacher needs to isolate and act upon key
moments in a lesson. Yet time to review a lesson is not the only requirement. How objective can one be at such close proximity and when one
is perhaps over-investing in success? How can one eliminate the vagaries
of mood in both teacher and pupil? How close to the surface are long-
held misconceptions of what a child needs to do in order to read, ready
to throw the teacher off a chosen course if all does not go smoothly?

The lesson began with Trevor innocently asking how to spell 'shoe'.
Though it was no part of my plan, it seemed obvious to link this
question with the work we had been doing on sounds the previous
week. I find the list of 'sh' words we had compiled and despite the
repeated miscues ('shilling, shutting, shape, self, shadow', read as
'shitting, shotting, sheen, shift, shawe') push him on to look at words
beginning with 'the'. I suggest he might like to use the dictionary to
help him and somewhat to my surprise he finds the relevant section
fairly quickly, humming loudly as he turns the pages. When I ask him
how he knows where to find the words, he ignores my questions
singing 'Ah, ha, ah, ha, ah ha'; delighting in withholding the secrets of
his skill from me. Instead of entering into the fun of the game, my
tone of voice grows flatter and soon I announce: 'That's enough of that
for one day.'

In fact this area of letter/sound correlation has always been prob-
lematic for Trevor and my refusal to exploit what could be seen by
others as a 'growth point' may have a very sure instinct guiding it.
There remains a conflict between my anxiety not to let Trevor run
away with the idea, at once too simplistic and too complicated, that
reading is to do only with sounds and letters, and my ambition to let
him experience success and mastery – in any field.

The lesson then moves at a leisurely pace through several topics
of discussion. I recall a story he dictated about a long jump he had
made. Trevor feigns indifference, denying vehemently that he ever

became excited about the telling of the story. This is immediately followed by an animated description of his form teacher's new motor bike (to
be disclaimed next week?). Trevor then gets up and operates his yo-yo
deftly a few times. It is at this stage that I bring the lesson to heel.

Me: Come and sit here now Trevor.

Trevor (eyeing *Paul, Hero of the Fire*): I'm not reading that book, Miss.

Me: You're doing very well with this book.

Trevor: I don't want to read that book.

Me: We'll go on from where we were before.

Trevor: No, we won't.

Me: You were doing so well, Trevor, come on.

Trevor: I don't want to read that book, Miss.

Me: You always want to give up just after we've begun. But I want to
go on because you were really enjoying it.

Trevor: I don't want to read that book. It's so boring.

Me: No, it's not. You don't know what's going to happen yet do you?

Trevor: I don't want to read that book. It's so boring. I'll read this
book here.

M: If you want, we'll go on to that book later but we can't just start
books and then abandon them otherwise you'll never know what it
feels like to get to the end of a story. Come on. We won't go from
the beginning but can you just remind me what it was about?

Trevor: I can't remember.

Me: Nothing at all?

Trevor: I don't want to read that book. It's boring.

Me: But you were getting quite involved in it. We talked a lot about it
last time.

Trevor: It's too boring now.

Me: We hardly begun. We don't know yet how he's going to make some
money? Do you remember he went off to see his friends, Alf the
coalman and Tom the butcher's boy and asked them their advice
and they both said, 'you must get a job'. Why did he need to get a
job?

Trevor: To earn some money.

Me: Why did he need some money?

Trevor: To help buy the house.

Me: To help?

Trevor: Save it?

Me: Yes, that's right. Well done [I then go on to recap the rest of the
story].

And so this defiant and most reluctant Trevor is slowly drawn into the reading contract. The above transcript covers nine or ten refusals to respond to my invitation to read. He sticks doggedly to his refrain 'it's boring' and none of my approaches — the 'firm line', 'praise', 'admonition', 'flattery', 'bargaining', 'appeals to his curiosity and his sense of puritanism' — affect his sure sense of his rights to reject what I am offering. It is only when I re-tell the story that Trevor becomes slightly involved but having set up such resistance, it is not lightly abandoned and one senses Trevor's resentment for some time to come. There are still outcries of 'it's so boring' and he only agrees to read when I offer to read alternate pages. Maybe those two things — my awakening of memories of the story in his mind and my offering the prospect of a speedier journey through the remaining tract finally brought us out of the impasse, but one wonders at what cost to Trevor's sense of dignity, his sense of his autonomy and his faith in me as his teacher. Trevor, however, as we have seen in earlier encounters, is a resilient child and just the openings he needed to restore his self-image occurred later on in this lesson.

I read several pages of the book to him (not the alternate pages I originally suggested) and when he did begin to read it was in a soft monotone, fully expressive only of his bitter sense of compromise. I tread very carefully, making few demands on him, supplying words he pauses at (rather too readily?), constantly re-phrasing and reinforcing the text. He does not, in fact, intersperse his own reading with any of his usual reflections nor with further protestations — he seems to have submitted passively and is offering the barest minimum. He reads flatly, with none of his emerging resourcefulness, but I warmly praise him for what he does achieve and take up the reading myself.

Still trying to find a way through for Trevor, I ask him what his parents would do if they found him missing at night. 'Don't know really,' he replies dully. I then reflect, 'In point of fact, the manager of the fair would have reported Paul's arrival there to the police.'

Instantly and in a voice totally animated again, Trevor asserts 'But that would ruin the story — there'd be no story if the manager just returned him home to his parents.' I fall gratefully on such a perception and enthusiastically agree with him. Later I reflected that where there is such disparity between a child's instinctive understanding of the devices of narrative and his ability to read fast and accurately enough to appreciate those devices it seems inevitable that the internal conflict will create tensions much like those of this session.

I am sure Trevor's verbalizing of this insight and my acknowledgment of it improved his morale. A few minutes later his self-esteem was further restored, when, *à propos* of the dwarf in the story teaching our hero various acrobatic tricks, Trevor tells me that he can stay up in a handstand for twenty seconds. I ply him with questions and he ultimately concedes that he is the best gymnast in his class.

His reading from this point on shows two or three quite distinctive changes from his earlier efforts. Firstly, instead of pausing before difficult words, he is willing to take the chance of being wrong (thus he says – 'please' for 'panic', 'such' for 'squashed', 'cows' for crowd'). Secondly, he repeats my correction before carrying on. Previously he had behaved as if he hadn't heard me, wishing to keep me and my charitable offerings at arm's length. Now he seems willing to accept me again. Thirdly, and this is the most encouraging sign, he voices his predictions aloud. 'He's remembered what he heard the boy saying – about the hole in the fence. He's going to take the children there.'

It would be delusion to claim that we finished the book with sweetness and light wholly restored. In fact as he reaches the last word, Trevor excuses himself and rushes out to the toilet and does not return. He may have felt himself the loser in the battle of that lesson – after all I achieved my objective of enabling him to experience the 'satisfaction' of finishing a book. His need to have the book recognized as 'boring' – was ignored. The growth points in the lesson were almost certainly submerged as far as Trevor was concerned and only visible to me after an interval of time and much reflection on the tape.

There are many points that this type of encounter (which must be familiar to many teachers of secondary school poor readers) raises. They would seem to fall into four broad categories; *organizational*, how could the lesson have been arranged to avoid such a confrontation? – *teachers' response*, – how do I cope with my feelings of dismay and frustration? – *pupil's motivation*, what is it that makes Trevor turn away from the help he so badly needs? – *text*, was Trevor's verdict on the book justified and if so, what makes a 'good' text?

And even when these issues have been thoroughly discussed, there still remains the peculiar, unpredictable, charged relationship of teacher and taught which obeys no laws and is full of surprises.

Lesson four – two days later

How did I view my task at the beginning of this lesson? Certainly there could be no discussion of *Paul, Hero of the Fire* which might normally have followed finishing a book. At all costs I wanted to avoid reminding Trevor of his final tussle with that book. I wanted to give him the experience of engaging with a reasonably sophisticated, plausible story with characters with whom he might identify, with a subject that interested him. *Spit Nolan* which I had read to him during the first of these four sessions, had been very much on Trevor's wavelength and he fell in eagerly with my plan to read the accompanying story in that book which was *The Goalkeeper's Revenge*. There was no question of my expecting Trevor to read any of the text (we had discovered *Spit Nolan* was beyond his capacity) and I wanted Trevor to relax and listen and feel the shape and pattern of a story again. I told him I was not expecting him to read at all this lesson and he settled down to enjoy the story.

Atypically he listened without interruption and as I was eager to have some feedback I suggested that he might like to tell the story back to me in his own words. At first he interprets this as a request to read and starts to turn back to page one but I repeat that I'd like him to tell it as if to someone who'd never heard it before and he asks me if I am going to write it down . (There had been a history of Trevor dictating his own stories to me, but he had never dictated a version of someone else's story before.) I immediately reach for his notebook and take down this version of the story.

Trevor's story

Once upon time there was a boy named Sim. His arms were long and wrinkly, his face was thin and his legs were tall and skinny. He was a goalkeeper – no balls could go past him. His Mum used to play with him. Sim used to stand by the middle door and his Mum had a ball and she used to boot it and Sim saved it (but once or twice he let a ball go through). At school he used to wait till four o'clock when he went down to the park to play goals for some team. The goal posts were made of children's coats and bags.

A few years later, when Sim was twelve, he was the school goal-keeper. Just when the school got into the quarter-finals, an inspector came and said to Sim, 'You have to tell your Mum that you are leaving the school. We will send a note to your Mum saying that you are a bit touched in the head. Sorry we have to say this but your work is very bad.'

Bob Thropper was the school football captain, and very jealous of Sim because he was getting a medal for goalkeeping. He was pleased that Sim was leaving and took his shorts, stockings, and boots from him. Sim felt especially sad when he had to take off his jumper. Bob Thropper grabbed his shoulders and said, 'Goalkeepers – I could buy 'em and sell 'em!' and Sim said, 'I'll never buy you; but I might sell you one day.'

A couple of years later when Sim was fifteen his Mum was looking for a job for him. He acted stupid and they all turned him down. When his Mum got him outside she said, 'Stop this at once – you are going on like a fool.' At the age of nineteen, Sim got a job at a Fair in the 'Beat the Goalkeeper' game. It was 3d a kick and if you win you get 6d back.

The owner of the Fair was an old lady. She had a wrinkly face and brown hair. She used to pat him all around to find out if he had taken any other money, but she never found any on him because Sim made special pockets inside his jumper. How he made it was like this, he got a piece of cotton wool and sewed it under his jumper, so that you couldn't see it, so even if the owner turned him upside down, she still wouldn't hear a jingle at all.

Six years later she was selling the Fair and Sim said he will buy it. She said, 'Bless you Lad.' Not realizing how he had managed to save up enough money.

One night, Bob Thropper was coming from a football match with his friends. They say he used to break goalposts and crossbars – he had a hard shot. He was the best footballer in that district. He wasn't very drunk that night and they saw the fair and they all said, 'Let's have a bit of fun at the Fair.' They saw the 'Beat the Goalkeeper' game and Sim saw Bob Thropper coming and said, 'Come here and try your luck. Let's have pounds instead of pennies.' So Bob Thropper said, 'All right then,' and one of his men said, 'Blast him to pieces.'

There was £11 on the orange box with a brick on top holding it down. Sim placed the ball near Bob Thropper. He stepped back and took a hard shot. It went flying in the air like a rocket. In a flash, Sim leapt up and caught it and slowly rolled it back towards Bob Thropper. One of Bob Thropper's mates said,

'Shall I go and get your boots?'

He ran and got his boots and brought them back. The ball was placed in the middle. Bob walked back and then ran forward and shot the ball. It went low, Sim dived for the ball. One of Bob's mates said, 'Goal, Goal!' but Sim had the ball tucked under his arm.

From that day Sim was asked by plenty of people to be the goalkeepers for their teams but Sim said, 'No, I would like to be a

Manager' and one day Bob Thropper saw Sim and Sim said, 'I can buy 'em and sell 'em and one day I will sell you. I will sell you now.' One of Bob Thropper's mates said: 'Bob, he means it, you better retire and find a pub somewhere fast,' and from that day Sim was known as the goalkeeper Bob Thropper couldn't beat.

Trevor Williams

It is impossible not to compare how Trevor takes on this task with his behaviour of the previous lesson. There is no prevarication, no resistance; he starts off with great confidence and is immediately at ease in the tradition of story-telling. Once upon a time it would be too cynical to conclude that he was consciously redeeming the situation of the previous lesson. I think he saw this as a challenge well within his limits which had ample scope for his creativity and an opportunity to work harmoniously with me.

To transcribe the tape at any length is unnecessary as Trevor's dictation was much the same as the finished version, but I would like to focus on moments where Trevor is aware of his powers of organization of the material or where he can clearly be seen to be shaping the experience for himself.

Half-way through the first paragraph he looks at what I have written so far and says, 'This is going to be a long story – lots of pages you know.' He's aware of how the story will have to be reduced proportionally.

Later we hear Trevor thinking aloud, 'One day Sim was twelve'; 'No, not "Sim was twelve" one day; No. I'll change it. A few years later, Sim was the age of twelve, he was the school goalkeeper. No. A few years later *when* Sim was the age of twelve he was the school goalkeeper.' In a rapid series of modifications Trevor has shifted the emphasis to where he wants it – cued the reader in chronologically and ended up with a neat, complex sentence.

The process of composition is nicely exposed. Later, when talking of Bob Thropper's behaviour towards Sim, he offers the word 'jealous' which in fact is not used explicitly in the original text. The motivation for the behaviour is clearly understood by Trevor.

When describing Sim's reluctant returning of his football kit we see Trevor anticipating confusion on his reader's part:

T (dictating): When he was coming near to his top – no, that doesn't make sense – 'coming near to his top'. He's taking off his top, he didn't want to take off his top see.

Both the words 'coming near' and 'top' are ambiguous in this sentence and Trevor cannot allow them to stand.

Sim's mother's exasperation with her wilful son seems well understood by Trevor. The expression 'You're going on like a fool' is Trevor's own but exactly in keeping with the spirit of the original story.

When he realizes that he has already used the expression, 'A couple of years later', Trevor offers 'At the age of nineteen' which fulfils his need to impose a time structure on the story but allows a variety of construction which pleases him.

At one point, I interrupt as I anticipate a crucial omission in Trevor's telling of the story but Trevor has everything under control and commands me to 'carry on just carry on', and indeed he proceeds to close the loophole most successfully by using an adverbial clause of reason.

Nearer the end of the story, as Trevor enters the spirit of the contest between Sim and Bob Thropper his language becomes more daring, 'flying in the air like a rocket'; 'in a flash'; and his short sentences effectively create a sense of suspense. (He had earlier hummed an appropriate mounting scale when Bob Thropper re-entered Sim's life.)

One could obviously endlessly analyse the narrative skills that Trevor effortlessly uses in re-telling this story. One could make further assumptions about the insights and perceptions necessary before a re-telling would even be possible.

Perhaps it is enough to say that the experience restored the balance and Trevor and I were both aware of his achievement and potential at the end of this lesson. It was a lesson where Trevor was at the helm but not manipulative, a lesson where I was a willing scribe, not a tyrannical master. It was a much needed lesson.

In transcribing the tapes of her lessons with Trevor, Judith makes all the main points about her actions and reactions and re-interprets Trevor's responses for the group. Judith keenly wants to ask why she swings between thinking that Trevor can read well and a conviction that he may still be unable to read above a bare minimum level. See how unsettled a lesson can be, even in the best circumstances. We discussed Judith's description of lessons three and four. Judith apologized for not transcribing all of the first section where Trevor asked how to spell 'shoe'. We agreed that her explanation was not only reasonable but right.

Eliz: The crucial bit is Trevor saying how bored he is.
Steve: Don't worry about the gaps. In a way you've already established

the readers' respect for your authority and the interest of the
audience.

Judith: I don't think a full transcript would have added much. Trevor
was so angry he wouldn't do anything.

Vicky: There's no law of sequence of prediction about what Trevor
will do.

We then agree that the story itself draws him back into the reading
situation. When Judith suggests that in real life the manager of the fair
would have reported Paul's arrival, Trevor defends the author: 'that
would ruin the whole story'.

Judith: When we were talking about this I thought it was a complicated side issue. All I wanted was some response because I'd failed
to engage him. Now I see that his reaction is more sophisticated
than mine.

Vicky: Is he scoring off you when he says, 'that wouldn't really
happen?'

J: I don't think he is, not here.

V: Are you wondering how much more he sees after all that stone-
walling?

J: Trevor may have intuited a great deal about that text. I now don't
think that's the right book for Trevor at all.

S: Are your rhetorical questions genuinely open in paragraph one? My
own reaction is that when something goes well in a previous lesson
I don't create it as a design.

V: It's *an* opening – a direction. We have to take what we can. We
haven't much choice of direction.

J: We discussed last time the difference between lessons one and two.

S: Are you offering a tentative answer?

J: I do think now that I could have done something to salvage that
lesson. I should have started with what we'd read of the previous
lesson. Trevor loves stories and had I been reading it when he came
in I'd have hooked him again and things could have improved.

S: You can't repeat happy chances.

V: No, but perhaps we should always assume, as Judith does, that every
lesson raises a lot of questions about the assumptions we make. You
can't always say, 'if I'd done this it would have gone right'.

We agreed that the lesson, for all its unsatisfactory outcomes at the
time and the account of it, gave Judith important issues to ponder and

comment on. Again, we looked squarely at the admonitions of those who write about what has to be done in the 'systematic instruction' of inexperienced readers, and we asked how these were related to the actuality of a lesson like this one. The overriding question still remains: does Trevor 'read' only in the context of school without any belief in the value of this activity in his life outside?

In discussing lesson four, Judith voices her worst fears for Trevor. These have been there since the early encounters: how can a volatile adolescent of his temperament *believe* that he can read when his best security seems to come from remaining a non-reader? As he read his version of the story, it became clear that Trevor's composition was that of a reader, someone who knows the conventions of narrative at a sophisticated level, who can cope with time sequences, embedded clauses, mediated inference and an organized pattern of main points and detail. Judith then asks the crucial question:

J: Do you think he can read?

M: In a sense, yes. With confidence. No.

E: The Trevor in my class won't take books home. His parents make him read and when he makes mistakes they shout at him.

J: Last week he read five chapters of *The Ear* silently. He thought it was a game, and said, 'I don't have to read everything.' Eventually, the story got hold of him. He asked me five words on one page. I was going to record today's lesson even if there had been ages of silence. But he didn't come. He won't let me record him now.

V: Tracy wouldn't either, after a long absence.

J: I told him how much I learn about his reading from these tapes but he doesn't believe in research. It doesn't appeal to him. He doesn't really like being taken seriously. It's too much responsibility. He still thinks there might be a moment when I say, 'Right Trevor, come down. I'll teach you now.' He still doesn't believe . . .

E: That you're not keeping the secret to yourself.

V: But you're watching Trevor watching you. You're watching and listening to his every move. You're listening closely to find out . . .

J: I feel there's a long wall — a kind of barrier between Trevor and reading. He rushes up and down the length of the wall when he needs to jump over it. He won't jump.

V: He doesn't know how to jump.

E: He still thinks there's some magic.

J: I think he's looking for a hole to climb through.

V: He wants to know, should he put his feet first or his hands . . .

J: He isn't brave enough to look up.

S: If he's fixed in his idea that you'll do it, you have to con him into a point of no return. Maybe you could say: 'I've told you that and that. You read the rest for yourself.' He still thinks the vital key is being withheld. We know there is no key in the sense that he means. He has to be conned where the impulse is – to read the story.

E: He's saying implicitly 'I'm doing a bit. Now you do your bit.'

J: Half of his teachers don't know he can't read.

Judith's four lessons are being discussed at the end of the eighth term. In the early design of the project they should have been done in the third or fourth term. But now, involvement in the discussion has shifted; it shows changes in the participants. There was no tape recorder for this session so Margaret acted as scribe, not opting out of the discussion, but altogether with less need to interpose. The others have confidence in their judgments, are hard on Judith from time to time, but they understand her dilemma. If Trevor is to go on having lessons he must trust her. If he is to learn to read, she must seem to abandon him.

From listening to the discussions and reading the transcripts one can educe something about the problem of what is all too easily described as 'motivation'. Trevor could be a good reader in a way that would intend what all reading intends. Yet the reading demands of school leave him little time for stories. Information comes less and less in narrative form as he goes up the school. What are designated 'intermediate skills' are not being overtly taught because there is no possibility of Trevor's tolerance of the kind of material on which they are usually exercised. He composes in a way that indicates a well-developed linguistic competence, yet lacks the matching skill to write for himself. Trevor demonstrates every facet and convolution of our problems. Anyone who thinks that Judith has not tried everything has no idea of what's involved in teaching a boy in his situation.

Elizabeth and Chris – progress exemplified

The group had known each other for three years when Elizabeth reported the lessons with Chris that were to exemplify progress. By now our listening was more sophisticated. Elizabeth could find something significant in Chris's worst attempt and she used a miscue analysis with great skill and insight. Now we were studying how far we had taken our pupils so that we could say something about where we had got to with them, and we were looking at ways of describing the gap between the progress our pupils made and the outside world's expectations of literacy. Here is Elizabeth's account.

In these three lessons, which took place in the middle of his fourth year, Chris was attempting to read three very different sorts of texts. In the first, he was reading a piece about the gearbox of the motorcycle engine. In the second he was reading from *The Terrible Things* in the Instant Readers series, and in the third he was reading his own story, called *A Win on the Pools: A Motorbike*. The fact that he had varying degrees of commitment to these three pieces brought into play both his attitudes towards reading and the various strategies he adopted to get through a text.

Chris had always been prepared to do almost anything rather than read in his reading lessons. Throughout his second year he spent much time trying to inveigle me into long conversations about anything and everything, and in the third year he wrote many stories (an activity which he also found very difficult) and used this as a reason for not reading. When he was prevailed upon to read, he would try to persuade me to read as much as possible, or he would insist on trying to read material that was too difficult for him (e.g. motorcycling magazines) on the grounds that it was all he was interested in, and I would again end up doing most of the reading.

When he was finally forced to come face to face with a page of print, his most noticeable reaction was panic. The attention to the meaning which enabled him to supply a missing word when listening to someone else read, vanished almost completely. In its place came a desperate, and almost random phonic attack, interspersed with appeals for rescue, 'what's that, what's that?'. The only time when all this did not seem to come into action was when he was reading a piece of his own writing and had a certain degree of confidence in his ability to work out what it said.

Lesson one

In this lesson Chris was working on his CSE metalwork folder – the material for his examination assessment. He had a very great commitment to this project. I think he realized that he had very little chance of succeeding in an exam, but felt that it was possible for him to do

gearbox

In a motor cycle engine ~~with~~
with a (four speed gearbox)
-like a BSA singles 250 it
Consists os.

① mainshaft sleeve pinion(top gear).
② mainshaft sleeve pinion thrust washer.
③ mainshaft.
④ mainshaft sliding gear(second gear)
⑤ mainshaft third gear thrust washer.
⑥ mainshaft third gear.
⑦ mainshaft bottom gear.
⑧ Layshaft bottom gear shim.
⑨ Layshaft bottom gear.
⑩ Layshaft sliding gear (third gear).
⑪ Layshaft second gear.
⑫ Layshaft.
⑬ Layshaft thrust washer.

A gear selector. Selects the
gear individually when moving the
gear change like this.

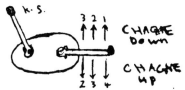

.f you are a metal worker you
should be-able to make some
of the parts on the laethre
like a bronze bush. it is indigenous
to this country. To make it for
the hiving Cut In the.

well in his course work. He knew a great deal about motor bikes, and felt that, with help, he would be able to set this down quite impressively. At any rate, his metalwork teacher later told me that Chris took a great deal of pride in his folder, tended to carry it around with him, and often showed it to other pupils, not something he usually did with his other exercise books.

I, however, was growing increasingly impatient with Chris's evasiveness about reading. It seemed that if he were not prepared to face at least some of the truth he would never progress any further. I felt, when I saw the first page of his folder, that this was a typically unrealistic exercise and I decided to challenge him on it.

Me: Can you read what you've written down there?
Chris: (inaudible).
Me: You can't understand it.
Chris: But I knew what it was about and all that and I just put it down.
Me: Yeah, you should also be able to read it. I mean, suppose they asked you to read it out? (pause) That's a word you've got down in almost every single one.
Chris: Man. (Pause.)
Me: Start from the top.
Chris: What, from here? 'In a motorcycle . . . in a, in a motorcycle engine with a four speed gear box like a BSA Starfire 250 it consists of am . . . am.
Me: You've put it down in almost every single item.
Chris: Man. What does that say, Miss? Main . . . Main.
Me: Main.
Chris: Str . . . strength.
Me: No.
Chris: Sh . . . main . . . shaft, mainshaft.
Me: Right.
Chris: Mainshaft.

I was fairly sure that he was not going to be able to read very much of what he had written down. I thought that he had copied it completely from a book and did not know what it meant and I decided to make him admit this by giving him very little help with it. Needless to say, I was unable to refrain entirely from interfering and was caught on the horns of a typical Chris dilemma. When he got stuck, he tried to get himself out by sounding out the words. I was torn between encouraging him in what he was trying to do (which was likely to fail with this vocabulary) and getting him to concentrate on the context (in which, as far as I could see, very few clues were to be found).

Chris: Thirst, thirst is that?
Me: No.
Chris: Th . . r . . ust.
Me: Yes, go on, you're good at that.
Chris: Thrust, thrust, thrust. What's that word? Was here her was her.
Me: Well, you can break it up to that can't you, but . . . you see, the reason why you can't read it is because you didn't know what it was when you wrote it down.
Chris: But I knew what it meant, Miss. I knew the gist of it.
Me: I don't think you did because . . .
Chris: I did.
Me: I can't see why you shouldn't be able to read *that*.
Chris: It was in the diagram, the numbers on the diagram.
Me: Where's the diagram?
Chris: At home, in the book.
Me: Well, that doesn't help you to read it now, does it?
Chris: I knew what it was then, Miss.
Me: What's that? Look, start from the beginning.
Chris: Main sh . . . Man
Me: You've got this word.
Chris: I know, I forgot it. I was looking at that one. . . . I forgot. Min, mainshaft.
Me: You know what this one is, don't you?
Chris: Pinion.
Me: Mainshaft something pinion.
Chris: Shaft pinion.
Me: No.
Chris: Sh.
Me: Sleeve.
Chris: Sleeve pinion.
Me: Do you know what all that means? If you, if you, I would've thought it would be obvious, if you could read 'mainshaft pinion' if you knew what it was all about, I should've thought you'd know the word 'sleeve', just from the meaning of it.
Chris: Mainshaft.
Me: I'm surprised you don't.

Despite the impression which the tape gives, of Chris thrashing desperately through a text which is far too difficult for him, he did actually cope with it remarkably well. He read through from (5) to the end with help on only two words. He was probably helped by the fact that, while he was reading this section, I was mostly engaged with other members of the group and so prevented from giving unhelpful advice:

Chris: Mainshaft tr . . . d gear, tr . . . ied gear.	(5)
Me: T h there.	
Chris: Thr . . . ied gear.	
Me: You've had second gear.	
Chris: Third gear.	
Me: Mainshaft third gear.	
Chris: Thruster washer. Thrust washer.	
Mainshaft third gear	(6)
Mainshaft. gear. Bottom gear.	(7)
Mainshaft bottom gear.	
L . . lay . . laystr . . . layshaft.	(8)
Layshaft bottom gear shaft. Shim.	
Layshaft top.	(9)
What's that? Dr. . .	
Me: Bottom that says.	
Chris: Bottom, yeah, bottom gear.	
Layshaft. Bottom.	
Layshaft. What's that? Sliding gear. The third gear.	(10)
Second, second gear.	(11)
Layshaft.	(12)
Layshaft third thuse.	(13)
Thrust washer.	

Chris: A gear, a gear selector, selects the gears, gears in in. What's that? in . in . . individually when mov . . moving the gears change like this.
Me: When *moving* the gear change.
Chris: Moving the gear change like this. Is that all right so far, Miss?

I think that, after this reading, I felt that it had been a disaster not to be repeated if at all possible, that the passage had been far too difficult for Chris and that he had panicked his way through it. In fact, a close look at the transcript does not bear this out. The text is 78 words long.

He gets 67 words right, not necessarily first time. I told him three words outright and helped him with five others. He omitted two words, and inserted correctly one word which he had originally copied wrongly ('Starfire' for 'singles'). The passage is difficult by any standards. Despite repetition of many of the words, there is ample opportunity for confusion – sleeve/sliding, third/thrust. It's clear that my accusation that 'you didn't know what it was when you wrote it down' was in fact not true. My 'tough' attitude was out of place and was probably the reason why he made more of a mess of the first half than of the second half, when I left him alone more.

The group discussed this strange lesson with great heat. Judith thought that Elizabeth's tone had been unnecessarily fierce, but Elizabeth countered with an explanation of why she thought the confrontation was necessary. Week after week she had seen Chris sitting with motorcycle manuals and magazines in front of him. When she suggested that he was only looking at the pictures, he'd say 'I'm reading it, I'm reading it'; so Elizabeth would then say, 'Well, read a bit to me.' Chris would stumble and stammer until Elizabeth operating on her trading agreement with Chris that people read books that interest them or because they need to know what they say, would do the rest of the reading until she thought it was his turn again. She explained how she once felt that she had found the best possible book for Chris; and they read some of it together in class. Chris asked to take it home. When he brought it back he said he had read it, so that when Elizabeth asked him to read some of it to her, he said he would not read something he had already read.

E: He had a sound argument from our point of view. But I'm sure he hadn't read it.

J: It's complicated. It's marvellous that he has done what we want – taken a book home and read it, and yet there's a level of anxiety in us that makes us think we can't let it pass at that; we've got to check it out. Are there times when you accept what he says? Could you have said 'That's good; it's the first time you've done that?'

M: Elizabeth's point is that unless Chris is prepared to face some of the truth he'll never get any further.

E: He was not pretending to read them, but that he could read them ...

M: It's a tricky moment – you're saying, 'should I challenge him now?' When he says he can do it, and Judith is wondering if this is the right moment – when things are going right, near the end. . . .

This is a point with some depth. Elizabeth saw Chris's having copied out this page as a meaningless exercise. Judith is hanging on to the idea that the reading had some significance for Chris. Only much later did it occur to Margaret that the list had a symbolic significance rather than a transactional usefulness, that to a devotee of motorbikes the words for the parts are not an ordinary list of words, but a special list of significant words, a litany for a different kind of recitation; a poem, in fact.[4]

Steve stuck with the main point of this argument and said that we were all faced with the problem of suggesting that sometimes we told our readers they were better than they actually were in order to encourage them, and at other times, we had to face them with the fact of their inability to read sufficiently well for it to count. They needed practice and encouragement while all the time we wondered if, in Chris's case, what he really had to do was to face the fact that he avoided working at his reading. Steve characterized Elizabeth's dilemma thus: 'You're saying what Chris has to do is to sit down and say, "I can't read by reading easy texts. But I'll get better texts because it's worth doing."'

Margaret was sure that Elizabeth was facing the panic that comes over teachers when they feel they have to confront evaders with their problems. Elizabeth agrees and says that the next lesson is worse.

Lesson two

In this lesson Chris was reading from *The Terrible Things*. In contrast to the previous lesson where he was reading something which I thought was too difficult for him and which I thought he was being unrealistic about, in this lesson I insisted on his continuing to read a book which he had grown tired of, but which I thought he could cope with. On both occasions I would have done better to trust his judgment.

We started the lesson badly with Chris very unwilling to read:

Chris: I don't want to read that, Miss.
Me: Yes, come on, you've got this far and . . .
Chris: (inaudible).
Me: Look Chris, what you seem to be saying is that you're not prepared to read, now that's a ridiculous thing to say.
Chris: I wanna read, I don't like, I get bored of that book going on, I don't like stories that go on and on.
Me: Well, you chose it [pause]. When I ask you to choose something ▸

else, you won't, because you say they're all boring and you don't bring things in to read. So what are we supposed to do? Come on, what are we to do? Give up reading?

Chris: No.

Me: Well then, you think of something that we can read. [Pause]. Come on. You haven't disliked reading this this much and we've got to page 39, nearly half-way through.

Chris: No, but it goes on quite a lot.

Me: Well, it's quite a long book. You did pick it, you could see how long it was. Do you want to pick something else?

Chris: No, I'd better get on with this.

With hindsight it is clear that I probably ought not to have insisted on Chris going on with this book. But it did not seem any more difficult than his motorcycling project, and he had time and again evaded reading to me with similar excuses. He expressed a desire to read only books about motorcycling and almost the only one I found that seemed to be at his level, he took home to read, brought it back a few days later saying there was no point in reading to me as he had finished it at home. We had reached a point where I felt I had to challenge his evasions even if it meant him reading something he was less than committed to.

After some discussion of the story so far, I read a page and a half and then asked Chris to read (page 39):

Chris: By this time Peter had got his br . . . breath back and went along s . . ., all sat. . .

Me: Go back to 'went' because it wasn't 'went' was it?

Chris: 'When', what? We all sat on the dark, deck in the sun. . .

Me: The sun? What does that sound, that s h, yes, go on.

Chris: Sunset.

Me: No, what sound does that s h make? Sh so sunsh . . .?

Chris: Sunshine.

Me: That's it. 'We all sat on the deck in the sunshine.'

Chris: With he.

Me: While.

Chris: While he told us what had happened to him. He had like. . .

Me: Yes, there's a comma there, so you go, 'He had . . . like. . .'

Chris: My.

Me: Yes.

Chris: Mys   myself , , got kept for, from. . .

Me: Go back to that.
Chris: Kept off.
Me: No, it's not 'kept'.
Chris: Closed, closed.
Me: He had, like myself got . . .
Chris: Cast off.
Me: Cut.
Chris: Cut off from his p . . .
Me: Party.
Chris: Party and had happened in the rain, run from a house . . .
Me: Now go back, 'got cut off from his party and had something in the ruins of a house . . .
Chris: Hided.
Me: Yes.
Chris: Hided in the ruins of a house until the dr . . .
Me: Dang . . .
Chris: Danger had pr, passed by.

Despite my efforts to remind him of the story and create a situation where he could make intelligent guesses, he was not really trying to make sense of the passage, just seeing words as individual hurdles to be cleared. I was clearly unsure about how I should help him. On the one hand, since he was trying to use his knowledge of phonics, I did not want to tell him that this was wrong, though in fact it was not helping him much. On the other, when I left a mistake uncorrected, in the hope that the lack of meaning would send him back to it, he got himself so bogged down that he did not notice he was not making much sense. In fact, what he often seemed to do was to exchange one mistake for another, and incidentally change the syntax so that an appalling mess developed, e.g. 'happened in the rain, run from a house' for 'hidden in the ruins of a house'.

Later on in the lesson, after I had read some more, he had another go (page 42):

Chris: Maybe we'll, maybe we'll find one somewhere and then we'll go. . . . What's that?
Me: Hunting.
Chris: Hunting. He ope . . opened the tr . . ., What's that?
Me: Throttle.
Chris: Throttle and speeded . . .
Me: Spun.

Chris: Spun the wheel, wheel so that the L . . . What's that?
Me: Luxor.
Chris: Luxor tr . . . tugged . . .
Me: Read on.
Chris: To the s . . . What's that?
Me: East. So that the Luxor . . .
Chris: Tugged.
Me: Turned.
Chris: Oh, I thought it was 'tugged', turned, what's that?
Me: Turned to the east towards . . .
Chris: Mortsea.
Me: Mortsea.
Chris: The big, the big, b . . ., bat, but . . .
Me: What are they on? Now come on.
Chris: Boat.
Me: Yes.
Chris: Started fr . . .
Me: Forward.
Chris: Sh . . . shooted forward . . .
Me: Yes.
Chris: Had tr . . ., turned . . .
Me: Her twin.
Chris: Twin engines thr . . . What's that?
Me: Throbbing.
Chris: Throbbing pr . . . p . . . ow . . . f . . . i . . .
Me: Powerfully.
Chris: Powerfully as she turned.
Me: Thrust.
Chris: Thrust first . . .
Me: Herself.
Chris: Herself at the girl . . .
Me: At the green.
Chris: Green sea.
Me: Yes.
Chris: I, it looked uz, looked uz, us, it turned us, told, took, took us
   for, from . . .
Me: More.
Chris: For more . . .
Me: It took us more . . .
Chris: Than three hours . . .
Me: Mmm.

Chris: To find Mortsea. Could you read some?

It was painfully clear by now that he was hardly attempting to make sense of the passage at all. He appeared to be operating two strategies only. The first was to make a desperate phonic stab at the word. He often added r to the first letter of the word, e.g. tr (throttle), tr (turned), fr (forward), pr (powerfully). It appears from this as if he had overlearnt certain consonant blends at some period of his life and was now desperately using his knowledge quite inappropriately. It is interesting in this context to recall the comment on the primary school profile that he had no grasp of sounds despite considerable help.

He also tended to say any word which began with the same letter, e.g. speeded (spun), tugged (turned), bat, but (boat), girl (green). It might have seemed better to let him go on rather than correct him continually, in the hope that he would go back and correct himself, but as I said before, in fact when I did this he merely got into a worse mess. A useful strategy discovered later by another teacher was that if one merely kept one's finger below the offending word, this would be a more calming way of concentrating his mind and preventing him from thrashing around among the print. However, that discovery was still in the future then.

His second strategy was just to utter cries of help periodically. He said, 'What's that?' six times in the course of this short extract, and twenty-eight times in the course of the lesson. On a good day, 'What's that?' could be a mere self-interrogation, but here it was a persistent and successful attempt to pass the problem over to me.

The last extract quoted contains fifty-six words. Out of these he read only thirty-nine correctly and significantly I told him sixteen and helped him with only one. I felt, probably mistakenly, that if I told him the words he would get up a bit of speed and read himself into the meaning of the passage, whereas if I discussed the meaning of the passage with him, he would get even more confused. In the event, I should have just abandoned the book, as it appeared to be the worst possible combination – a difficult text in which he had no interest.

Chris's final comment, as the tape ran out and the pips went, was 'I've got a headache, Miss, that's why I didn't feel like. . .'

When they discussed lesson two the group agreed with Elizabeth's assessment; it was a painful lesson. Chris did not want to read the book and the result was very bad indeed. This led to a discussion, not about Chris's reading, but about the kind of books that are produced for poor readers. Elizabeth was convinced that Chris understood enough of the story to carry on. The group were persuaded that the text gave him no help as it was poorly constructed, had no authentic 'voice' and no detailed particularity by which the characters and the action could be considered or empathized with. Chris had done very badly; Elizabeth had been cast down. But the general opinion was that part of the problem lay in the book. Margaret reminded the group of the success that all poor readers had with *The Iron Man*. Judith added *The Shrinking of Treehorn*. But Chris had chosen the book because it was about motorbikes – a theme well worked over by producers of teenage reading material.

At this point we discussed Applebee's *The Child's Concept of Story*, to see if the developmental research could help in seeing what Chris brings to his reading. We wonder if Chris does not know how to deal with the story world, how to 'take both of his feet into the story . . .'. He still tries to operate story from his stance in the world where he is. Young children learn early to make the leap. Chris can do this when he makes up his *own* story. So, to that Elizabeth now turns.

Lesson three

In this lesson, Chris was reading a typed copy of the story he had written in his English lesson, *A Win on the Pools: A Motorbike*. Here, finally commitment and an accessible text come together. I did a miscue analysis on this text, rather than a transcript and this is on the following page. The text is approximately 746 words long and he made forty-seven miscues. He corrected twenty-eight of these. Out of the nineteen uncorrected miscues only one really foxed him, and that was the one on line 58. None of the others made any very significant difference to the meaning. More significant perhaps is the overall 'feel' of the reading. He did not say 'What's that?' once, or engage in his usual phonic stammering. Eighty-four per cent of his miscues stemmed from graphic similarities in the words, as opposed to 42 per cent from sound similarities. One would expect this from his previous performances, but it is clear from the fact that these miscues were corrected when they did not make sense that his eyes were scanning the line ahead as he read.

In this reading Chris had gone a long way towards being a fluent and independent reader. It is clear that confidence about his ability to read the passage plays a major part in this. Although the text is syntactically simple, it does contain a number of difficult words which in this context

A WIN ON THE POOLS

A MOTOR BIKE

1 On Thursday there was a knock on the door. It was the
2 pools. The prize was a motor bike. It was an N.V.T.
3 moped. It was a month before my birthday and I was
4 sixteen. I wanted a moped. I gave the pools man the
5 money and coupon and he gave me the change. I said
6 "Thankyou" and he said, "Tata." In bed that night I
7 thought about the moped. I could not sleep for thinking
8 of it. At breakfast that morning I asked my dad,
9 "Would you let you have a moped?" My dad said, "Yes.
10 I would let you have a moped but how would you buy
11 one?" "But dad, if mum wins the pools she would win
12 a moped. But a moped is no good to mum, is it dad?"
13 "No, it is no good to mum." said dad. "But you have
14 no chance of winning the pools." "But lots of people
15 win the pools, but we are unlucky." "Yes..."
16 Dad and I went to school. Some mates have mopeds
17 already and that's all they talk about. I kept quiet
18 about my moped because I did not know if I would get
19 it - but I had a feeling that I would get that moped.
20 Every day I waited for the post, until one day there was
21 a letter from the pools. I woke up my dad and told him
22 that mum had won the pools and my moped. That day I
23 did not go to school and me and my dad went to collect
24 the moped. I could not ride it because I did not have
25 my license. So I got my insurance and sent off for
26 my license. On Monday my mum said that a letter
27 had come for me. It was my license. On the way back
28 from school I swapped a sheath knife for a crash helmet.
29 When I got in I got a coat on and went out on my moped.
30 I did not go fast because I was running it in.
31 The next day I went to school on my moped. I pulled up
32 at school. I was there before anybody. I put my crash
33 helmet in a locker and I went to the class. The kids
34 said what a good moped it was outside (it is an 'R'
35 registration). I said that it was mine. 'Where did you
36 get that moped?" "My dad got it for me." "Do you
37 want to come out for a ride?" "I might go."
38 That night the boys came round for me and I went out
39 for a ride. I am glad I got that moped. It is a way of
40 life to me. The boys asked if I wanted to come out
41 camping. I said that I did not know if I could go. I
42 asked my dad and he said. Yes. I could go camping,
43 and on Friday I got my gear ready to go camping.
44 On Saturday Jim and Tony came around for me. I was
45 still eating my breakfast and when I had finished I got
46 my moped and got my gear and put it on my moped and
47 I was ready to go - and we went.
48 We were going to Brighton but we did not know if we
49 would make it to Brighton on our mopeds. It was a
50 good ride to Brighton but you used a lot of petrol to
51 get there.
52 We did make it to Brighton on our mopeds. It is good
53 there at the seaside the sea smells fresh. Then we
54 put our mopeds up in a motorbike bay and then we had
55 some fun on the slot machine, and other things. It was
56 good. We had to find a place to camp. We found a
57 place. We were woken up by a noise. It was a rump-
58 ling. We were worried and I looked out - it was a
59 load of cows. We were in a field. We packed up the
60 tent on the moped, then we went off. Tony had a
61 puncture. I thought it was funny, but he did not. We
62 done it and we were off. We got to Crawley then I
63 had a puncture and we laughed at me. I said, "Me
64 and my big mouth!" Then we were off again and
65 before I knew it, we were home and Tony went home
66 and Jim went home.
67 "Tata Tony. Tata Jim."
68 That was one of our adventures.

Miscue Number	Reader	Text	DIALECT 1	INTONATION 2	GRAPHIC SIMILARITY 3			SOUND SIMILARITY 4			GRAMMATICAL FUNCTION 5			CORRECTION 6	GRAMMATICAL ACCEPTABILITY 7	SEMANTIC ACCEPTABILITY 8	MEANING CHANGE 9	COMPREHENSION				GRAMMATICAL RELATIONSHIPS			
					Y	P	N	Y	P	N	Y	P	N					No Loss	Partial Loss	Loss	Strength	Partial Strength	Weakness	Overcorrection
3-1	pods	prize			✓			✓	✓		✓			Y	Y	Y	N	✓						
4-2	the man	the pods man			✓	✓			✓		✓			Y	Y	Y	N	✓						
5-3	change	coupon			✓				✓		✓			Y	Y	Y	N	✓						
6-4	to	thank you	✓			✓			✓		✓			Y	N	N	Y	✓						
6-5	I	in			✓				✓		✓		✓	N	N	N	Y	✓						
8-6	we're	we are			✓			✓			✓			N	Y	Y	N	✓						
9-7	said Dad	Yes					✓		✓		✓			N	Y	Y	N	✓						
10-8	will	went			✓				✓		✓			Y	N	N	Y	✓						
11-9	crept	kept			✓			✓			✓			Y	P	P	Y	✓						
14-10	had no my	I did not have my home			✓	✓		✓			✓		✓	N	N	N	P			✓				
14-11	because I had no li	"			✓			✓			✓			N	Y	Y	N	✓						
15-12	and sent	and I sent			✓					✓	✓		✓	Y	Y	Y	N	✓						
15-13	off my license	off for my license			✓			✓			✓			Y	Y	Y	N	✓						
16-14	pushed	pulled			✓				✓		✓			Y	N	N	Y	✓						
4-15	it	I			✓			✓			✓			N	Y	Y	N	✓						
39-16	a	an			✓			✓			✓			N	Y	Y	N	✓						
6-17	I said that was mine	I said that it was mine			✓			✓			✓			Y	Y	Y	N	✓						
50-18	I said that is was mine	I said that it was mine			✓			✓			✓			Y	Y	Y	N	✓						
51-19	went for a ride	went out for a ride			✓				✓		✓			N	Y	Y	N	✓						
48-20	then the boys	the boys			✓				✓		✓			Y	N	N	Y	✓						
40-21	would	wanted			✓			✓			✓			Y	N	N	Y	✓						
41-22	didn't	did not			✓			✓			✓			N	Y	Y	N	✓						
42-23	come	came	✓			✓			✓			✓		N	P	Y	Y	✓						
45-24	then	when			✓			✓			✓			N	N	N	P			✓				
45-25	will	"			✓				✓		✓		✓	N	N	N	P	✓						
47-26	were	went			✓				✓		✓			Y	N	N	Y	✓						
49-27	wouldn't	were					✓		✓		✓			Y	P	P	Y	✓						
47-28	in	to					✓			✓	✓			Y	P	P	Y	✓						
49-29	Brighton. On our mopeds	Brighton on our mopeds.		✓	✓				✓		✓			N	Y	Y	N	✓						
50-30	use	used		✓	✓				✓		✓			N	Y	Y	N	✓						
52-31	there at	there, at		✓	✓				✓		✓			Y	Y	Y	N	✓						
53-32	something	some fun			✓			✓			✓			N	Y	N	N	✓						
55-33	machine	machine					✓			✓	✓			Y	Y	Y	N	✓						
55-34		it			✓						✓			Y	N	N	Y	✓						
51-35	went to	were			✓			✓			✓			Y	N	N	Y	✓						
52-36	anything	anything			✓				✓		✓			Y	N	N	P			✓				
52-37	wondered	worried			✓				✓		✓		✓	Y	N	N	Y	✓						
52-38	wondered	"			✓				✓		✓		✓	N	N	N	Y			✓				
52-39	wondering	"			✓			✓			✓			N	Y	Y	P			✓				
64-40	mopeds	moped			✓			✓			✓			N	Y	Y	P	✓						
62-41	Tom	Tony			✓				✓		✓			Tow	P	Y	N	✓						
62-42	did	done	✓		✓				✓		✓			Y	Y	N	Y	✓						
64-43	I	he					✓		✓		✓			N	Y	Y	N	✓						
64-44	went	were	✓		✓				✓		✓			N	P	Y	N	✓						
65-45	was	were			✓			✓			✓			N	Y	Y	N	✓						
7-46	Tom	Tony			✓			✓			✓			N	Y	Y	Y	✓						
62-47	episodes	adventures					✓		✓	✓				N	Y	Y	P	✓						

		COLUMN TOTAL	4	5	38	3	4	19	17	9	36	1	8					COLUMN TOTAL	41	6	0				
		PERCENTAGE			84	7	9	42	38	20	80	2	18					PERCENTAGE	87	13	0				
		QUESTION TOTAL			48			45			45							PATTERN TOTAL	47						

MISCUE ANALYSIS

Summary of Results

Measure	Y	P	N	T	% Y	% P	% N
1 Dialect	4						
2 Intonation	2						
3 Graphic Similarity	38	3	4	45	84	7	9
4 Sound Similarity	19	17	9	45	42	38	20
5 Grammatical Function	36	1	8	45	80	2	18
6 Correction	28		19	47	60		40
7 Grammatical Acceptability	29	6	12	47	62	13	25
8 Semantic Acceptability	27	2	18	47	57	4	39
9 Meaning Change	27	5	15	47	57	11	32
10 Comprehension	0	6	41	47	0	13	87

did not throw him. The question to answer, of course, is how can one lead him gradually from this sort of reading to the unseen text, which is what both pupils and the outside world see as 'real reading'?

Before anyone discussed Elizabeth's question there was a general rejoicing. Suddenly Chris is reading much faster. He makes intonational sense. Vicky says, 'It's so well written and memorable'; and Elizabeth is clearly pleased:

E: For once, he's reading what's something he has written for himself. He knows what's coming; he can make use of that. He uses it, he looks ahead to remind himself of what he has said. In a book he wouldn't do that . . . He really resists being told to look and read the next bit . . . as he then goes into an orgy of phonics.
J: The whole thing is persuading him he's got it there if only he can see it *beyond* the printed word . . .

We agreed at the end of listening to Chris that we had learned a significant lesson. Here we have Chris intending what reading and writing intend. He is taking literacy in hand for his own purposes – even of fantasy – which reading makes possible, so that he can sort out a version of his consciousness. Reading and writing are part of his own situation – to sort himself out. Readers do this all the time, and for once, Chris has known what readers do and what reading is actually like. This must be progress.

Small steps forward

Readerly behaviour is learned less by specific instruction than by personal discovery, and the process is neither clear not straightforward. But much of the spontaneous activity that can lead to taking the reading task in hand is inhibited in poor readers or not developed in inexperienced ones. Tracy has very little idea that the word in her head can become a symbol on a page. She has no picture of a word. John in his early lessons was making onomatopoetic sounds and dramatic gestures, the illustrations of the story he was telling, because he could not see the picture in his head as words on a page. Trevor was persuaded that his story-telling, apparently so ordinary, spontaneous and pleasurable, could have no relationship to reading, which *had* to be difficult and specific word-calling. Chris could not see or believe that the story on the page could ever become the story in his head, or vice versa. Competent, experienced readers never think about these things; they have come to know them as part of the reading process as a whole and certainly the operation was not explained to them in these terms. But inexperienced, failing readers need encouragement to do what they think will not help, and therein lies the teacher's dilemma. To what extent can you face the bad lessons really to see what you have to know and understand, as well as what you have to do?

We think that each of these sets of lessons shows a pupil's progress, but so minimally in terms that the outside world would understand. Yet, from our point of view, we think that Tracy, Trevor and Chris all encountered radical alternatives to their view of the task at a time when they had to decide, even if unconsciously, to face up to the consequences of their new awareness. Tracy became more rhythmical and learned to anticipate seeing in print what she knew in her head. Trevor reluctantly acknowledged that he had to be the reader in his own right, and Chris had the success of authorship and fluency. All were, in one way, giving us grounds for hope. Who else would recognize our fragile optimism and nourish these tenders buds of new growth?

As for our own progress, we learned to recognize the occasions on which our instinctive decisions (e.g. Elizabeth's being tough) were right, and wrong (Elizabeth's first judgment of Chris's first lesson). We discovered when we collude with the pupil's view of himself as a failure (Trevor) and thus have a harder time pulling ourselves out of this situation. As we read these notes now, we see that we could not have changed at the time (the wrong book, the unsuitable text). We understand that 'new' text does not mean unfamiliar content (Chris) and we are more than ever persuaded that literacy is the power of production that comes from reading something you have written. And we are alerted to our need to be successful, to *see* progress in our pupil especially when the evidence, visible to us alone, needs to be confirmed by others. Even at that moment we know we have to be challenged.

Steve and Tom − a very special case

From time to time a reading teacher is in very deep water. A pupil comes for lessons and before long it is clear that his failure to read is the surface manifestation of an extensive private disarray. Other responsible people, housemaster, tutor, educational psychologist, treat or ignore, as seems to them best, that part of the overall problem that is within their scope. Extra reading lessons help to solve the time-table puzzle of 'what to do about' the pupil in school time. The reading teacher may or may not have access to confidential information. In the case of Tom, there were things that Steve should have known sooner about his early school experience, but he picked him up as he might have done any other pupil.

At first Tom came for lessons as a member of a small group. When others in the group read in turn, Tom preferred to listen rather than to take his turn at reading aloud, and he often asked Steve to read his piece for him. When he came for his first lesson on his own, Steve chose an elementary book about aeroplanes in which Tom had shown some interest. This led to a general discussion about Tom's past and then about reading. Steve brought to the group the tape of the entire lesson, but he also transcribed this part for us to discuss Frank Smith's assertion that the teacher should ask the pupil what kind of help is really helpful. This is Steve's transcript from that first encounter, the paper as he presented it to the group. After a little reading and then some conversation about Tom's childhood and former schooling the dialogue ran like this:

Me: Did you find that . . . did you find coming here that in fact most people can read quicker and faster than you can, which makes it a bit difficult for you I should think (yeah) in the lessons, doesn't it?

T: Yeah.

Me: Yeah, why do you think that is? Why did you think . . . did you . . . why do you think you're not as quick a reader as they are? Is it just lack of practice? Is it (yes) having (yeah, yeah) having not enough practice? (Mmm.) Perhaps they didn't give you enough reading at your other school?

T: Yes, that's true. You only had reading practice once every week.

Me: Really? Just once a week?

T: Yeah.

Me: Oh, I see. And what sort of books did they give you?

T: 'Peter and Jane' books . . . *babyish* books —

Me: Babyish books . . . ? Oh, not very interesting? Can you remember any book you've read that really was interesting . . . that you really liked?

T: Comics, I suppose.

Me: Comics . . . yes . . . they're fun, aren't they?

T: I suppose I can read 'em books only if I try really hard at it.

Me: Yes . . . you find it's a big effort?

T: Yeah . . . no, not a big effort, but I just don't try *reading* them . . .

Me: Yeah. The thing is, of course, that the more you practise, the easier it gets (yeah) doesn't it, really? Do you read at home (yeah) at all? Do you read the newspaper, or . . . ?

T: Not the newspaper. I usually pick up a book and read to my Mum.

Me: Do you?

T: 'Cos she knows I have reading trouble, so she says, you know, she doesn't say anything, she doesn't say I *have* to read to her, but she just says she'd like it if I read to her, so I read to her (that's nice) and if I don't know any of the words she helps me.

Me: Well, that's good, yes, that's quite right. What sort of books have you got at home, for that?

T: War annuals, comics . . .

Me: Oh, that's good. And you like those, do you? You like reading them?

T: Yeah . . . you get bored with them after you've read 'em all.

Me: I should think if you've read the same ones again and again, you would, yes. . . . Can you think of anything . . . I mean can you yourself tell me anything that might make it a bit easier . . . getting to read? Is there something that you think is a . . . particular problem? Or is there anything that you find particularly difficult?

T: No. Not unless, um . . . no, not necessarily, no.
(Interruption.)

Me: Right, where were we? Um, you don't think, um . . . is there anything which is particularly useful to be told? If you're trying to read something and it's difficult, what's the most useful thing to be told?

T: The word, I suppose.

Me: To be told what the word is . . .

T: No . . . or, sometimes my Mum tells me to sound it out.

Me: She tells you to sound it out . . . (yeah) . . . do you find that helpful?

T: Yeah.

Me: So how would you do it? I mean supposing you'd come across this word here; the first time that you read that you read it wrong in fact.

T: I said pilots . . .

Me: But if I said to you . . . you said it? (Mmm.) Yes. You said what, Pirates?

T: Pilots!

Me: Oh, Pilots, yes, of course, because you were thinking of people who . . . (joint − indecipherable) . . . pilots, yes. Why do you think you said 'Pilots'? Because it begins with P I suppose . . . ? (yeah) . . . and so does pilots, yes. But if I said to you, right, now sound that out, what would you do?

S: Per . . . ler . . . a . . . P . . . A . . . L . . . A . . . N . . . S . . . E . . . well I wouldn't really . . . S . . . well I wouldn't spell it out like that, I'd just sort of (yes) per . . . ler . . . you know . . .

Me: Yeah − per . . . ler . . . a . . . (yes) . . . but that doesn't sound very like PLANES does it?

S: But I know how to (yes) sound it out like . . .

Me: Oh I see. So, I mean, you know it, so you can do it straight away, it's always so much easier if you can do it straight away, isn't it, really? Yeah. Let's read a little bit more . . .

When we heard this we were delighted that Steve had found such a promising pupil, but already Steve was highly self-critical, as he remained throughout, and said: 'I didn't give him a chance to say what he wanted to say. I kept putting all the things I want to hear into his mouth.' This admission alerted Margaret who was editing the earlier tapes at this time. She transcribed the part that Steve summarized as 'some conversation about Tom's childhood and former schooling', and hoped to discover more about how a reader like Tom coped with the information that the book offered him.

Transcribing tape is a slow business. In this case Tom's painful progress through the words on the page was dragged out longer, as was Steve's gentle urging. Tom says 'rough' for 'runway' in a sentence about planes landing. He uses the monotonic unphrased word-recognition of the inexperienced reader who 'calls out' the words in order without combining them into the texture of written text. We knew by now that we cannot judge from a performance like this how much the reader understands. Some fluent readers have very little comprehension; some hesitators understand very well. Margaret wanted to find out what Tom knew about aeroplanes and what the book told him that he could make use of. This is what she heard when Steve, exhausted by Tom's struggle, pauses for reflection. Both seem quite relaxed and ready for conversation. In fact, they are both tired.

Steve: Do you know what happens at Heathrow? Have you ever been on a plane? Where've you been? (The questions go straight on without a pause.)

Tom: Yes, America. I used to live there.

S: *Did* you? I didn't know that.

Tom: I used to live in Connecticut.

S: Connecticut. How long for? D'you remember?

Tom: I was born in England and I lived in Connecticut for four or five years.

S: Four or five years. Oh I see. You were born here and went straight over there?

Tom: Yes.

S: Can you remember very much about America?

Tom: Yes; good memory. I remember well [This line is spoken very clearly. The rest is softer and needed greater attention to transcribe it].

S: Did you . . . were you old enough to go to school in America?

Tom: Yes [something indecipherable].

S: What was that like?

Tom: All right. Bit stricter than this one.

S: I think it must have been. How old were you when you left America?

Tom: About four or five.

S: And then you came back here. Where did you go to school here? Did you come to London straight away?

Tom: Yes. I went to . . . that was only the juniors. I mean the infants — then I went up to the top then I just came here . . .

S: At the usual time?

Tom: Yes.

S: And that's the only school in London you've been to?

Tom: Yes.

S: It seems quite a long time you were there; six years.

Tom: When you were about twelve and a half you had to leave the school . . . it's only a little school . . . for little boys . . . you had to leave . . .

Here begins the part that Steve transcribed and you have already read.

Steve is not counting the years of Tom's childhood. He confesses to the group that this is the last lesson on a Friday at the end of a hectic week. There have been many interruptions which offer a break in Tom's painful reading. The transcription has gaps that we cannot fill from Tom's soft speech.

Steve accepts the American story and does not question it, although there are signs that it is somewhat muddled. Because Tom was emphatic that he was interested in aeroplanes as the result of this journey, Steve continued to discuss flying with him. But the book is a disaster, confirming all of Margaret's prejudices about the baleful influence of this kind of 'topic' information on beginning readers. In order to glean as much as she could from this part of the tape Margaret played it many times, and, in the end, was convinced that Steve is, by his own account, putting in 'what he wants to hear'. Instead of waiting for Tom's answers, Steve has helped Tom to make up an alternative version of his past.

When we discussed this as a possibility the group agreed that Steve should not go back over it, but cast forward to see what happened. In so doing, Steve investigated one of the classic problems of the non-reader, eyesight. Tom seemed to squint at the page, screwing up his eyes. But there was nothing the matter with his sight. Elizabeth said Chris did the same from time to time. She taught us to call this 'taking the page by surprise'.

Tom and Steve return to the aeroplane book for their second lesson. You can tell from the tape that nothing seems to go right. Tom reads even more slowly and his tone falls into the depressed word-by-word utterance that indicates little or no engagement with the subject. (It can also indicate over-concern, but not here.) Steve then reads seven pages of our favourite *Flat Stanley* to Tom who then reads the next page, after which Steve takes up the story again. At his next turn Tom reads more quickly. The hesitations decrease and he is clearly moving into a different strategy. His eyes now run over the ends of sentences and his intonation is at odds with his search for meaning. He reads, 'Mrs Lambchop said she thought Stanley's clothes would have to be altered by the tailor now' in such a way as to show he expects 'now' to be the beginning of a new sentence, but he can explain clearly what is happening.

At the beginning of the third lesson Steve and Tom have to sort out the fact that Tom had failed to appear when Steve expected him. There had been a troublesome incident that Tom clearly did not want to discuss so Steve let Tom start again with the aeroplane book. He is much more confident, so that when Steve asks him how gliders get up into the air, Tom can tell him. When he meets 'winch' in the text he says it easily and familiarly. But he can't get 'warm air' in the sentence 'Gliders use the warm air around us'. The text has little cohesion and less redundancy so the reader is forced back into a word-by-word decoding position until he can take a sentence at a run. Tom's pace increases and his hesitations decrease as Steve gives him clues about the pictures he should look at, and offers a kind of commentary on the text once Tom has got it right. Tom feels he is reading because Steve keeps a firm focus on the meaning and discusses the topic.

He is, in fact, teaching Tom that to understand this kind of text he needs his action knowledge of the world to fill in what the words do not tell him, so that he then knows what the words mean.

At a natural break, Steve asks Tom about his reading strategies: 'What d'you do when you're stuck?' Tom's reply is: 'Sound it out or go on.' There is very little taped evidence of his doing either; he mostly waits to be told, or pauses and then says something, often far wrong or sometimes nearly right. He gives no clue as to what he does when he is silent. The feedback Tom gets from Steve is mostly in the form of 'extension'; Steve expands the meaning of what Tom says, sometimes with the effect of over-anticipating what Tom is about to say or might have said. Listening to the first two lessons, the group debated how long the teacher should wait for the reader to get the next word before offering help.

Elizabeth: The kid's thinking . . . they need space to think.

Vicky: You're giving them space by talking more.

E: No. I don't think that. . . . I think you should sit quiet for a bit sometimes. I know I do that . . . then there's a silence, then I say something five times as long as they're looking at and that just confuses them. They're working it out.

Margaret: There's our time and their time. When we listen to answers on the tape recorder we scarcely give them time to draw breath.

E: That's true.

Steve: What I've written is that Tom seemed to have faith in his sounding out strategy but wasn't very good at explaining how it was done. But (a) he doesn't get a chance to explain how it's done, and (b) why should he have to if he knows?

V: In early encounters you're both under strain.

S: The paramount thing in your mind is: will he come next time? You're only looking at the next session.

Judith: All these searching questions (about strategies for getting over difficulties) are a bit irrelevant . . . if you're creating an atmosphere he'll find congenial.

S: We talked a lot about aeroplanes.

M:We all speak so quickly and anticipate their thinking. We keep them from tangling with the text which is what they're pleased to put off.

Steve is oppressed by the lack of scope in the aeroplane text. He thinks that Tom's predictions are not being helped by the writer who confuses small segments of text with easy reading which comes in fact when the reader has enough help from extended or redundant text. So they agreee to go back to *Flat Stanley*. They take pages or paragraphs in turn. Then Tom reads slightly faster. He does not seem to make so many intonation errors, but his habit of repeating everything that is not clear to him means that he still seems to go slowly. Here is a paragraph on p. 8 with Steve's miscue markings.

\\But Stanley was not hurt.^(c)In fact he\\would
still have been sleeping\\if he had not been
                  shoot
woken by his\\brother's shout.^(p)
      gone   in
'What's going on here?' he called out
cheerfully from\\beneath ^(c) the enormous board
                            the
Mr and Mrs Lambchop hurried to lift it
from the bed.
'Heavens!' said Mrs Lambchop
\\'Gosh', ^(p) said Arthur.\\'Stanley's flat'

Tom reads 'Gosh' with encouraged enthusiasm. The pace is still slow but the pause between the words is shorter. When he tries he invites Steve to read, and together they arrive at this paragraph on p. 18

One day Stanley got a letter from his friend
Anthony Thomas Jeffrey, whose family had
moved recently to California. A school holiday
was about to begin and Stanley was invited to
spend it with the Jeffreys.

'Oh boy!' Stanley said. 'I would love to go!'

Mr Lambchop sighed. A✓ round trip or aeroplane
ticket to California ^{costs (c)}\\is very expensive',
he said. 'I shall have to think of some cheaper
way.'

When Mr Lambchop came home from the office that
evening, he ^(c)\\brought with him an enormous brown-
paper envelope.

'Now then, Stanley', he said. 'Try this for size.'

The envelope fitted Stanley very well. There was
extra (p)
\even   room(for)left over, Mr Lambchop discovered,
for an egg-salad sandwich made with

By now Tom is reading much more fluently and is clearly attending
to the story. The members of the group noted how he did not stumble
at the expressly American features: 'round trip ticket', 'California' and
'the egg-salad sandwich'. He did not stumble at California, but he also
rushed over the pause to 'A', without its seeming to make sense, righted
himself and went on. From his intonation it is also clear that his eyes
and voice are doing something different from his thinking. He then
baulks at 'brought' where the sentence takes a new turn, but when he
gets it, nothing else is difficult.

As we listened to the tape no one claimed that Tom was now safe, or
even better, but the whole group was convinced that the tone of the
reading was *readerly*. The change was perceptible in that short space,
and we described this very small shift to ourselves as a change in Tom's
attention. He is now focused on 'what happens next'. He is reading
extended text. His success makes him successful. He is at ease with
the situation – the text and Steve.

This latter point is crucial because Tom, we thought, must now
know that his story about his childhood in America had been exposed
as a fantasy. He had never been farther than the locality of his present
school except on holiday. He had spent his primary years in a school
for maladjusted children and had been in fairly constant trouble that
involved the school and other authorities. Steve had caught up with his
record *after* he had allowed Tom to reconstruct his past on fairy-tale
lines and Steve had never gone back on this, keeping the factual version
to himself. We suggested that, as a result of a series of growing threats
from his peer groups whom he had seriously tricked, Tom had moved
out of the playground world, which was full of danger for him, into the
fairly secure ambience of the reading room and his contact with Steve,
the world of books, aeroplanes and Stanley. As his confidence increases, so does his reading become that of a reader, encouraged by
Steve's tact and reticence about what he clearly knows is happening
elsewhere. At this point it did not occur to us to think that Tom could
read and was concealing the fact. He read, as all poor readers do, not
knowing how to make the text mean. Here now was Tom involved
in the story. We felt that was enough explanation for the change in

his confidence. The story was going *inwards*. At this point we should
have known to encourage him to read silently.

In their end-of-lesson chat, Tom tells Steve that he can read his
mum's books, 'them sort of murder books'. Steve asks if silent reading
or reading aloud is easier, then runs over Tom's response and answers
his own question – another teacherly habit – to say that reading aloud
is easier 'because you can get help'. The group thought that Tom,
uninterrupted, might have said silent reading is easier. Tom's hesitation
shows he might have been going to say 'on my own', but this would
have implied that he did not value Steve's help. Tom leaves the third
session with Steve telling him that he is getting better. Tom says, 'It's
getting easier.' The group think that he has had a safe introduction to
the idea that reading is something you do on your own, and we wonder
how to get Tom's mother to help him so that he confirms his confidence at this stage.

Just after this lesson Tom was suspended from school for his part in
the incident to which Steve made no reference. A week later, he is
with Steve in the small group of pupils who have 'extra English'. Steve
and Tom both know that this little group is not Tom's platform
because he has his special lessons at another time. So Tom listens to
the other pupils. Amongst them on this day is Michael, not enthusiastic or interested, whom Steve is urging to compose a story about a
new race of special people. Steve is ready to type Michael's story as
he composes it, but as Michael has no idea where to begin, Steve offers
him the notion of a new creature called The Chog. Michael is entirely
disinclined, so Tom offers to take on his story. With the rest of the
group listening, Tom launches into this narrative, interpreting The Chog
as a creature from outer space. He composes 147 words straight off,
and stops only when the bell goes for the end of the lesson. He does
not even recap his story then, but leaves it with Steve.

That same afternoon when Tom has his own lesson with Steve they
go straight back to his text. Steve asks Tom to remind him of where he
had got to, and they enter on the collaborative venture that results in
this story which, when it was finished on the last session before Christmas, Tom read into the tape recorder, all four pages (A4 paper) with
no more than three or four stumbles, hardly a miscue, and in a voice
which would not have disgraced a competent, experienced reader.

The text, as it stands, has had some revisions, mostly by Tom. His
repetition of 'rather large' was edited out; 'all of a sudden' was changed;
'the bloke never came out' became 'and he was never seen again'. The
text is now as he composed and revised it for Steve, in dictation units

of about eight words at a time. He carries the meaning units in his head, even when he is waiting for Steve to catch up with him on the typewriter. When Tom reads it back, his voice is strong and confident. There is still a trace of the earlier reading voice, as if the calling-back ritual were too important to be abandoned, but the entire impression of Tom reading is quite different.

The most remarkable thing about 'The Chog' is its rhetoric – the forms of written language, the kinds of phrases that people know from what they have *read*. As you read this part of it, ask yourself if you would have expected a composition of this kind from all that you have heard of Tom so far.

The Chog

In the year 2001 there was a French fishing trawler in the middle of the Arctic Ocean, when suddenly there was a strong wind and it blew it off course. And the fishing trawler hit a rather large iceberg. They thought they were sinking when they heard a noise coming from within the iceberg. Suddenly the iceberg cracked open and the chog come out. It was enormous you could say, it was a thing nobody had ever seen before. It was forty feet high, and twenty feet wide, and it looked horrifying. It was green and slimy. Suddenly it picked the trawler up. Twenty men dived overboard. The captain shouted, 'You traitors!' Then he turned round to the wireless operator and ordered him to send an SOS message. Then he told the gunner to bring several sub-machine guns and several extra magazines. He came back with them. They tried to hold it off but the bullets just went through. Suddenly it picked up one of the crew and tossed him into the sea. And he was never seen again. The captain took a megaphone and tried to communicate with it but it was no use. They were stranded in its colossal paw. The captain shouted 'It looks like we're going to have to swim for it', and one man tried to shoot himself. Another man dived overboard but before he could touch the sea the thing picked him up and threw him onto an iceberg and he screamed a horrifying scream and lay there motionless. The captain thought that the wireless operator should try again as he thought nobody heard when suddenly they saw a gunboat coming through the mist. The monster carefully put the ship onto a large iceberg and with one giant hit of his paw he split the gunboat in two. There were no survivors. The gunboat sunk immediately. The captain shouted, 'Now's our chance!' But before they could throw a ladder down the beast came over, picked the ship up and started to swim across the ocean with it. They thought they were all going to die when as if a light bulb had struck in the captain's mind he ordered the armsman to bring up several large grenades from the emergency box which was normally meant to be used for if they were stranded on large icebergs. The captain had made a wise decision. For he had aimed to blow up the creature when suddenly a wise petty officer decided that he couldn't let the captain do it because it might baffle the scientists. For millions of years they tried to communicate with the outside world, but now the armsman came back with the large box of grenades and the captain ordered each and every one to take two grenades and on the captain's command they were to pull the pins out and lob them at the beast. But before the armsman had a chance to give them out the wise petty officer ran forward and told the captain his plan. And the captain agreed to go along with it on one condition: that if the creature causes any more harm to the crew, then he will have to use the grenades. The petty officer agreed, but the beast just kept on swimming.

The beast swam for two days and two nights. The captain was getting fed up because there was no way they could escape. He was getting short tempered and started shouting 'Why don't someone come?' One of the crew said 'Maybe they didn't hear us' and because the captain was short tempered he had the man lashed. The crew didn't like this. They swore they'd get their revenge. The captain was cursing and shouting at everybody. Just then he picked up a harpoon and threw it at the monster. It stuck in the monster. The monster was in agony. It took it out, got hold of the captain and ate him.

The mate took over the ship. The beast just kept on swimming. All of a sudden from out of nowhere there were seven large fighter planes. They started to shoot the monster. The monster put the ship on a sand bank and started fighting the planes, the planes dropped bombs and fired machine guns. The men thought that the monster was helpless, but all of a sudden it spat fire and hit two large fighter planes. They melted in seconds. The pilots were burnt to ashes. Two other planes which were small and manoeuvrable dived at it. Like razor blades the monster shot its claws and hit the other two planes and stuck in them. With the weight of the claws it brought them down and they crashed in the sea. The men gave up all hope and the other three planes turned round and went back. The men were disgusted at the way the navy and air force acted.

The monster just kept on swimming and swimming. The mate made them all go on rations. because there wasn't enough food to go round for all of them now. All of a sudden the men turned nasty. They thought the mate was being a bit greedy as he had a lot more than they had to eat and drink, and they threatened him with knives. He agreed that he was greedy. Then they let him go.

And all of a sudden they reached shore. The monster threw the ship a mile and it smashed to pieces. There was no survivors on the ship for it was just a bundle of scrap metal. The monster came ashore. The place was Japan. It was horrifying, it picked up a large mono-train, tore the doors off and picked up a boy. The mother shouted, the passengers panicked. It threw the train to the ground which made a large explosion. Then all was silent.

The story was composed over a period of four lessons. At the beginning of each lesson Tom could pick up where he left off and continue, while Steve typed what he dictated. When we listen to Tom composing and Steve typing we are struck by the reversal of their roles. When Steve makes a spelling error in 'megaphone', Tom corrects him. We are all staggered, first by Tom's fluency and assurance in dictating, then by his confident tackling of the text, as a reader, although he still goes slowly.

Now there is no magic about reading, except that everything about it is magical. But in Tom's case we were all thrown back on our analytical ingenuity to explain his performance. We examined his miscues, and could not find the explanation because Tom corrects himself throughout from the context and Steve's recapping of the story up to that point. In any case, this was not a reading for miscue analysis. Tom is reading *his* story. We noted that 'manoeuvrable' gave him not the slightest trouble.

Judith: Is there a possibility that children get bored with simple words?
Elizabeth: I think so . . . especially when they've written it themselves and they think they've put in a good word. They relish the feeling . . .
Margaret: The order of difficulty of 'simple' words is not the same order of difficulty of 'unknown' words . . .
J: There is no challenge ⎰ in simple writing . . .
E: ⎱ they enjoy writing things that have big words . . .
Steve: He reads a lot of war comics. I know that now, but at the time

I didn't think that it counted . . . that gives him 'sub-machine guns' . . .

J: That could account for the vocabulary.

S: 'Wireless operator' and things like that.

E: A kid was dictating a story to me today and he asked where you get a driving licence. I said 'the post office' and he says then, 'Let's put "the town hall".' He just wanted something grander.

The simplest explanation is that Tom could read all the time and had concealed the fact. But no one who hears the tapes or who knows Steve's competence would think so. His reading aloud still has some of the features of the classroom ritual. He was also too close to the text to be recalling what he had made up, and he made too many mistakes for someone who had learned a piece by heart. It may not strike you as a splendid composition, but its coherence and cohesion are strong. Look at 'The captain thought/ that the wireless operator should try again/ as he thought/ nobody heard/ when suddenly they saw a gunboat/ coming through the mist'. This is literary language. When Tom reads it the chunking is sensible. He possesses the text as any author would.

As he saw his prose appearing on the page, Tom said, 'That's all my story, mostly,' presumably to hold on to it as his own, to claim it from Michael who had been invited to begin it. Tom then wants to know if it is any good. He said he got the idea from a film and did all the rest in his head. No one had ever done this kind of work with him before.

Success like this is as difficult to explain as failure. Clearly Tom now intends what reading intends — a story and a reader, Steve. The following term the story was continued for a further three pages of typescript, given a climactic conclusion and published in two instalments in the school magazine with illustrations by Tom himself.

What had happened? We suggest that it was nothing magical, just the coming together of a number of things. Tom did not fail in Steve's company. We had already seen him pick up the story in *Flat Stanley*, and he knew from television and films that the stories you see can become the stories you tell. We have heard Judith and Vicky talking about the strong fascination exerted by stories over Trevor and Tracy. Here is Tom composing his story and finding his voice when he looked again at the words. We remembered James Britton's assertion that no one has looked very much at the child's motivation to make the language of books his own. When Tom reads 'The Chog' he is *in* that other language. When he does school reading he tries to get the words right. When he reads his own prose he makes very few mistakes and corrects them at once. To be a good story, the tale of Tom needs a happy ending. We have no such thing. The problems of his life inside and outside school became too complicated. The authorities claimed that the attempt to give him normal schooling had failed and he was sent to boarding school before 'The Chog' appeared in print. The exact details of his subsequent career were not known by Steve at the time and were outside our discussions.

But Tom was our star performer when Frank Smith paid us a visit. We were discussing these three lessons and he joined in. He said of Tom reading *Flat Stanley*:

> The things that struck me are, I'm sure, the things that struck you. His intonation. His intonation is perfect. When he makes a mistake or when he slows up it's not because he's battling to make sense, but . . . because he's reluctant to take a chance. . . . I was impressed by the sense he was making. . . . He's not one of those readers who stumble along trying to get this word and this word. . . . Does he really have a lot of problems?

Margaret: No one up to that point construed him as a reader. Steve did. He had been pretty fiercely told he couldn't read . . . so whatever else was true about him that was how he saw himself.

FS: The kid isn't doing anything wrong at this point. He may be able to do it in silent reading outside school.

Steve confirmed that war comics and detective stories are in Tom's home. Then we played the tape of Tom reading 'The Chog', and asked for comments. Our guest assured us that the chunking is essentially skilful and the composition is genuine.

There are many unanswered questions. We noted Tom's lack of self-consciousness as he composed his story and his complete inability to write even three-letter words with confidence. We should have examined his composing process in greater detail. But not even the experts have fully accounted for Tom's performance with 'The Chog', except to say that Steve, who inadvertently had given Tom a revised version of his past, had treated him as a reader when no one else had done so.

Tom confirmed our growing awareness of the disadvantages of hearing pupils reading aloud without knowing or examining what we are hearing. He also taught us that once readers are thought to be poor, even the best teachers may expect too little rather than too much. For Steve, the outstanding problem remained. If Tom had stayed with him, what would he have done next?

8

Reflexions

We need to remember that effective teaching is aimed not so much
at the ripe as at the ripening functions . . .

Arthur Applebee

The elusive joy

We hope that you have become concerned enough about Sharon and
Tracy, John and Tom, Trevor and Jamie, Chris and Andy to wonder
what happened to them. We kept in touch with them until they left
school, or like Sharon and Tom, went elsewhere. We did not have last
lessons as we had first encounters. Reading lessons may drift to a stop
at the end of one term and not be renewed at the beginning of the next
unless someone takes the initiative. You remember that our concern
was not to keep our pupils, but to lose them as soon as they thought
they could cope with the ordinary curriculum lessons.

Trevor asserted that he could manage in his examination year, but
he kept coming to see Judith when he needed help and reassurance.
The initiative had passed to him. As long as they read books with
Vicky, Tracy and Sharon knew what reading was like. At other times
it retreated to the edge of their lives and they did as little as possible.
Chris got his motorbike and, eventually, a job and his self-respect,
thanks to Elizabeth. At the end of the third year of our work together
we stopped recording lessons and taped only the discussions of our
stock-taking.

Was it all worth it? Look first at the pupils. Trevor willingly and
sometimes spontaneously took up a book and read it for his own purpose or pleasure. We have no evidence about the others. Even so, the
limited progress they made was more than worth our joint longitudinal
efforts on their behalf because so much more was involved than the

reading process itself. We now know, in great detail, that inexperienced readers in secondary school who want to learn to read have to subject themselves to a particular kind of metaphysical distress. Nothing written about it can fully convey the strain of what, hitherto, has been superficially described as 'reluctance', 'failure', 'poor motivation'. The real condition of these pupils was not lack of desire to learn, or poor basic skills, but absolute conviction that they could not be successful no matter what they did.

Perhaps we learned most. Doubtless *what* we learned is contained in all the good advice that is so abundantly offered to reading teachers, but *how* we learned it is the more important lesson. We confirmed our conviction that reading has to be taught as the thing that it is, holistically. To break it down into piecemeal activities for pseudo-systematic instruction is to block the individual, idiosyncratic moves that pupils of this age make to interact with a text and to teach themselves how to *make it mean*. When we began, our pupils had one reading strategy. They held it in common because they had all been taught it when they first had reading lessons in school. They were efficient sounders and blenders and decipherers of initial consonants; so efficient, indeed, that words they could have recognized 'at sight' were subjected to the same decoding as those they had never seen or heard before. When these early reading lessons failed them, they believed that they were to blame because they were different from other learners. 'Thick', is what they said we thought they were. The hardest task of all was to dispel this belief. It was not that they had a 'poor self-image', as texts for training teachers glibly say. Their view of themselves was sound enough; but the view they thought we had of them was what made them angry, depressed, rebarbative, frightened.

One of the most significant lessons we learned was that expert readers, like us, are competent by virtue of what we were never taught in lessons. From the books we had read we knew how to 'tune' the voice on the page, how to follow the fortunes of a hero, how to tolerate the unexpected, to link episodes, to read a joke, to relate fictitious events to the world outside the book in a 'hierarchy of veracity'.[1] All this tacit competence, we, as English teachers, maintain as part of our stock-in-trade. We learned it when we first read for ourselves the popular literature of childhood. Our pupils read comics, but as the skills they had learned in this reading had not been validated in school, they never went about reading anything else with the same active involvement.

We saw Jamie discover the relationship of his own opinions to

events in a novel. We speculated about Chris reading his motorbike list
as if it were Auden's litany of sacred objects. We had glimpses of Tom's
powerful brain fictions[2] by which his real life was sometimes ruled. Andy
could read when he was no longer angry about school. Tracy, Sharon
and John had to be urged into understanding that they could 'make up'
the story with the author. Trevor came to know that the voice in himself and the one in the page are in dialogue. He paid dearly for this
knowledge, as we shall show.

We kept up right to the end our acquired habit of asking them to
comment on what we were reading together. If they hesitated, it was
from their surprise at being asked for an opinion. We knew that reading
could not change for them until we could awaken this active response.
Trevor found this a genuine conflict. He was convinced there was a
secret about reading that Judith kept to herself. Nevertheless, with her
help he battled through to CSE and the oral examination in English for
which he successfully gave a talk on 'How I learned to read in the
secondary school.'

There is a late tape (May 1978) that shows us working towards an
understanding of what we had done, exactly three years after our very
first encounter.

Margaret: Most of the material designed for poor readers reinforces
their poor view of themselves.
Vicky: A number of children 'cross over' yet are not very good at the
beginning – then they become firm readers. Some can't spell or
write, but they still read a lot or are happy with books. There are
enough coming over . . .
M: What keeps the view of reading as something difficult to learn? Is
it the child's view of the teacher as someone with a little bag of gold
from which you get another nugget – a piece of information about
reading – in return for good behaviour, a reading lesson? You can
tell that Trevor thought that information about reading was withheld or doled out when he said, 'Are you going to teach me to read
now, Miss?'
Judith: Trevor's attitude has changed. He's become quite submissive.
He reads a lot in the lesson; he's reading better, but he no longer
comments. His critical tendency has gone.
  He says things like, 'After half term I've got exams. What's the
point of my coming in to do them? I can't even read the paper,
and even if I can I can't write quickly enough to answer the

questions. The only one I'm coming in for is technical drawing. Otherwise, I'm going to have a leg problem.'

Then I say, 'Why don't you ask if you can tape the answers', and he says, 'Others don't do that; it's an admission of failure.' But he's being more curious than assertive, so I try again and say, 'These exams are five weeks away. Anything can happen in five weeks.'

Then Trevor: 'Oh yes miss, who are you kidding? I've been coming for three and a half years with you. . . . I'm not going to read in five weeks.'

Then I say: 'I know someone who learned to read in a fortnight. . . .'

Trevor: 'Oh well, miracles don't happen like that to me.'

Then I say: 'Trevor, why do you think I *go on* – that I have such faith that you will learn to read? What do you think makes me go on trying to teach you?' He was momentarily nonplussed by that. He'd never thought of it. He'd never thought of it from that angle. He could have said something bitter like, 'You're paid to be here', but he knows, in fact, I'm not obliged to teach him. He knows I teach him in my free time.

For a moment I thought that things were turning – that he had begun to see that for him to be defeatist in the face of my optimism was a perverse thing to be doing. Then things improved a bit. But he has got hold of the idea that it can't happen now to him, that it is too late, that although he recognizes that he now reads more easily I think he knows that the *elusive joy* of reading is gone, and he can't get it back. He would agree that technically he could improve, but he has seen the disparity between technical competence and enjoyment of reading. He has seen that gap widen recently, almost as his own confidence has increased. It troubles me; I don't know what I can do. On the other hand, I'm quite positive that he can read; he certainly now reads easily at subsistence level . . . he can get around London now. I remember how once he came to visit me and landed miles away. . . . He can cope with life, if not absolutely at the 'civic-national' level. Another part of me is distressed that he is no longer commenting on stories. He's not putting up any sort of fight. He's lost all that delightful tearing apart of style that he had not very long ago . . . the fourth year exams are coming up . . . he's been withdrawn into himself in those last weeks . . . he's much less interested.

I'm sure this fits in to what you said but it seems to me that a poor reader just starts off on a different path. Some of them, according to Vicky, cross over . . .

V: I can't prove it. I don't see them between five and eleven. . . .

M: It must be true, or there would be more poor readers than there are . . .

Steve: The question is: what do all the kids who can read perfectly well do when reading isn't part of their lives? How do they do it when they never actually read?

M: Margaret Clark says there's a stage called 'beyond the risk of failure. . . . when it's possible to believe you can and never forget how . . . like swimming . . .

S: I'm trying to think of kids for whom reading has never been part of their lives and how they came by this competence. . . . Some children achieve technical competence by what we consider inappropriate methods . . .

V: Are you sure there's a distinction between technical competence and actually enjoying reading? You make it sound that there's reading, and what he was reading was not significant. He [Trevor] was reading better and better but he wasn't interested in what he was reading. How can that happen at the same time? If he's reading something like *Spit Nolan*, is he being mechanical?

S: There are children who do learn to read on *Ladybird*. They become 'free readers'. I'm just trying to get at Margaret's theory . . .

M: Indeed. But I think their view of reading is different if *Ladybird* is the end and not the means to another end, *their* end, in becoming readers.

J: Do any children learn to read and then forget how to?

M: It's doubtful, not if they make reading do what *they* want. The difference is between 'doing reading' according to the teacher's prescription, and making it serve your own intentions.

J: I've suggested to Trevor that he can read better than he wants anyone to know. He wouldn't have that at all. You'd think that he would collude with that idea of himself . . .

E: Some kids just need to grab at that . . .

J: Trevor can't entertain that as a likely way of behaving. I think he'd say, 'If I could really read I'd get the hell out of here.'

M: What do you think he thinks he still has to do to be able to read?

J: He has to *want* to. He doesn't read at all unless he comes to me. The Goodmans said we build in dependence. Do we? But he doesn't know how to push himself. If you were to say to Trevor 'What do you want to do more than anything else?' he'd say, 'I want to *want to* read.' He gets angry with me for not pushing, and all the time I'm thinking I'm withdrawing support too rapidly.

E: I don't know that many people really want independence. I have colleagues who are free to make decisions and they won't. . . . . It's so much easier to be told than to accept autonomy, for learning or anything else. . . .

We then went back to our early stage of trying to see the pupil in his reading situation at home, and the persistent problem of the pupil's lack of practice, of being *in* the book. We push and push, and push against the idea that books are simply external objects. We agree that successful reading aloud is no exact measure of reading competence, although intonation, running over sentence boundaries, line skipping, all give us some more certain awareness of what is happening in the reader's head. Anticipating the story, retelling, discussing consequences − engagement in that kind of activity seemed so much better a way to estimate progress. M reads to the group from Josipovici[3] 'What the sophisticated reader needs to recognise is what every naive reader instinctively knows, that symbolic systems, including novels are not repositories of meaning but invitations to take part in certain kinds of activity.'

We had kept open the invitation to join us in this activity because its earliest form had been overruled by persistent teaching of irrelevant behaviour. We had diversified the kinds of reading activity and we had offered guidance through unfamiliar territory. We believe that 'One book, one little story . . . can sink so deep that it alters our lives, and we know . . . that its reverberations will never cease to be felt until the day of our death.'[4] We agree that the significant move for beginners is to get to first base as independent runners. The metaphors for the action are not lacking. But the significant ones are about struggle and risk.

In the early days of our meeting we thought that if we made analyses of our pupils' miscues, taught them, then did later analyses we should be able to tell what 'works' for them and what does not. At least we would have 'hard' evidence of the kind that other teachers could pay attention to and then perhaps they would say, 'So that's the way to teach reluctant readers in secondary schools.' Perhaps all that we have shown in these many pages is that it is not as simple as that, and you can make something of this kind of evidence when you meet it in inexperienced readers.

For nearly two years we were caught in a double bind. When we invited our pupils to behave like readers they saw this as another deceit, a 'con'. For them, the reality was that they could not read, and that we were foolish to believe they ever could. As special lessons are a kind of a rest, they colluded with us, at least for as long as each lesson lasted. Thus the Goodmans were able to show us that we were falling into the very mode of teaching that we wanted to avoid and the pupils were still, successfully, evading the real task. They were still, in Bruner's terms, 'dependers'.[5]

We made our pupils into 'copers' by increasing the length and the difficulty of lessons. In one exact sense they became literate: when they composed stories of their own and were the authors of what they read. In doing this they discovered a way out for the voice within, the power of production that lies with the writer. They showed, yet again, that literacy is a function of language development allied to the purposes of the user. The narratives of Andy, Chris, Tom and Trevor are forceful statements. They are learning to look at what they mean. Because of their inexperience, stories have to do still for all their modes of thought[6] but as long as the writing stays on the page, they can revisit it as theirs. They own it; they do not rent it.[7]

Where else, we asked each other with some passion, are they encouraged to do that? In many lessons, if they have a choice they do not read, and few subject teachers take the trouble to scribe for them. Instead of real books, they have worksheets where reading and writing are reduced to a minimum. The expanded redundant text that they need is reserved for the skilled. Instead of being shown how to read it, they are given something simpler, so the circle of failure revolves again. They cannot tolerate that the special lesson is the *real* thing unless it helps them to do what the skilled actually do. When we showed them that they too could be writers, our pupils, for a time, broke out of captivity.

We now teach their successors, and this is where we confidently begin. Like our pupils we had to rid ourselves of all that was not helpful, and to find reasons for doing what we instinctively had known at the start, that literacy is reading *and* writing. Indeed, the books we all like best are the ones we wish we had written.

Two years after he had stopped, one of these fortuitous accidents that all teachers know about let Trevor read Judith's published account of one of their lessons.[8] He was furious. Judith, sympathetic to what she thought was his view of a breach of confidence, explained that she wanted other teachers to learn from their pupils as Trevor had taught her. Despite their long, good relationship Trevor could not accept the idea that he was no less of a success because Judith had explained his case to others. Nor could he see, when they examined the article together, that it puts him in a good light and Judith in a bad one. Although the evidence is all around us, we doubt if there is enough general understanding of just how deeply wounded these inexperienced readers are, and the extent to which they believe school fails them.

Implications and implementations

Teachers, like other folk, set their own bondage where they choose to establish their convictions.

George Kelly

As a group we met regularly for three years while we kept record of lessons. Thereafter we tried to turn our observations and discussions into analyses and judgments that might help us to improve our pedagogy and understanding. Meanwhile, the output of reading research had increased. Its emphasis was changing as developmental studies of children's language showed that reading could not be understood apart from other language activity, including the language of teaching.[9] With help from teachers' centres, pupils were producing materials for others to read.[10] Concern about reading problems had become less pessimistic and the reading lobby less strident. The Open University reading course was revised. All of these, in one way or another, impinged on what we discussed.

We agreed that, if we had had trained observers in our lessons or at our discussions, this last chapter would present 'results' in a more systematized, more conceptually and theoretically coherent form. They would have discovered more of what we still take for granted as obvious, and found recurrent stable patterns in even the most fleeting lessons. Professional observers can be hidden like spies at the back of a normal classroom or inside the multifarious operations of group work. But in a one-to-one encounter their role is a severe constraint on both teacher and pupil. (Margaret was never actually present at a lesson.) We wish we had made more videotapes, but pupils like Trevor, who resent the intrusion of even the tape recorder, refuse to collaborate if they suspect outside interference. So we had to be both teachers and observers and to make as explicit as we could in our group discussion the latent theorizing of our practice.

We are open to all kinds of criticisms: that the books we gave our pupils covered our culture and not theirs, so that their inability to read was a resistance to us and what we offered them; that what we interpret as a kind of 'coaching' is in fact an unwarranted burden of sustaining a teacher's undivided attention for an hour at a time. Others will bring their constructs to our evidence. Even so, we claim that in these lessons we were trying to make away from the single authoritarian dominance of the classroom teacher in order to share the task with the pupils in such a way that they could take it on for themselves with a new view of it. We wanted to make them 'consociates'.[11] If, in our attempt to revise our relationship, we still took more control of the operation than we really wanted to, the reasons for this are interesting in themselves.

Reading is regarded as a 'basic skill' or subject about which options do not really exist, either in our literate society or in school. The reading teachers' authority is socially sanctioned so that they are obliged to make all children literate. In no other area of education does the same constraint exist and the work of other subject teachers has traditionally been built on this assumption: learn to read, then read to learn. The reading teachers' frame of reference seems absolute. Only since the Bullock Report has the responsibility for literacy been officially widened to include every teacher. Negotiations with pupils can go on about *how* they are to be taught and *what* they are to read, but they cannot opt out of literacy in the same way as they may be disinclined to encounter the Romans in Gaul.

In the lessons we have reported you find us trying to negotiate new relationships with our pupils and to pass the initiative for learning over to them. We try to relinquish a measure of our control over how the lesson proceeds, to make the pupils' talk less restricted and our (still too many) questions more open-ended, all within the tacit assumption that the pupil has to learn. We think we worked hard to give our pupils more meaning potential. One piece of evidence pleases us. In all the third-year tapes the pupils speak more than the teachers, partly because the lessons are now a familiar ritual that needs no explanation, partly because they are secure enough to initiate discussion and ask questions that are not simply challenges to authority. We can trace this feature from the early group discussions about teachers' interventions. We notice that, after we talked about them, the number of interventions in the next set of lessons fell by a half, and the pupils were being encouraged to go on as long as they could or to read silently.

The most delicate negotiation involves the nature of *collusion*: allowing the pupil to make a decision that lets him or her avoid a genuine reading problem; agreeing that a difficulty can be tackled 'next time'; accepting an explanation that is partly false or at least dubious. In one sense Steve in his haste colluded with Tom, but the outcome was a successful new relationship. The remedy for collusion is not aggressive confrontation. Yet we all knew that headaches, excuses, the prolonging conversation to avoid reading, while offering temporary relief from the pain of tackling what we are uncertain about, only extend the uncertainty and never remove it. For both pupil and teacher, to face what you know you must is to expose your ignorance.

As we went back over the early lessons again we became more aware of signs of change in our pupils and in ourselves. We saw ritualistic exchanges for what they were, and, with group support, learned how to turn frustration and failure into insights. (Reading is more difficult to teach in the weeks before school examinations; the less experienced are more at risk.) We began to look for what we could set against test scores, readability formulae, and even miscue analyses and close procedures that have always been the 'hard' evidence of reading ability. In this way we learned that the school's view of literacy and how it should be taught, the negotiations of teachers and pupils in the early lessons, the kinds of reading from which both draw their view of the task, all deserve notice as kinds of evidence. We no longer left unquestioned statements about 'poor motivation' which excuse both the pupils' reluctance and our own to investigate what we know: that no child reads well if he doesn't want to, or can see no point in it, or hates his teacher, feels cheated, subdued or devalued by the whole reading business. 'Poor motivation' now means for us that we have failed to harness the pupils' intentions because we have led them to believe that they have none.

And so we came to see, in the way that outside observers rarely do, that longitudinal studies of this kind can demonstrate more of the dynamic nature of teaching-learning interaction. The teacher's approach cannot be the operation of fixed sets and structures. Genuinely to support our pupils' learning we have to be open to what we receive from them that will help them reconstrue their view of the task, yet strong in our development of theoretical understanding. The rationale for the teaching of reading is always in evolution for every teacher.

Within the dynamic change of our view of the task certain things emerged that have important implications. All of our pupils were in search of personal and social meanings in what they did in school. In this they were no different from other adolescents. But we were expected to intuit these, to know what these meanings were, to understand and to make allowances *even when the pupils said nothing about them* in a situation where it was open to them to do so. Trevor reproached Judith, Andy was angry with Fiona for what they thought was a failure of understanding of the consequences of their illiteracy. Reading lessons were not 'special' to our pupils because they were about reading, but because they crystallized their hopes and fears, their anxiety and doubt about themselves. As we tried to make them more responsible for the reading task, so we seemed to be throwing them back on resources within themselves that school, for six years, had told them they lacked. In their role as non-readers they had always seen themselves as severely restricted. We were now trying to link life-understanding as relevant to what they persistently saw as something to be done only in school.

This was the hardest thing to change. Reading, for our pupils, was solely a school task, done there, for the teachers' reasons. They were to do what they were told in order to learn. In our lessons you see them searching for clues as to what the teachers want, with the result that they cannot understand the teachers' desire that they should come to intend what reading intends. Hence the difficulty, pinpointed by Steve, that Frank Smith's question 'what can I tell you that would help you?' is utterly meaningless to them. Our most persistent action is to persuade our pupils to behave like readers, in school and out, to commit themselves to reading.

We were too late. For all our concern to choose pupils whom we might successfully help, we found those whom school had disappointed. They had not been ill-treated or neglected; they just did not see the point of much that happened. Trevor, Chris and Andy reproached their teachers in their criticisms of themselves. Others had periods of bamboozlement that later occupied long tracts of discussion time. No remedial exercises or special materials would have solved their problems. For them a reading laboratory is an elaborate competitive game, more school exercises. They had rarely been in a genuine resource-based learning situation that gave them significant tasks where one of the resources was a teacher to support the inexperienced reader to pursue genuine inquiry. We learned this from Chris with his metalwork folder.

Although we read together books that reflected what our pupils claimed were their interests, (i.e. those things that school had so far legitimized), we stuck to our belief that extended text for inexperienced readers should be narrative. In Steve's encounter with Tom, the difference between his *Starter* book on aeroplanes and his productive

capacity in 'The Chog' makes our point clearly, as does Culler's view
that 'fiction can hold together within a single space a varieties of languages, levels of focus, points of view, which would be contradictory
in other kinds of discourse organized towards a particular end'.[12]
Strange as it may seem, this is what we recognize in *Flat Stanley* and
The Iron Man. It is the summary of the untaught lessons that confident,
competent beginners know by the time they are eight or nine. At that
age, they possess narrative skill that shows them how reading is worth
the trouble it takes to learn. Our pupils lacked this conviction, this
freedom. Their frame of reference was *Janet and John*.

At our last meetings we asked each other what we had learned. You
find this in what we have chosen to report: that remedial lessons, as
generally practised, work against those pupils they are intended to
help. The teacher's view of the task has to become explicit items of
knowledge, as does the readers' reading behaviour and their tacit awareness of what reading means to them. The early resolutions where
collusions begin, interventions that keep the teacher in authority,
weaknesses of linguistic understanding in both text and treatment
on the part of pupil and teacher, all these we talked about in as open a
fashion as we could. Where the tapes showed that we persisted in doing
what we knew wasn't helpful, at least we became conscious of it.

Our pupils learned to read when we made it seem worthwhile, and
to the extent that we expected them to be able to. They learned best
when, instead of grinding away at unfamiliar text with intermittent
success, they *composed* the text. Then the roles were reversed; they
were the authority for what was said and their frame of reference
became the dominant one. In addition, when an inexperienced reader
reads what he has written he discovers the vital secret — that readers
tell themselves what the author says. The basic knowledge or skill is
not the ability to decode print, but literary competence in the written
language — an extension of the primary socialization into speech —
the ability to make it mean.

We have taught other pupils since we worked with those you have
met and we have worked with teachers and students who soon get over
their surprise at being told that the most successful role for a reading
teacher is that of the scribe for what the pupil has to say. Then collaboration becomes, not a simulation, but esssential. ('Let me just
check this with you where you say . . .'; 'Read this to me and see if it
says what you want'; 'Have we done the best we can with this bit?'
'Could we go through this together before we type it?')

Our pupils taught us many things. The most unexpected, perhaps,

was the anatomy of boredom, that constant condition of all inexperienced readers. 'Aw miss, it's *boring*' is a threat to any teacher. Our
pupils used this as a warding-off device, implying that their teachers had
no right to bore them. It is said with special urgency when the story
begins to draw them into it, when they know they will want to go on.
After all, to offer the young the chance to become competent readers
is also to give them the freedom enjoyed by expert readers of sometimes choosing *not* to read. Teachers tolerate this idea with difficulty,
('we must get on') but tolerate it they must. Because they had always
been told what to read and when, our pupils never understood that even
as a possibility.

We think that we broke down some of the 'severe functional restric-
tions on what pupils can say because what they can mean is normally
bounded by what the teacher considers relevant'.[13] They confronted us
with an inescapable challenge. Each one, at different times but in the
very same words said: 'You think I'm thick, don't you'. They had
every right to ask, for that was the implicit message that came with
every school lesson where reading was involved. Both 'yes' and 'no'
in answer would be a confirmation of their fears – that it was true or
that we could deceive them; collusion again. We learned to say 'is that
what *you* think?' to which the answer was always 'no'. Whatever the
fear we could always go on from there. The question haunts us still,
but we had made it possible for them to ask. It is a kind of evidence.

Notes

1 A view of the task

1 Cf. Margaret Clark, *Young Fluent Readers*, London, Ward Lock, 1974.
2 The following pages explain what some of these things are. No school day passes without extra incidents. Most teachers acknowledge that 'time to do what you hope to' is the greatest problem where the school day is rigorously divided into lesson 'periods'. But now our response to 'there's no time' might be that this is also our most recurrent excuse.
3 We missed Rebecca Barr's 'Case study of the effect of instruction on pupils' reading strategies'; *Reading Research Quarterly*, 10(4), 1974-5, pp. 555-82. Readability studies had not yet fully emerged. Reports from the Schools Council: E. A. Lunzer and K. Gardner, *The Effective Use of Reading*, London, Heinemann, 1979, and Vera Southgate, Helen Arnold and Sandra Johnson, *Extending Beginning Reading*, London, Heinemann, 1981, were still in preparation. We should now acknowledge Clem Adelman (ed.), *Uttering, Muttering*, London, Grant McIntyre, 1980.
4 M. Stubbs, *Language and Literacy: the sociolinguistics of reading and writing*, London, Routledge & Kegan Paul, 1980.

2 Features of the starting point

1 This extract is taken from *If the story ain't so good*, a magazine published by the English Department of Langdon School, London in 1975 when the Bullock Report was being discussed.
2 Reported in *Talkshop*, a collection of studies including the teaching of reading by teacher-students on the Role of Language in Education course at the Institute of Education, London, in 1975.
3 J. F. Reid. '*Learning to think about Reading*', *Educational Research*, vol. 9, 1966, pp. 56-62.
4 M. Stubbs and S. Delamont (eds), *Explorations in Classroom Observation*, Chichester, Wiley, 1977.
5 E. A. Lunzer and K. Gardner, *The Effective Use of Reading*,

London, Heinemann, 1979.

6 The recommendation in *A Language for Life*, London, HMSO, 1975 (the Bullock Report), that has been implemented with money and expertise is that which led to the setting up of the Assessment of Performance Unit to monitor reading nationally and to devise new tests.

7 Ibid., p. 271 18.12(2) The Report has a very positive approach to the problem in this chapter.

8 Most teachers dislike investigations of reading standards, official or unofficial because they do not give a complete picture of a child's reading ability. At the same time, they use the results to make comparisons between children.

9 This is no longer true. The use of the tape recorder has revolutionized studies of language development. It is widely used and greatly valued.

10 There are frequent references to this 'window on the reading process', as Kenneth Goodman calls it, throughout this study. You will see it used later. The basic idea is that when children read aloud their 'miscues', or the words they say that do not match the text on the page, are neither haphazard nor random but can be used to show what language processes the reader is counting on to make the text meaningful. We read Kenneth S. Goodman, 'Analysis of oral reading miscues: applied psycholinguistics', in *Reading Research Quarterly*, Fall 1969. Later we read Kenneth S. and Yetta Goodman, 'Learning about psycholinguistic processes by analysing oral reading', in *Harvard Educational Review*, vol. 47, no. 3, August 1977.

11 We are indebted to our colleague Phillida Salmon for the beginnings of this valuable insight.

12 Judith contributed 'A Lesson with Trevor' to the *English Magazine*, no. 1, 1979 (Spring) and Elizabeth wrote 'How I stopped testing and learned to live wthout it', in the *English Magazine*, no. 2, 1979.

13 *The London Reading Test* is published for the Inner London Education Authority by the ILEA Learning Materials Service.

3 The compromise

1 A. F. Watts, *Holborn Reading Scale*, London, Harrap, 1948. The test consists of thirty-three sentences in order of difficulty in terms of word-recognition and it is claimed, understanding. It is easy to use. The norms are out of date.

2 M. D. Neale, *Neale Analysis of Reading Ability*, London, Macmillan, 1957-8. A series of stories, increasing in length, followed by questions. This test has long been popular with teachers for measuring 'comprehension'. The questions are not altogether satisfactory.

3 D. Young, *Group Reading Test*, London, Hodder & Stoughton, 1968. A test of word-picture matching and reading comprehension.

Elizabeth consented to the use of this test in the early days because it made certain that no pupil failed to get some of the answers.

4 Margaret's concern here is to suggest that there are progressive moves in remedial education which should not be neglected. Our dissatisfaction with some practices comes across strongly but it should not be interpreted as a blanket condemnation of those who have given their teaching lives to the service of children whom others neglected.

5 F. J. and F. E. Schonell, *Schonell Reading Tests*, Edinburgh, Oliver & Boyd, 1942-55. These are a battery of tests for the assessment of reading attainment — word test, simple prose, silent reading tests A and B etc. — for both group and individual testing. They are the most prevalent tests, especially the *Schonell Graded Word Reading Test*. J. C. Raven. *Standard Progressive Matrices*, London, H. K. Lewis, 1943. A non-verbal test.

6 The booklet was published by the school as *The Learning of Reading*. We are concerned here to indicate the value of discussions that take place in schools about reading. We do not want to draw attention to a particular school.

7 Roger Gurney, *Language, Learning and Remedial Teaching*, London, Arnold, 1976.

8 A quotation from Caroline and David Moseley, *Language and Reading Among Underachievers: a Review of Research*, Windsor, NFER, 1977. Most books about remedial reading suggest well-ordered reading schemes, well-run classrooms and more consistent teaching would 'make' poor readers better. There is a certain air of unreality about them in that they suggest children like to come to lessons to be done good to. In fact, poor readers stay away more often than any other group in school so that the best laid schemes to teach them are often awry.

9 We owe this to Douglas Barnes whose work on group discussion has meant a great deal to us. D. Barnes and F. Todd, *Communication and Learning in Small Groups*. London, Routledge & Kegan Paul, 1977.

4 Reading, without tests

1 We have long been indebted to Elizabeth Cook's *The Ordinary and the Fabulous*, Cambridge University Press, 1969 (second edn 1976). The title is a quotation from Edwin Muir.

2 We spent a great deal of time in these inquiries and we are not dismissing the topic as either irrelevant or trivial. Our impression was, however, that when a child was diagnosed as 'dyslexic', a great weight of guilt was removed from both child and parents. Most people would rather have a medical report of an illness than the suggestion of a failure of intelligence or intellect.

3 D. Tobin and P. D. Pumphrey, 'Some long term effects of remedial teaching of reading', in *Educational Review*, University of Birmingham. See also P. D. Pumphrey, *Measuring Reading*

Abilities: concepts, sources and applications, London, Hodder & Stoughton, 1979.

4   L. John Chapman and Mary Hoffman, *Developing Fluent Reading*, Milton Keynes, Open University Press, 1977.

5   Ibid.

6   D. Moseley, *Special Provision for Readers: when will they ever learn*, Windsor, NFER, 1975. The second quotation in the paragraph comes from C. and D. Moseley, *Language and Reading among Under-achievers*, Windsor, NFER, 1977. The authors' criticism of James Britton can be offset by reading Britton's theory in his *Language and Learning*, Harmondsworth, Allen Lane, 1970.

7   Joan Tough, *Listening to Children Talking: a guide to the appraisal of children's use of language*, London, Ward Lock, 1976; *The Development of Meaning*, London, Allen & Unwin, 1977.

8   Gordon Wells, 'Language use and educational success: a response to Joan Tough's *The Development of Meaning*', in *Nottingham Linguistic Circular*, vol. 6, no. 2, October 1977.

9   Connie and Harold Rosen, *The Language of Primary School Children*, Harmondsworth, Penguin, 1973.

10 Britton, op. cit. The work of George Kelly, *A Theory of Personality*, New York, Norton, 1963, its implication for learning theory and personal growth is discussed by Britton. LATE is the London Association for the Teaching of English, founded in 1947.

11 In Alan Davies (ed.), *Problems of Language and Learning*, London, Heinemann, 1976.

12 M. Clark, *Young Fluent Readers*, London, Ward Lock, 1974.

13 Jane W. Torrey, 'Learning to Read without a teacher: a case study', in Frank Smith (ed.), *Psycholinguistics and Reading*, New York, Holt, Reinhart & Winston, 1973.

14 John and Elizabeth Newson, *Perspectives on School at Seven Years Old*, London, Allen & Unwin, 1977.

15 Kenneth Goodman, 'Reading: a psycholinguistic guessing game', in *Journal of the Reading Specialist*, May 1967, College Reading Association, pp. 259-64, 266-71; Frank Smith, *Understanding Reading*, New York, Holt, Rinehart & Winston, 1971; *Reading*, Cambridge University Press, 1978.

16 Ronald Morris, *Success and Failure in Learning to Read*, Harmondsworth, Penguin, 1972.

17 Elizabeth Goodacre, *Hearing Children Read*, University of Reading, Centre for the Teaching of Reading, 1972.

18 Cliff Moon and Bridie Raban, *A Question of Reading*, London, Ward Lock, 1975.

19 Helen Savva, 'Reading development in a fifth year girl', in *Becoming Our Own Experts, studies of language and learning made* by the Talk Workshop Group at Vauxhall Manor School 1974-9, published by the authors, obtainable from The Englsh Centre, Sutherland Street, London, SW1. This book is another of example of teachers generating their linguistic and educational theories from their practice.

230 *Notes to pages 55-65*

20 Margaret Donaldson, *Children's Minds*, London, Fontana, 1978.
21 Marie Clay, *Reading, the patterning of complex behaviour*, London, Heinemann, 1973.
22 Roger Gurney, *Language, learning and remedial teaching*, London, Arnold, 1976.
23 The studies have been extended in 'Aspects of Discourse in the Story Reading and Reading Development of Young Children', PhD thesis, University of London, 1982.
24 F. Whitehead, A. C. Capey, W. Maddren and A. Wellings, *Children and their Books*, London, Macmillan, 1977.
25 C. Harrison, 'Assessing the readability of school texts', in E. A. Lunzer and W. K. Gardner (eds), *The Effective Use of Reading*, London, Heinemann, 1979.
26 David Mackay, Brian Thomson and Pamela Schaub, *Breakthrough to Literacy*, Teacher's Manual, London, Longman, 1970.
27 E. B. Huey, *The Psychology and Pedagogy of Reading* (reprinted from 1903), Cambridge, Mass.: MIT Press, 1968.
28 G. Dennison, *The Lives of Children*, Harmondsworth, Penguin, 1971.
29 This is the central idea of *The Cool Web* edited by Margaret Meek, Aidan Warlow and Grizelda Barton, London, Bodley Head, 1977.
30 James Moffett, *Teaching the Universe of Discourse*, New York, Houghton Mifflin, 1968.
31 Arthur Applebee, *The Child's Concept of Story*, University of Chicago Press, 1977.
32 B. Bettelheim, *The Uses of Enchantment*, London, Thames & Hudson, 1978; J. L. Singer, *The Child's World of Make-Believe*, New York, Academic Press, 1973.
33 Judith's school document: *The Meaning of Reading*.
34 The distinction between 'new' and 'known' text is explained by Daniel P. and Lauren B. Resnick in 'The nature of literacy: a historical explanation', *Harvard Educational Review*, vol. 47, no. 3, August 1977, pp. 370-85.
35 Ibid.
36 M. A. K. Halliday, *Learning How to Mean*, London, Arnold, 1975.
37 As the study progressed, we looked to writers who were adding insights from language and linguistic studies to literary criticism. We were pleased to final Jonathan Culler in, *Structuralist Poetics*, London, Routledge & Kegan Paul, 1978, say that 'a theory of literature is a theory of reading'. George Craig's 'Reading, who does what to whom' in Gabriel Josipovici (ed.), *The Modern English Novel*, London, Open Books, 1976, explained for us many things we thought we understood but needed to talk about.
38 Margaret Spencer, 'Handing down the magic', in *Coming to Know*, ed. Phyllida Salmon, London, Routledge & Kegan Paul, 1980.

5 Early encounters

1 In the third year of our study we saw the early stages of the programmes about reading made for the Inner London Education Authority by the Centre for Language in Primary Education. The 'raw' tape of early reading lessons in a primary school was especially helpful to us. We should have made more videotapes than we did.

2 John and Elizabeth Newson, *Perspectives on School at Seven Year Old*, London, Allen & Unwin, 1977, ch. 6. 'Already at seven years old there is a chill in the air. Too many of the tender leaves of hope will have withered by the end of the summer of childhood.'

3 A phrase used in a talk by James Britton.

4 John Holt, *How Children Fail*, New York, Dell Publishing Co., 1964.

5 W. Labov, 'The logic of non-standard English', in *Georgetown Monographs on Language and Linguistics*, vol. 22, 169.

6 W. R. Jones, *Step up and Read*, London, Hodder, University of London Press, 1965.

7 Sara Delamont, *Interaction in the Classroom*, London, Methuen, 1976.

8 H. B. Grice, 'Logic and Conversation', in *Syntax and Semantics*, vol. 3, *Speech Acts*, ed. P. Cole and J. L. Morgan, London, Academic Press, 1975.

6 Two sources of evidence

1 Peter Trudgill, *Accent, dialect and the school*, London, Arnold 1965.

2 Elizabeth Goodacre, *Hearing Children Read*, University of Reading, Centre for the Teaching of Reading, 1972.

7 What progress looks like

1 Paul A. Kohlers, 'Three stages of Reading', in Frank Smith (ed.), *Psycholinguistics and Reading*, New York, Holt Rinehart & Winston, 1973.

2 Iona and Peter Opie, *The Oxford Dictionary of Nursery Rhymes*, Oxford, The Clarendon Press, 1951.

3 J. N. Britton, *Language and Learning*, Harmondsworth, Allen Lane, 1970.

4 This was not a random guess, but the kind of reference that suggests itself to English teachers. In 'Making, Knowing and Judging' (in *The Dyers Hand*, London, Faber, 1963) W. H. Auden explains the nature of 'sacred objects'. Likewise, in 'Freedom and Necessity in Poetry: my Lead Mine' he says, 'Any secondary world

he may imaginatively construct necessarily draws its raw materials from the Primary World in which we all live.' (in *Play*, ed. J. S. Bruner, A. Jolly and K. Sylva, Harmondsworth, Penguin, 1976).

8 Reflexions

1 'Gradually and intuitively, the child seems to learn that there is what might be called a "hierarchy of veracity". Some classes of fiction are "truer" than others. Some narrators are more honest and better informed than others. Some types of story allow people to travel on magic carpets and animals to talk, while others do not. Some stories invite "verifiable belief", while others require "imaginativeness" (a distinction made by I.A. Richards). The conventions of one class of story do not apply to others. Different sorts of fiction bear different relationships to life as he knows it' (Aidan Warlow, 'Kinds of Fiction: a hierarchy of veracity', in *The Cool Web: the pattern of children's reading*, ed. Margaret Meek, Aidan Warlow, Grizelda Barton, London, The Bodley Head, 1977).

2 R. L. Gregory. 'Psychology: towards a science of fiction', in ibid.

3 Gabriel Josipovici, *The Modern English Novel*, London, Open Books, 1976.

4 Ibid.

5 Jerome Bruner, *Towards a Theory of Instruction*, Harvard University Press, 1966.

6 James Moffett, *Teaching the Universe of Discourse*, New York, Houghton Mifflin, 1968. 'Whereas adults differentiate their thought with specialized kinds of discourse such as narrative generalization and theory, children must, for a long time, make narrative do for all. They utter themselves almost entirely through stories – read or invented – and they apprehend what others say through story.'

7 Donald Graves, 'Renters', in *English Magazine*, no. 8, 1981.

8 Trevor came to see Judith at work and found on her desk a copy of her article in the *English Magazine* called 'A lesson with Trevor'.

9 A. D. Edwards and V. J. Furlong, *The Language of Teaching*, London, Heinemann, 1978.

10 The English Centre where our work began has published many books of writing by children for children, including *Our Lives: Autobiographies of Young People*.

11 The term is used in Edwards and Furlong, op. cit.

12 Jonathan Culler, *Structuralist Poetics*, London, Routledge & Kegan Paul, 1978.

13 Edwards and Furlong, op. cit.